D1490904

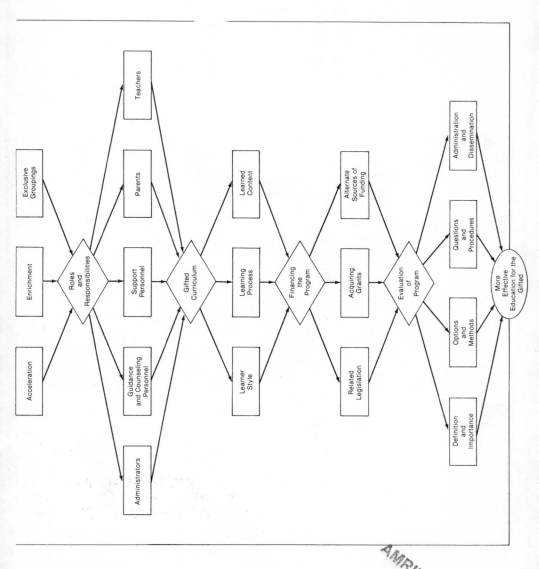

GIFTED EDUCATION

A Comprehensive Roadmap

Patricia A. Alexander
Texas A & M University
College Station, Texas

Joseph A. Muia
Educational Consulting Services
McGaheysville, Virginia

AN ASPEN PUBLICATION®
Aspen Systems Corporation
Rockville, Maryland
London
1982

Library of Congress Cataloging in Publication Data

Alexander, Patricia.
Gifted education.

Includes bibliographies and index.
1. Gifted children — Education.
I. Muia, Joseph.
II. Title.
LC3993.A397   371.95   81-12707
ISBN: 0-89443-383-0   AACR2

Library of Congress Catalog Card Number: 81-12707
ISBN: 0-89443-383-0

Printed in the United States of America

1 2 3 4 5

To my gifted students and to J.F.,
whose uniquenesses have never ceased
to amaze and enlighten me.

P.A.A.

To Lil and Kristen
for helping me to experience love
and happiness.

J.A.M.

Table of Contents

Preface ix

Acknowledgments xi

Chapter 1—Gifted: Historical Perspective and Definition 1

Historical Perspective of the Gifted Movement 1
Comparison of Recent Definitions of Giftedness 10
Summary 17

Chapter 2—Identifying the Gifted 21

Strategies and Models in the Identification Process 21
Behaviors of Typical and Atypical Gifted 42
Nontraditional Assessment Devices 52
Procedures and Participants: Who Makes
the Decision? 56
Summary 60

Chapter 3—Needs Assessment: Clarifying Program Focus 65

Needs Assessment 65
Areas of Assessment 69
Levels of Program Planning 89
Summary 96

Chapter 4—Establishing Program Goals and Objectives **99**

Unit-Specific or Program Goals 100
The Group-Specific Objectives Level 109
The Learner-Specific Objectives Level 120
Summary 125

Chapter 5—Determining the Program Format **127**

Principal Factors Affecting the Structuring
of Gifted Programs 128
Categories of Gifted Program Formats:
Description, Analysis, and Implications 144
Summary 160

Chapter 6—Outlining Roles and Responsibilities **163**

The Administrator 163
Guidance and Counseling Personnel 173
Support Personnel 186
Parents of Gifted Learners 189
Teachers of the Gifted 194
Summary 214

Chapter 7—The Gifted Curriculum: A Holistic Approach **217**

The Holistic Curriculum: Its Purpose and
Its Parts 218
Learning Style 220
Learned Content 233
Summary 248

Chapter 8—Financing the Gifted Program **249**

Gifted Legislation 250
Acquiring Funds—A Necessary Headache? 256
Summary 268

Chapter 9—Evaluating the Gifted Program **269**

Evaluation: Its Definition and Its Importance 270
Evaluation: The Options and the Methods 273
Evaluation: Questions, Methodologies,
    and Procedures Related 280
Evaluation: Administration and Dissemination 284
Summary 287

**Appendix A—The Renzulli-Hartman Scale for Rating Behavioral
            Characteristics of Superior Students** **289**

Appendix B—Alternate Sources of Funding **295**

Index **307**

Preface

The major premise of this book is that gifted learners need and deserve an educational program commensurate with their abilities and uniquenesses. Too little attention has been paid to the complex aspects of gifted program development organized within a systematic and comprehensive framework. That is the purpose of this book—to consider the who, what, when, where, and why of gifted programming. The authors have attempted to look at this process with an eye toward thoroughness and orderly progression. Certainly no text can provide all the information required to initiate instructional programs for the gifted and, certainly, no text can anticipate the exact sequence in which aspects of a specific program must be undertaken. Yet, the authors of this text have sought to furnish the reader with what they perceive to be the information most pertinent to program development and have done so in as systematic and orderly a fashion as possible—understanding only too well the complexity and scope of such an undertaking.

It is also the purpose of this book to provide a balance between theoretical and practical concerns. For a gifted program to function adequately, it must bridge the gap between theory and practice. To serve gifted learners well we must have some understanding of their mental processes and cognitive development. We must also be familiar with related research that provides guidance in the establishment of an educational environment conducive to learning for gifted individuals. On the other hand, educational planning for the gifted cannot disregard the practical issues that are a part of the daily functioning of an instructional program. Therefore, along with theoretical principles we have furnished practical examples, and along with research findings we have presented functional information.

The authors hope to bring about improvement in educational environments for those learners capable of reaching great depths of thought and great heights in achievement. Our audience, then, is anyone and everyone who shares that aim, whether they be educators, administrators, specialists, parents or students. We are sincerely grateful for the opportunity this book affords us to reach our goal.

P.A.A.
J.A.M.

Acknowledgments

The authors wish to extend thanks to the following individuals for their assistance in this undertaking:

To Curtis Whitesel, Editorial Director for Aspen Systems Corporation, for his comments and advice throughout the development of this book and for his deep concern for the gifted. To Jane Coyle, Anne Hill, and Darlene Como of Aspen Systems for their help in making this a better project through their editorial assistance. To Lisa Beck for her assistance in obtaining pertinent research for the project. To Dr. Doug Coulson for his expertise in and reactions to Chapter 9 on evaluation. To Drs. Louise Berman and Jessie Roderick for sharing their knowledge of underlying curricular processes. To Dr. Melvin Ladson, Director of the Office of Gifted and Talented, for providing information when needed. To Ms. Gail Beaumont, Office of Gifted and Talented, for furnishing information on program funding. To Patty Williams for her help with graphics for the book. To Mary Lou Glick for typing the chapter drafts. To William and Rose Mullins for their undying patience and support of this project.

Chapter 1

Gifted: Historical Perspective and Definition

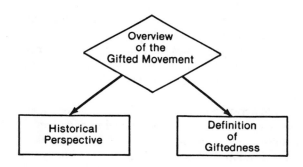

Before beginning the task of examining comprehensive educational programming for the gifted, it would seem appropriate to concern ourselves, briefly, with the roots of the gifted movement. This introductory consideration of relevant past occurrences should be undertaken for at least two reasons. First, by developing an awareness of how gifted education has progressed and what factors have influenced its growth, we may view the entire subject of education for the gifted and its current directions from a more accurate perspective. Certainly, the steps taken in our current programs for the gifted should, at the very least, benefit from the steps taken in the past. Second, such background information is a constant reminder that interest in the gifted is not a recent phenomenon. The search for a greater understanding of the human mind and individual differences within the cognitive system appears throughout recorded history. Even as far back as the writings of ancient philosophers, the question of human intellectual growth was raised and thoughtful explanations were offered.

HISTORICAL PERSPECTIVE OF THE GIFTED MOVEMENT

Philosophical-Rationalistic Phase

One philosopher who considered the question of human intellectual growth was Plato. In a translation of Plato's discourse (Nettleship, 1966), the human mind was envisioned as growing from a state of intellectual darkness into varying stages of intellectual illumination or knowledge. Plato theorized that there were four such stages and that all minds must pass through them sequentially. He further speculated that individuals progress to different distances through, and attain differing heights within, these stages. It was also Plato's belief that a more perfect social order could be achieved if the people selected to govern were chosen from among the most intellectually capable of available individuals. However, throughout many succeeding ages, this Platonic philosophy was never to be fully realized. From ancient times to recent centuries, outstanding potential was generally overlooked or not even considered. Surprisingly, there were some early attempts made at measuring individual differences through scientific observations. Around 2200 B.C., for example, the Chinese had devised a form of civil service examination to scrutinize individuals seeking various government positions. For the most part, however, training, position, and power were awarded to individuals as a consequence of their class, or as the luck of their birth, rather than as a result of their abilities or potential.

Within this early historical phase, ancient philosophers attempted to explain the existence and uniqueness of man in rationalistic terms and seemed less concerned with implementation of their philosophic beliefs. As an illustration, a definition of giftedness that was developed around the Platonic philosophy would be a rather abstract, metaphorical description of how the mind develops and how differences in such development might be envisioned. It could be postulated from Plato's writings that the gifted individual would be one who passes through the stages of knowledge more quickly than others, reaches a higher level of understanding within each stage than most, and is able to progress through all stages, attaining what Plato calls total illumination or understanding. At this period in history no more precise definition was required.

Fixed Intelligence Phase

As the importance of scientific inquiry into natural phenomenon was expanded, there was a phase reached when scientific methodology was applied to human behaviors and human intelligence (see Figure 1-1). As the age of scientific inquiry into the social sciences approached, philosophical questioning of man's intellect and abilities would no longer suffice. Consequently, there was a movement toward defining, in terms of measurable and observable behaviors, what it was that philosophers had so eloquently described as man's uniqueness.

Also, with the advent of Darwinian theory, there came a desire to obtain more conclusive evidence concerning the nature of heredity. The combination of interest in intellectual measurement and heredity was mirrored in the work of Galton, an English biologist, who sought to develop methods and techniques to measure human abilities. Galton's studies produced a conceptualization of intelligence as

Figure 1-1 Schematic Representation of Historical Developments Related to the Gifted Movement

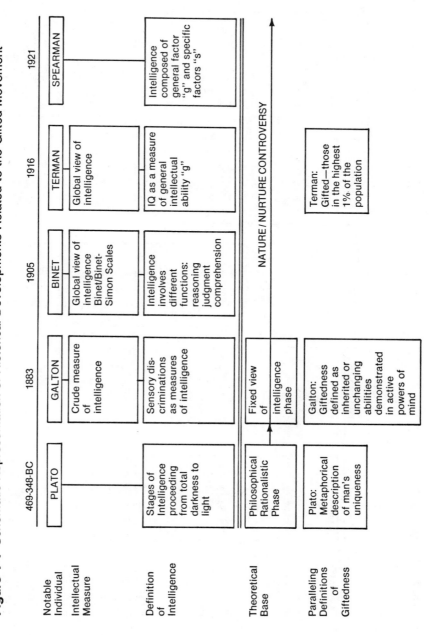

Figure 1-1 continued

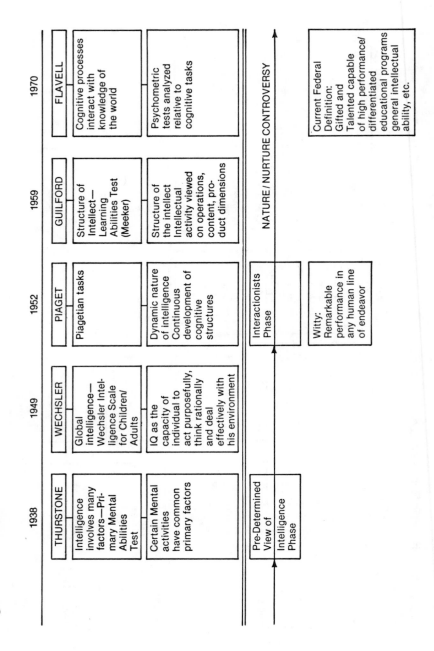

an inherited, fixed ability, and his efforts resulted in a crude, but influential, measurement scale of intelligence. Galton's interpretation of intelligence as an inbred, unchanging quantity had ramifications on the view of giftedness that predominated well into the 1950s. Galton's efforts to produce an instrument capable of measuring this quantity called intelligence had at least equal impact on the gifted movement, as demonstrated by the thrust in the psychometric evaluation of intelligence that ensued (Galton, 1883).

Growth of the Psychometric Movement in Intellectual Evaluation

Some years later, Galton's attempts to devise an instrument capable of measuring human intelligence were repeated and refined by Binet. Binet was commissioned by the French government to produce a scale able to distinguish students of intellectual extremes for instructional purposes. Binet, along with his colleague, Simon, later developed the *Binet-Simon Intelligence Test* (1905), a test which measured a wide variety of behaviors. The *Binet-Simon* scale stressed verbal skills, except at the early age levels at which motor responses were predominant.

Terman (1925), best known for his longitudinal studies of the gifted begun over a half century ago and still being updated, can also be credited with the revision of the Binet scale developed for use in the United States. This scale was entitled the *Stanford-Binet*, and, except for some minor modifications, it was quite similar to the original *Binet-Simon* scale. By applying the *Stanford-Binet* scales, which have undergone several normings, Terman sought to define the gifted as those individuals within the highest 1 percent in general intelligence.

What Galton, Binet, and Terman collectively exemplified was the move from philosophical into scientific inquiry of the differences in the human intellect. However, during this period the predominant view was that intelligence was a global construct and that the intelligence score was the unalterable representation of that construct.

Through the research of many psychologists, attempts have been made to unveil the intellect and view it as a far more complex and interrelated phenomenon. In order to broaden and more fully understand the intellect and the influence of the environment on its growth, researchers have sought to more precisely define the factors or aptitudes that are characteristic of the intellect. In order to describe more fully the importance of these multiple-factor theories, a brief explanation is warranted.

Two-Factor Structure Theory

One of the earliest theories attempting to define the concept of intelligence factors was Spearman's (1904) two-factor theory. In his theory, Spearman postulated that there were two types of intellectual aptitudes or factors. There was the general aptitude common to all intellectual activities, which Spearman referred to as the "g" factor, and there were specific, or "s," factors unique to the particular task being performed.

As illustrated in Figure 1-2, given a series of specific instructional tasks in the areas of reading, science, or math, an individual must possess aptitudes specific to each area in order to successfully accomplish each task. However, there will be that aptitude that underlies performance of and is common to all tasks. This is the "g" factor referred to by Spearman. The purpose of testing, as Spearman rationalized it, was to determine the amount of "g" in each person. He further reasoned that "g" measurement could best be accomplished through tests of abstract relations. *Raven's Progressive Matrices* and the *Cattell Culture Fair* are two intelligence tests developed as measures of "g" factor (Raven, 1956; Anastasi, 1976).

Multiple-Factor Structure Theory

As psychologists continued to refine the notion of aptitudes related to intellectual structure, it became more evident that there were many additional aptitudes or factors not accounted for in Spearman's simplistic two-factor theory. In addition, these aptitudes varied in their degree of importance within various tests. It was no longer sufficient to speak simply of specific or common factors. What became necessary was an analysis of the factors that played a role in the relationship of various tasks. Thurstone (1938) produced a list of abilities that he felt could account for the apparent relationships among tasks. These seven factors were used as the basis of Thurstone's *Primary Mental Abilities Test* and included:

1. number factor
2. verbal factor
3. space relations
4. memory
5. reasoning
6. word fluency
7. perceptual speed

As demonstrated in Figure 1-3, there may be aspects or portions of certain factors or aptitudes that create a link between reading tasks and math tasks.

Guilford's Structure of the Intellect

While the multiple-factor theory added much to the expanding notion of the complexity of intelligence, it still held several disadvantages. For example, the multiple-factor theory was significantly limited in its ability to explain divergent thinking abilities, as well as social intelligence. Special abilities in areas such as

Figure 1-2 Representations of Spearman's Two-Factor Theory

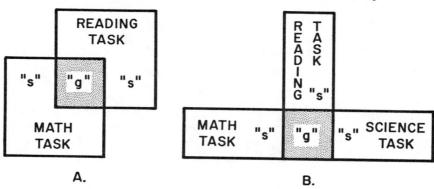

A.   B.

Figure 1-3 Representation of the Multiple-Factor Theory

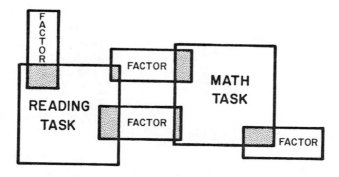

athletics, music, drama and oratory, and mechanical intelligence were also given little consideration (Divesta & Thompson, 1970).

In 1959, Guilford described a factor analytic model of intelligence that identified and classified 120 cognitive abilities along three dimensions: operations, contents, and products (see Figure 1-4).

According to Guilford's definition, the *operations* are intellectual activities or what the organizer does in processing information. *Contents* are the types of information on which the operations are performed, and *products* are the outcomes of the organism's processing of the information. Evident from this model is a broadening of the multiple-factor theory to include factors that earlier were given little consideration.

Social intelligence, which, as mentioned above, warranted little attention in other psychometric measures of intelligence, was an area of concern in the

Figure 1-4 Guilford's Structure of the Intellect Model

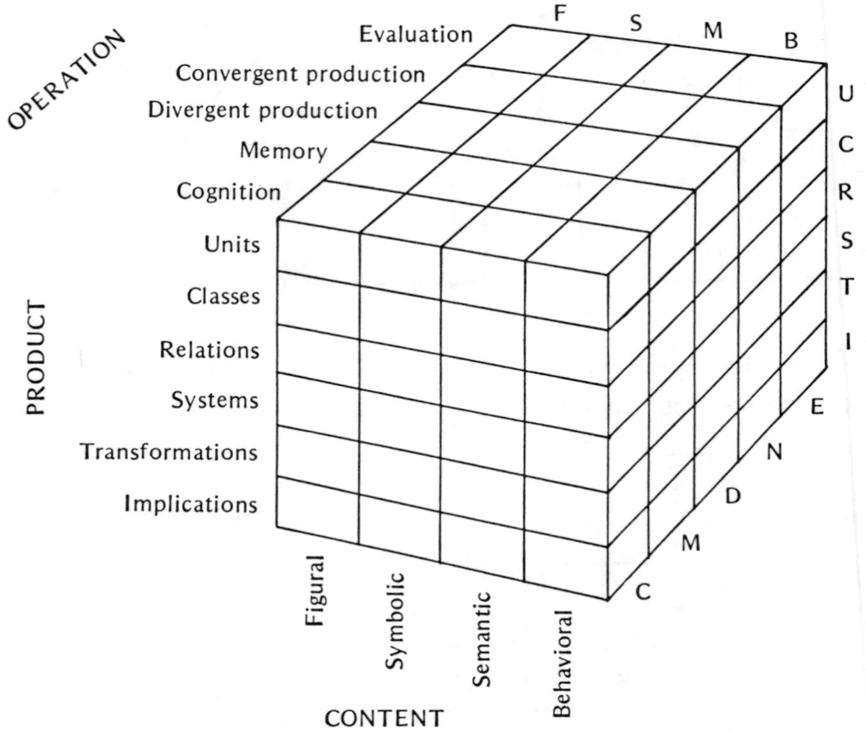

Source: From *The Nature of Human Intelligence* by J.P. Guilford. Copyright © 1967, McGraw-Hill Book Company. Used with the permission of McGraw-Hill Book Company.

Guilford model. This area provides an excellent example of how Guilford's notion of intelligence broadened earlier conceptualizations. In the divergent production of behavioral classes, for example, the individual might be asked to look at a series of drawings depicting body parts expressing various emotions. The individual must then organize the drawings into as many groups that express some common thought, feeling, or expression as possible. In the divergent production of behavioral transformations, the individual is asked to look at an incomplete cartoon strip and invent different endings for it (Guilford & Hoepfner, 1971).

Since Guilford's development of the *Structure of the Intellect Model,* there have been additional attempts by others to construct measures of cognitive abilities based on this model. Meeker and Meeker (1976), as one example, have developed the *Structure of the Intellect-Learning Abilities Test (SOI-LA)* around the work of Guilford. Tests of creativity, such as the *Torrance Tests of Creative Thinking* (Torrance, 1966), are also offshoots of Guilford's research endeavors.

The Interactionists Phase

As new ways of assessing intelligence emerged, there continued, and still continues, to be much controversy in determining answers to such questions as what is intelligence and how do we explain its development. The genetic and interactionist theories were postulated to explain the concept of intelligence. Presently, the most accepted of these theories is the interactionists' view, in which intelligence is seen to result from an interaction between the learner's inherited capabilities and the nurturance provided by the learner's psychological, social, emotional, and educational environment. Much of the impetus for the interactionists theory has come from the work of Piaget (1952), Inhelder (1969), and Flavell (1977). Although presented earlier under the heading of psychometric evaluation, Guilford's model of intellectual structure also portrays this interactionists' view.

The research of Piaget deserves special consideration for the focus it provided on intellectual growth and development from two perspectives. First, we were exposed to the concept that individuals play active roles in their own cognitive development. In order to progress through the various stages of cognitive development—sensorimotor, preoperational, concrete operational, formal operations—individuals must submit to pressures from their environment. This submission results in an assimilation and accommodation of the information that comes from these environmental interactions. Second, Piaget demonstrated the vast importance of the preverbal development period. The experiences accumulated by the learner long before formal schooling were shown to be crucial to optimal development.

As schematically presented in Figure 1-5, the interactionists theory of cognitive development can be described as consisting of three interrelated dimensions: (1) inputs, (2) intellectual structure, and (3) outputs. In essence, stimulations that arise from the environment and are experienced by the individual are inputs into the intellectual system, interact with that system, and are manifested in outputs unique to the individual.

Within this very brief overview of past events relevant to the education of the gifted, we have seen how individual differences in the intellect were first explored as philosophical questions. Centuries later, intelligence became looked on as a fixed, and accurately measurable, entity, the level of which could be designated by a score on an intelligence scale and the parameters of which remained relatively unchanged by educational experiences. In time, although educational dependence

Figure 1-5 Integrated View of Cognitive Development

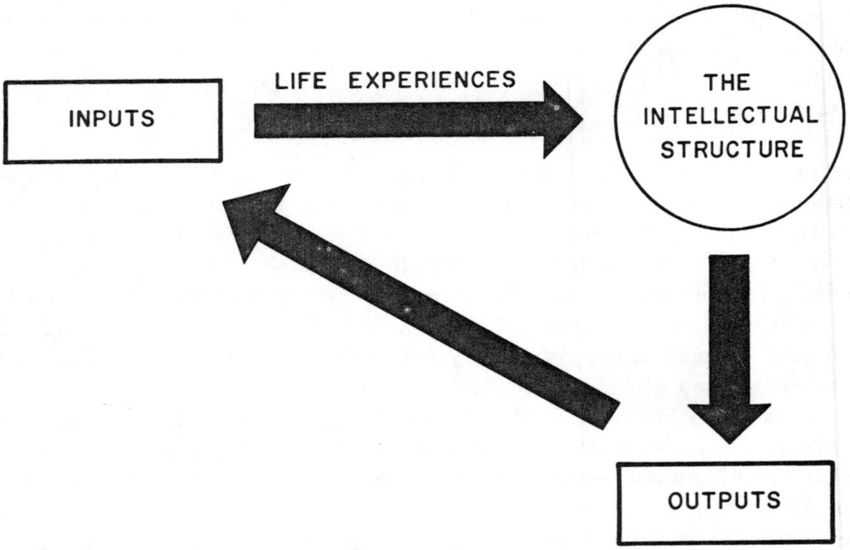

---

on testing continued to flourish, the accuracy of the unchanging, and infallible, intelligence score was brought into question. The countering of this view of intelligence was fueled, in part, by the work and writings of many, including Piaget (1952), Spearman (1904), and Guilford (1959). These investigations into intelligence continue and are paralleled by attempts to answer the question what is giftedness?

COMPARISON OF RECENT DEFINITIONS OF GIFTEDNESS

As shown in the schematic representation of the history behind gifted education (Figure 1-1), definitions of giftedness in the early and mid 1900s focused on IQ or intellectual ability as the main indicator of giftedness. The gifted individual was viewed as one possessing a high level of intelligence, which, in turn, was seen as a fixed and measurable quantity. Correspondingly, the gifted could be easily defined as a person with an IQ at or above an established point. Although this may be conceived by some as the narrowest interpretation of giftedness, it is one that can still be found in operation in some schools today.

However, during the period when IQ was conceptualized as a global ability measured by psychometric instruments, there were attempts by educators to broaden this narrow conceptualization. What was added to some definitions of gifted to broaden their scope was reference to achievements or performances as well as IQ. The frequently cited definition of Witty (1951) refers to this achievement factor: ''a potentially gifted child is considered as any child whose performance in a worthwhile type of human endeavor is repeatedly or consistently remarkable.''

In addition, some definitions attempted to demonstrate that the gifted child was not only cognitively but socially superior as well. ''The Gifted is one who has a high order of ability to handle ideas, to produce creativity and to demonstrate Social leadership'' (NSSE, 1958).

The difficulty with these broadened definitions, however, was the inability to quantify or explain in practice such phrases as ''remarkable performance,'' ''facility with ideas,'' or ''creative production.'' Furthermore, the resounding impact of Terman's research and its emphasis on IQ continued to exert influence on gifted education.

In the late 1950s and 1960s additional changes occurred in the notion of giftedness. While IQ continued to be an essential element in defining giftedness, other dimensions in which individuals could display their giftedness were added. In 1957, DeHaan and Havighurst made reference in their definition to such areas as leadership ability, artistic talent, and mechanical and physical skills.

What was noteworthy about definitions arising in this period was their acceptance of less traditional indicators of giftedness (i.e., music, graphic arts, creative writing, dramatics), which could be demonstrated and evaluated within the school setting, and their emphasis on the importance of adequate school programs for gifted learners.

> The gifted are those students whose potential intellectual powers are at such a high ideational level in both productive and evaluative thinking that it can be reasonably assumed they could be the future problem solvers, innovators, and evaluators of the culture if adequate educational experiences are provided. (Lucito, 1963)

The 1970s proved to be another period of turning points in gifted education, in part because of the revealing Marland report (1972). In his report to Congress, Commissioner of Education Marland painted a bleak picture of gifted programming in the United States.

On the basis of Marland's intense investigations, the federal government produced guidelines for state gifted program development. These guidelines included a rather elaborate and encompassing definition of giftedness:

> those identified by professionally qualified persons who by virtue of outstanding abilities are capable of high performance. There are chil-

dren who require differentiated educational programs and/or services beyond those normally provided by the regular school program in order to realize their contribution to self and society.

Children capable of high performance include those with demonstrated achievement and/or potential ability in any of the following areas, singly or in combination:

1. general intellectual ability
2. specific academic aptitude
3. creative or productive thinking
4. leadership ability
5. visual and performing arts
6. psychomotor ability (Marland, 1972)

However, Renzulli (1978), in an examination of the current definition, points out four major difficulties inherent in its design.

1. It fails to include motivational factors.
2. It attempts to separate the six aptitude areas by presenting six categories that represent process abilities and two that focus on performance areas. Renzulli indicates that the process abilities do not exist apart from the performance areas.
3. It is advocated by many people in theory, but the use of intelligence or aptitude test results predominate in practice.
4. It ignores task commitment, which research has shown to be directly related to giftedness.

Renzulli's model (see Figure 1-6) defines giftedness as the interaction of above-average ability, task commitment, and creativity (shaded area). This giftedness is then demonstrated, according to Renzulli, in general and specific performance areas such as math, art, sciences, and music.

There can be little doubt of the broadening of the definition that has occurred when we compare the currently used description of gifted to earlier ones focusing exclusively on IQ. One objective of these broadened interpretations of the term "gifted" would appear to be a desire to expand the philosophical base of programs established on this interpretation. In turn, it may have been felt that by expanding the philosophical base for gifted programming a greater diversification in the populations served would also result. This diversification in gifted populations does not appear to have taken place to any great extent, however. The profiles of students served by the broader definitions of gifted do not differ markedly, in terms of socioeconomic level and cultural background, from the profiles of the gifted students in Terman's study conducted approximately 50 years ago. Why this might

Figure 1-6 Renzulli's Ingredients of Giftedness

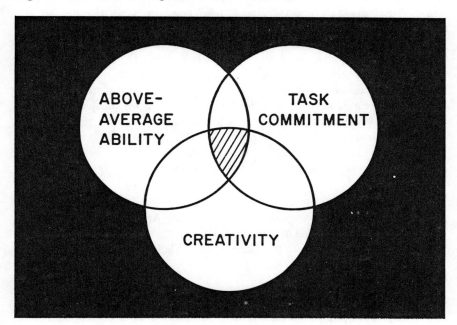

Source: Reprinted from *What Makes Giftedness* by Joseph S. Renzulli by permission of Creative Learning Press, © 1978. This material is from a booklet entitled *The Revolving Door Identification Model: A Comprehensive Approach to Identification and Programming for Gifted and Talented Students,* by Joseph S. Renzulli, Sally M. Reis, and Linda H. Smith. Published by Creative Learning Press, P.O. Box 320, Mansfield Center, CT 06250.

have occurred could be explained perhaps in part by the continued reliance on traditional, narrower identification procedures without regard for the scope of the population considered in the definition. In addition, clarification of the meaning of giftedness may be confounded by the inclusion of other unclear concepts. When we have not yet arrived at a clear understanding of the word ''gifted,'' we are asked to deal, as well, with such concepts as ''creative'' and ''talented.''

Solidification of the Gifted Movement

As described in the historical overview of the gifted movement presented at the outset of this chapter, the focus on the human mind progressed from philosophical analysis to scientific inquiry into individual differences in intelligence. Initially, this scientific investigation centered around intelligence as a fixed quantity that remained unchanged by outside forces. In time, however, many researchers came to view intellectual growth as greatly dependent on environmental stimulation and the attempts one made to adapt to that environment. Those currently involved in gifted education no longer feel it is sufficient to talk of the stimulation of the human mind and the important role of life experiences. Consequently, gifted education has now evolved to the point at which it is necessary to systematically plan and organize programs within our educational institutions that will adequately provide those appropriate and intellectually stimulating experiences.

The solidification of "gifted" from philosophical question to an educational movement has also been spurred by several related factors: (1) egalitarianism, (2) specialization, and (3) governmental interest and support.

Egalitarianism

Egalitarianism is the concept of equal rights for all. Applied to our schools, this doctrine represents the belief of many that all individuals are entitled to receive an education commensurate with their abilities and needs.

Specialization

As the field of education, itself, became a specialized area of study apart from its origins in philosophy, so, too, has gifted education begun to develop as a more specialized area of study within education. Such a focus in study may well have come about for two reasons. First, as the body of research relevant to the gifted expands and continues to expand, the need for analysis and synthesis of the research becomes more important. What is required is someone to interpret or translate the information available into understandable patterns with implications for practice. Second, as the demands on the educational system to meet the specific needs of each individual student increase and as teachers and administrators become more accountable to the public for their actions, educational specialization may serve as a partial solution. Classroom teachers, as a group, can no longer be expected to have the expertise to deal effectively with all the special needs encountered without some support. Therefore, as information pertinent to the gifted accumulates, and is refined, as pressure is brought to bear on the educational system to accommodate the needs of the gifted population, and as the educational personnel becomes more accountable for actions taken, the need for specialization in gifted education will result.

Governmental Interest and Support

As long as the government expresses an interest in the education of the gifted and continues to back up such interest with monetary support, the number of gifted programs should increase. The consideration of educational programs for the gifted cannot arise solely for monetary gains, but monetary support can assist in better, broader gifted programming. Educational institutions may be more willing to conduct research and establish experimental programs with the financial backing of state and federal government. Government, which fathered several educational programs following the launch of Sputnik in the 1950s, has apparently broadened its scope in gifted programming. Earlier its emphasis seemed to center on the location of students of demonstrated abilities especially in the areas of science and math. In the 1970s, the Marland report, referred to previously, laid the groundwork for additional federal support for the development of gifted programs. As a result of this report, federal interest in the gifted was expanded to include the recognition of potential achievement in the arts, as well as performance in the more traditional curriculum areas.

Giftedness: Defining the Concept

Through all ages and within every generation there have been those individuals who stood apart from the others. Their thoughts, actions, and creations distinguished them from their contemporaries. Such persons (the Brontes, the Michelangelos and the Beethovens) garner recognition for their extraordinary achievements and wear easily the title of gifted. However, the recognition of such outstanding ability may be far easier than its definition. Defining any abstract such as gifted is, at best, an uncertain and difficult endeavor in which we are bound by semantics and syntax to produce a concise, correct, and meaningful description of some concept.

If defining the word "gifted" is so difficult, as has been suggested, why should it be attempted at all, much less carefully pursued? Composing or choosing a definition of gifted should be thought of as one of the crucial beginning tasks of effective education for the gifted for three reasons:

1. It provides the base for further discussions and actions in the organization of gifted programming.
2. It demonstrates the philosophical focus of the educational program.
3. It determines the direction to be taken in identification procedures.

A Base for Further Discussions and Actions

Before any serious organizing on any topic can take place, it is essential to know about what one is organizing. Frequently, at the district or school level, gifted programs are initially conceived by one or a few highly interested or highly motivated individuals who organize others or who involve others in their organization. When these interested parties come together, it is sometimes erroneously assumed that they share not only a common interest in improving education for the gifted but also a common view of what "gifted" means. This may not be the case. By putting the individual's or group's feelings into writing, the springboard for additional communication and clarification is provided. To some extent, the organizational framework that may need to be developed around such a definition is signaled.

Philosophical Focus

For those within and those outside the program, the definition of "gifted" also serves to highlight the philosophy of the program to be undertaken. For example, if "gifted" were defined relative to a score on an intelligence test, it could be speculated that the conception of giftedness and the resulting population would differ markedly from that of a program that defined "gifted" on the basis of demonstrated or latent potential. Simply speaking, it displays to the public our beliefs about the meaning of giftedness and the emphasis we choose to place on certain aspects of the gifted process. This parallel between definition and philosophy can best be demonstrated by the change that has taken place in the definition of "gifted" over the years.

Direction of Identification Procedures

The definition selected to serve the gifted program answers the question "who" and is related directly to the procedures for locating the gifted population, which subsequently answers the "how" (Anastasi, 1958). Procedural strategies for the identification of the typical and atypical gifted learner will be discussed in detail in Chapter 2.

Choosing a Definition of Giftedness

Although the selection of the definition for program development should ultimately rest with those directly involved in program planning at the district or school level, two points should be taken under advisement when choosing the definition to be implemented.

First, the more abstract the terminology in the definition of gifted the more carefully delineated the identification procedures should be. Following the years of scientific inquiry and quite emphatically with the rise of the behaviorist movement in education, it became and still is, to a large extent, important to operationally define the terms used. Operationally defining is the process of including within our definition the method of identification or means of measurement. Certainly, the Platonic concept of intellectual differences as a progression through various stages of light (knowing) presents the reader with a vivid image of intellectual growth but with no information on how such growth can be identified. Conversely, the definition of the gifted as an individual with an IQ score at or above 130 on the *Stanford-Binet* scale not only tells us who but also puts forth, in very definite terms, the method for measurement. This is not to imply that abstract definitions should not be applied. The point here is that, should we choose to operate a program on a definition that does not pinpoint the measurement or identification procedures, then these procedures must be carefully delineated elsewhere.

Second, the more reliant on a specific test range or score the definition may be, the less variant the population may be. It is important to remember, also, that the scope of the definition chosen will probably have a direct or indirect effect on the scope of the population it will ultimately serve. Although this topic is a controversial one and will be addressed in more detail later, it should be briefly stated that the more dependent a definition is on a specific score or test, the less flexibility there will be in identification and the less variance there may be in the population identified. As an illustration, if we define our gifted as all those whose overall performance on the *Wechsler Intelligence Scale for Children-Revised (WISC-R)* is 120 or above, the more likely we are to select students who are highly motivated and more than likely possess the types of experiences crucial to success in school learning. Less likely to be identified by this procedure, however, are culturally different learners who, because of their diverse experiential background, may not demonstrate their potential on such measures.

What might prove useful in creating or choosing an appropriate definition of gifted is to ask ourselves a series of questions such as those that appear in Exhibit 1-1. When these questions have been answered to the satisfaction of those involved in the initial stages of planning, it is possible to progress to the next stage of program development—the identification procedures.

SUMMARY

In this chapter three important areas were stressed. The historical development of the gifted movement was presented first. Important in this section of the chapter was the understanding that giftedness is not a recent phenomenon but rather a concept that has been thought about throughout the ages. The concept of giftedness was initially thought about in more philosophical or rationalistic terms; however, as the desire to measure human potential led to scientific inquiry in testing, so, too, the gifted movement focused on the use of quantifiable data to measure giftedness. Throughout the testing movement, intelligence was viewed more as a global ability, both fixed and unchanging; however, through continued research of such individuals as Spearman, Thurstone, and Guilford, the intellect was unveiled as far more complex than had been previously thought.

In the second section of this chapter, a chronology and comparison of the definitions of giftedness were discussed. Evident from the chronology and com-

Exhibit 1-1 Questions Related to Gifted-Definition Selection

Question	Yes	No
Does this definition express the beliefs/ opinions of the program organizers?		
Would this definition tend to favor any specific cultural/socioeconomic group?		
Does this definition coincide with the district, state, or federal program guidelines being followed?		
Does this definition include or suggest any specific procedures or measures of identification?		
Does this definition have the support of those who will implement the program?		

parison was the important notion that the early perceptions of giftedness focused exclusively on IQ. While that is still somewhat true today, there has been a gradual broadening of the definition that enables individuals to display their giftedness in other dimensions and areas.

Intelligence has always been the focal point of the gifted movement. To understand current happenings in gifted education and the direction in which it is headed, it is necessary, historically, to look back at the changing notion of intelligence and its impact on the gifted movement. Those engaged in educating the gifted should have a fuller view of the gifted movement so they can more readily see how they fit into this emerging picture.

REFERENCES

Anastasi, A. Heredity, environment and the question "how." *Psychological Review*, 1958, *65*, 197-208.

Anastasi, A. *Psychological testing*. New York: Collier-Macmillan Publishing Co., Inc., 1976.

Binet, A., & Simon, T. Methodes nouvelles pour le diagnostic du niveau intellectuel des anormaux. *L'Année Psychologique*, 1905, *11*, 191-244.

DeHaan, R. F., & Havighurst, R. J. *Educating gifted children*. Chicago: University of Chicago Press, 1957.

Divesta, F. J., & Thompson, G. G. *Educational psychology, instruction and behavioral change*. New York: Appleton-Century-Crofts, 1970.

Education for the gifted: Fifty-seventh yearbook of the National Society for the Study of Education, Part II. Chicago: University of Chicago Press, 1958.

Flavell, J. H. *Cognitive development.* Englewood Cliffs, N.J.: Prentice-Hall, 1977.

Galton, F. *Inquiries into human faculty and its development.* London: Macmillan, 1883.

Guilford, J. P. *The nature of human intelligence.* New York: McGraw-Hill Book Company, 1967.

Guilford, J. P. Three faces of intellect. *American Psychologist,* 1959, *14,* 469-479.

Guilford, J. P., & Hoepfner, R. *The analysis of intelligence.* New York: McGraw-Hill Book Company, 1971.

Inhelder, B. Memory and intelligence in the child. In D. Elkind & J.H. Flavell (Eds.), *Studies in cognitive development: Essays in honor of Jean Piaget.* New York: Oxford University Press, 1969.

Lucito, L. Gifted children. In L. Dunn (Ed.), *Exceptional children in the schools.* New York: Holt, Rinehart, & Winston, 1963.

Marland, S. *Education of the gifted and talented.* Report to the Congress of the United States by the U.S. Commissioner of Education. Washington, D.C.: U.S. Government Printing Office, 1972.

Meeker, M., & Meeker, R. *Structure of the intellect-learning abilities test.* El Segundo, Calif.: SOI Institute, 1976.

Nettleship, R. L. The four stages of intelligence. In A. Sesonske (Ed.), *Plato's republic.* Belmont, Calif.: Wadsworth Publishing Company, 1966.

Piaget, J. *The origins of intelligence in children* (M. Cook, trans.). New York: International Universities Press, 1952.

Raven, J. C. *Guide to the Standard Progressive Matrices: Sets A B C D and E.* London: H. K. Lewis, 1956.

Renzulli, J. S. What makes giftedness? *Phi Delta Kappan,* 1978, *60,* 180-184.

Spearman, C. General intelligence—objectively determined and measured. *American Journal of Psychology,* 1904, *15,* 201-293.

Terman, L. M. *Mental and physical traits of a thousand gifted children.* Stanford, Calif.: Stanford University Press, 1925.

Thurstone, L. L. Primary mental abilities. *Psychometric Monographs,* No. 1, 1938.

Torrance, E. P. *Torrance Tests of Creative Thinking: Norms–technical manual.* Lexington, Mass.: Personnel Press, 1966. (Revised, 1974.)

Witty, P. (Ed.). *The gifted child.* Boston: D.C. Heath, 1951.

Chapter 2

Identifying the Gifted

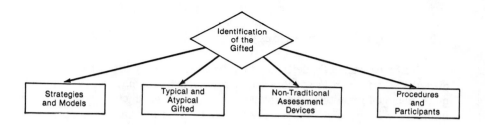

Now that the historical groundwork for the adventure into gifted programming has been laid, it is time to take the first step from paper to practice. That first step involves the determination of how those designated by program definition will be identified. The ultimate success of any gifted program must relate directly to the population of learners it will serve. Careful consideration, organization, and implementation of identification procedures, therefore, will keep the program on course to its goal of more effective education for gifted learners.

Within this chapter, several aspects of the identification process will be outlined and analyzed, including strategies and models of identification, materials and sources of information employed within these strategies, and current controversies and questions about the identification process.

STRATEGIES AND MODELS IN THE IDENTIFICATION PROCESS

The information accumulated and analyzed to make decisions about who will participate in gifted programs falls into two general categories: objective and subjective data. Objective data are those types of information of a test nature that can be quantified and are frequently standardized or norm-referenced. Sources of objective data most often employed to distinguish the gifted from the nongifted include group and individual intelligence tests, achievement tests or test batteries, and academic grade-point averages. Subjective measures, on the other hand, include behavioral checklists, recommendations, and referrals that are characterized by personal judgments about an individual's performance and capabilities.

These objective and subjective categories of information can be employed singly or in combination to produce three strategies or approaches to the identification process. In the first strategy, emphasis is solely on objective information. Conversely, the second strategy employs only subjective data in locating the gifted population, while the third strategy looks at elements from both the objective and subjective domains in the selection of the gifted population. The various subjective and objective components most often applied in identification procedures are detailed in Table 2-1. How might a program be set up under these three strategies and what are the advantages and disadvantages of each?

Objective Information Strategy

In this first strategy, the definition of gifted, as previously explained, is often an operational definition in which a score, percentage, ranking, or other similarly quantifiable information is specifically referred to and in which the source of such information is specified. Examples of objective type information are presented below.

Sources of Objective Information

Individual Intelligence Test Scores. Intelligence tests can be classified as either individually or group-administered measures. The most widely used and most respected individually administered intelligence tests are the *Stanford-Binet* and the *Wechsler Intelligence Scales*. The *Wechsler Intelligence Scales* include the *Wechsler Preschool and Primary Intelligence Scale (WPPSI)*, the *Wechsler Intelligence Scale for Children-Revised (WISC-R)*, and the *Wechsler Adult Intelligence Scale (WAIS)*. Within recent years there has been much controversy over the reliance on these intelligence tests for placement of students in special programs. Much of this concern has focused on the behaviors measured and on the interpretation and the suitability of these instruments, especially for diverse populations. Because of the importance of these instruments in the identification process and because of the growing controversy related to their use, these individual intelligence tests will be considered in depth later in this chapter.

Group Intelligence Tests. The second type of intelligence measures are those that are administered in a group setting. Examples of such tests are *Kuhlman Anderson, Otis Lennon,* and the *Primary Mental Abilities Test.* When large numbers of students need to be screened for possible inclusion into the gifted program, the group IQ test is a frequently selected assessment device.

Although these instruments provide a relatively quick method of assessing intelligence, there are some serious limitations to such tests. One major difficulty

Table 2-1 Overview of Procedural Components in Gifted Education

	OBJECTIVE					SUBJECTIVE				BACKGROUND INFORMATION
	Traditional Intelligence Tests	Culture-fair Intelligence Tests	Tests of Creative Ability	Academic Achievement Tests	Behavioral Checklists	Teacher Nomination	Parent Nomination	Peer Nomination	Self Nomination	
Initial Emphasis	✓	+	✓ +	✓	✓ +	✓ +	✓ +	✓ +	✓ +	✓ +
Comprehensive Information Strategies										
1. Weighted	xx		✓ **	xx +	✓ **	✓ **	✓ **	✓ **	✓ **	xx **
2. Alternate	xx	**	✓ **	✓	✓ **	xx +	✓ **	xx +	+ xx	xx **
3. Equivalent	✓ +		✓ +	+	✓ +	✓ +	✓ +	✓ +	✓ +	✓ +

✓ Information is considered in identification decision

xx More emphasis placed on this factor in identification

+ Information is considered in identification decision of culturally different

** More emphasis placed on this factor for cultural different

with group intelligence tests is their heavy reliance on proficient reading ability and competence in standard English. As a result, group intelligence tests become poor measures of intelligence for children who may be underachievers in reading or who may be from culturally diverse backgrounds. While the authors do not advocate the use of such group tests, there are a number of important questions program planners must consider if it becomes necessary to use such devices:

- Do any of the students have reading difficulties that will influence their performance on such tests?
- Do any of the students have difficulty in concentrating or attending to a task when working independently?
- Are there any students who demonstrate classroom behaviors that would seriously affect their performance in this type of test-taking situation?
- Are there any students whose cultural experiences lie outside the realm of experiences assessed by this test?

Achievement Tests. Achievement tests are periodically administered to students to determine specific knowledge or skill acquisition within various curricular areas. Success in standardized achievement tests, as in group intelligence tests, depends largely on the students' competence in standard English. Because the individuals' reading ability influences their performance on such tests, it is difficult to get an accurate view of ability. Another concern in using standardized group achievement tests, as with any group-administered test, is the inability of the examiner to effectively observe students' behavior and adequately assess attitudes during the test-taking session.

Academic Achievement. Some gifted children will be easily identified because of their outstanding academic achievements. However, there are a large number of gifted children who are not identifiable by their school performance. Several factors may account for this. First, certain gifted learners come to school with experiential backgrounds markedly different from the norm. Because of the experiential gap, they may not be able to demonstrate their potential in academic-related areas. Second, many gifted learners "turned off" by the educational irrelevancy of the curriculum will "mentally drop out," losing interest in school and often refusing to demonstrate their abilities. For these individuals, a "motivational" gap may prevent their accurate assessment by means of academic achievement. If academic achievement is to be used as a criterion for identification, it is necessary to evaluate those factors described above when making decisions for placement.

Culture-Fair Instruments. Various instruments have been developed to assess the potential of children who come from economically or culturally different backgrounds. These instruments are designed to minimize cultural or linguistic influences. Examples of these tests are discussed in the section on atypical gifted learners.

Tests for Creativity. The most widely used of these nontraditional measures of creativity are the *Torrance Tests of Creative Thinking*. These tests, which assess auditory, verbal, and pictorial areas, are designed to measure the divergent-productive abilities of the learner, an area frequently overlooked by more conventional instruments.

A Closer Look at Intelligence Tests

Currently accepted in the field of intelligence testing is the notion that intelligence tests measure different behaviors, each of which represents different mental abilities. There have been several attempts to anaylze these behaviors that appear in intelligence instruments and to determine the mental operations required for their successful completion. For example, Newland (1971) describes intelligence test items in two categories: (1) *process items,* which are fundamental psychological operations only slightly influenced by experiential background; and (2) *product items,* which require the application of accumulated knowledge. Newland's process-product categories are similar to the *fluid* and *crystallized* terms coined by Cattell (1963).

While it may seem obvious to the reader that intelligence tests do measure different behaviors, the knowledge of what specific behaviors are measured has important implications for education of the gifted. Very often in education we become so overwhelmed and concerned with the cumulative test scores that we lose sight of the fact that the learners had to demonstrate certain behaviors in order to obtain those scores. It is the analysis of these specific behaviors that enables diagnosticians to make more accurate inferences about a learner's performance and more accurate decisions about the individual's potential. Knowing the nature of the test items will also enable planners of gifted programs to select tests or portions of tests that are appropriate for the population for which the gifted is a member. In addition, if traditional-type tests must be used for selection of the gifted, knowing this information will enable diagnosticians to make appropriate recommendations for any future testing that may be required.

Few difficulties arise in the interpretation of a student's test profile when all of the student's scores fall neatly into the gifted range. However, such is not the case when the individual produces scores with wide discrepancies among the various behaviors. In these cases, correlating background information with an item analysis assists the diagnostician in understanding the reasons for the student's performance.

The following example will demonstrate how an item analysis might assist in making future educational decisions about a particular individual.

Case 1

Maria is a nine-year-old, third-grade child who was raised in a bilingual home. She was born in Italy and started school there where she studied English. During her first grade, Maria's father was transferred to the United States. She completed first grade in the United States, but the following year was retained in first grade.

Maria's father has minimal English skills and prefers to speak Italian at home. Maria's mother was born in America but speaks fluent Italian. English is used infrequently in the home, especially when the parents are communicating.

Background information reveals that Maria spends a great deal of time with her mother because her father often works nights and weekends. Maria's mother has difficulty devoting time specifically to Maria since she also has a two-year-old infant to care for. Maria has some friends, but because of her insecurity with the English language she does not spend much time with them.

Maria is presently reading at the first-grade level, with demonstrated difficulty in acquiring and utilizing word attack skills. Maria's teacher reports that she gets along well in school but does not seem to have the same background or perspective as other children her age. Informal assessment indicated that Maria tends to be very shy and is reluctant to enter conversation.

Maria's regular classroom teacher indicated that Maria enjoys working with her hands and demonstrates ingenuity and creative abilities.

The administration of the *WISC-R* produced the profile shown in Figure 2-1. Maria's verbal and performance scores were 108 and 128 respectively. Her overall IQ was 119.

It is evident from the case study presented above that due to the wide discrepancies in Maria's scores it is more difficult to make a clear-cut decision as to whether she is gifted. Certainly her scores do indicate a potential for giftedness.

In order to gain a fuller understanding of Maria's performance, a comparison of her background information to her subtests scores should be made. A closer analysis of the subtest scores indicates that Maria has difficulty in tasks that rely more heavily on experiential background and verbal abilities, that is, information, similarities, and vocabulary subtests. On the other hand, Maria's strengths were reflected in an extremely high capability in math, as well as in areas requiring nonverbal reasoning ability, visual-motor coordination, and planning ability. Based on the wide discrepancies in Maria's subtest scores, an appropriate recommendation would be to retest with an alternative instrument, such as the *Raven's Progressive Matrices* or the *Columbia Mental Maturity Scale,* which requires less verbal ability and experiential background.

Figure 2-1 Sample WISC-R Profile

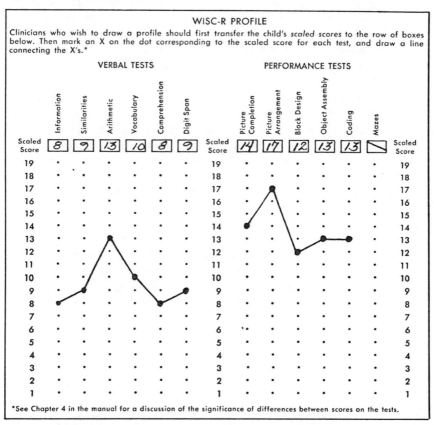

Source: Reprinted from the *WISC-R Intelligence Test* by David Wechsler by permission of the Psychological Corporation, New York, © 1974.

As has been demonstrated through the previous example, the analysis of intelligence test items can be a valuable tool in making recommendations about placement in gifted programs. Salvia and Ysseldyke (1978) identify the following 13 types of behaviors sampled by intelligence tests. These can be used to assist planners of gifted programs in making appropriate test selection and placement decisions:

1. *Discrimination.* Figural, symbolic, or semantic discriminators are presented in which the individual must find the item that differs from the others.

2. *Generalizations*. In these items the individual is presented with a stimulus and various choices from which he or she must choose the response most like the stimulus. This may be presented at the figural, symbolic, or semantic level.

3. *Motor behaviors*. These include walking, throwing objects, and similar behavior at the lower levels and visual-motor ability at higher levels of difficulty.

4. *General information*. The general knowledge acquired by the individual is assessed by these item types.

5. *Vocabulary*. The forms of these items include definitions of words, identifying pictures, or reading definitions and selecting the appropriate word.

6. *Induction*. These items require the individual to induce a general principle after observing a series of examples.

7. *Comprehension*. The individual is asked to demonstrate an understanding of directions, societal customs, or reading material.

8. *Sequencing*. The student must identify the progressive sequence pattern and identify the correct response that continues the pattern.

9. *Detail recognition*. Items require the individual to attend to details such as locating missing parts in pictures or to details involved in drawing a figure.

10. *Analogies*. In these items the learner is given three stimuli (A,B,C). A and B are related. The student must locate the item that relates to C in the same way as A and B relate.

11. *Abstract reasoning*. These items sometimes involve interpreting the meaning of a proverb or solving an arithmetic problem.

12. *Memory*. These items assess the ability of an individual to repeat a sequence of digits or stimulus sentences, to reproduce geometric designs, or to reconstruct the essential meanings of paragraphs and stories.

13. *Pattern completion*. This type of item requires the student to complete the pattern or matrix, identifying the choice that completes the missing part.

Owing to the the increased workloads of school psychologists and the time involved in the administration of either the *Stanford-Binet* or *Wechsler Intelligence Scales,* it is highly unrealistic to assume that these instruments could be employed as screening devices for giftedness on any large scale. This is especially true when the number of students to be evaluated increases or the number of qualified diagnosticians decreases. One alternative approach in such instances would be the administration of the *Slosson Intelligence Test.* This instrument is often substituted for other more reliable and valid measures of intelligence for two reasons: (1) it is easier to administer than the *WISC-R* or *Stanford-Binet* and can be given by regular school personnel and (2) it can be given in less time than other individual intelligence tests.

Again, it must be cautioned that the *Slosson* test and comparable instruments are not as valid or reliable for assessing intelligence as the *Stanford-Binet* or *Wechsler Intelligence Scales*. In addition, tests such as the *Slosson* primarily measure verbal skills and their results are highly influenced by the individual's background experiences. If the *Slosson* or similar instruments are used for selection of students for the gifted program, it will be beneficial to analyze the individual's responses, as was suggested for other IQ tests. Information on the *Slosson* item analysis is presented in Table 2-2.

By grouping the individual's positive and negative responses, the examiner can determine the pattern of strengths and weaknesses demonstrated. If, for example, the student does poorly on items that place a heavy emphasis on background of experience (i.e., information, comprehension, and vocabulary) but shows strength on items such as arithmetic, visual-motor, digit span, or memory for sentences, then it may be necessary to administer a less traditional intelligence test to determine potential.

Advantages of Objective Information Strategy

The advantages of strict reliance on objective measures lie in their definitiveness, their level of acceptance, the streamlining of the identification process that seemingly results, and the factor of their compliance with many state and federal guidelines.

Definitiveness. One of the advantages of an objective information strategy would appear to be that either the score, rank, percentage, or other criterion is attained and the individual included in the gifted program, or it is not attained and the individual is not included. From the administrative point of view, it seems that this might make the inclusion or exclusion of the individual student more justifiable. The decision, in essence, is made by the score and not by the person.

Acceptance. It often appears in our educational system that quoting the name of a test or producing a test score adds credibility to the process or procedure of which it is a part, at times regardless of what the test purports to measure or the reliability of the instrument. This same phenomenon exists in gifted programming as well. The program that specifies the employment of a popular or well-known standardized measure may well garner more support than the program that employs a lesser known objective instrument or more experimental, more subjective procedure for identification.

Streamlining. When the results of group testing serve as the main criteria for program participation, the identification process may seem to require less time and cost investment. Although this factor of time and cost differential is an often-quoted reason for the dependency on group-standardized measures in the identification process, recent research by Renzulli and Smith (1977) has demonstrated that the cost differential between traditional and more case-study identification

Table 2-2 Analysis of Slosson Intelligence Test Items

Item Type	What the Item Measures	Sample Item
Information (I)	General information in long-term memory from background experiences and school learning	What is paper made of? How many days in a week?
Comprehension (C)	Understanding of daily experiences and displaying common sense	What is the principal kind of work done by a pharmacist?
Arithmetic (A)	Arithmetic reasoning and abstract concept formation skills	If I cut an apple in half, how many pieces will I have?
Similarities and differences (SD)	Verbal reasoning and abstract concept formation skills	How is a submarine different from a fish? In what ways are a submarine and a fish the same or alike?
Vocabulary (V)	Ability with word definitions and expressive language	What does "tremendous" mean?
Digit span (DS)	Auditory sequential memory and attention to task	Say these numbers forward for me. . . 9 3 5 2 8 6.
Auditory memory of sentences (AMS)	Auditory memory of contextual information	Say exactly what I say: "I go to the store to buy bread, butter, and milk."
Visual-motor (VM)	Visual-motor integration and eye-hand coordination skill	Draw a kite for me like this. . . .

Source: Reprinted from the Item Analysis for the Slosson Intelligence Test by Slosson Education Publications, Inc., East Aurora, N.Y., by permission of the publisher.

methodologies may not be as significant as previously believed. It would appear, however, that the effort needed to assemble the results of group tests and to list the names of those who meet the established criteria may be less than that of procedures employing more subjective data analysis.

Compliance. For many school programs, the inclusion of an objective test measure is necessary to comply with district or even state guidelines for gifted programming. It is, therefore, important that the gifted program guidelines, if any exist, be carefully considered and satisfied when procedures are being outlined. However, these guidelines do most often allow some degree of flexibility in the selection of objective measures even when the inclusion of such objective data is required. Furthermore, some school districts find a percentage cut-off level on a quantifiable measure useful to comply with the current level of funding available from the state or federal government.

Disadvantages of Objective Information Strategy

Even with the advantages just described in the use of the objective information strategy, there are several disadvantages of this approach that must also be considered. Among these advantages are test availability, test selection, test administration, and the nature of the testing process.

Test Availability. For certain segments of the population from whom our gifted must be drawn, there are few, if any, appropriate or accurate measurement instruments available. There are few objective measures, for example, that have been constructed for, or normed on, culturally different or subdominant cultural groups. This shortage of appropriate testing instruments is even more acute for certain subdominant cultural groups, such as Native Americans and Asian Americans. Suitable measures are also in short supply for use with the young, preschool child, although the need for early identification of gifted potential is well documented in the literature.

Test Selection. Another problem arises in the method of test selection that might operate in some school systems. How are the measures to be used, how are the sources of objective data to be chosen, and what are the criteria for their selection? All major decisions in the development of gifted programming should consist of criteria that should be satisfied by any instrument under consideration (see Exhibit 2-1). Too often, measures are employed in the identification process primarily because they are already available. Accessibility, in itself, may serve effectively as one criterion for test selection, but it should not become the single determining factor.

Test Administration. No matter how carefully chosen a particular test or objective instrument may be, the information derived from it may be of no use if the test is not accurately administered. If special training is required by the

Exhibit 2-1 Sample Test Selection Criteria

1. What does this test purport to measure?
2. For what ages is this test appropriate?
3. For what grades is this test appropriate?
4. What is the format of the objective measure?
   a. Group or individual
   b. Norm-referenced or criterion-referenced
   c. Verbal or nonverbal
   d. Supply or select response pattern
5. Who can administer this test?
6. How much time is required in administration?
7. How are the results reported?
8. Did the standardization sample have similar acculturation to the population being tested?
9. Is this test appropriate for the identification of the gifted (according to established definition)?
10. What is the cost per pupil of this testing procedure?

examiner, then such requirements must be adhered to. Lesser problems may arise in the area of test administration, however. Among these problems are such concerns as:

- Was there sufficient privacy or quiet during the test?

- Was there adequate space and time allotted?

- Were the directions, especially of standardized instruments, followed specifically?

Many factors may arise during test administration that could have an effect on the test results and yet that are not under the control of the examiner.

Nature of the Testing Process. What is important to remember in the objective information strategy is that should an objective instrument be carefully chosen on the basis of specified criteria, and should the instrument be carefully administered, the results may still not be accurate for some individuals. No test is totally accurate or without its limitations. There is always error present in measurement. In addition, the test results may be affected by unreliability of the test or a particular individual's physical or emotional condition at the time of testing, cultural background, attitude toward the test or the tester, or any number of other intervening factors. Therefore, to place total reliance on such test results to determine inclusion or exclusion in programs for the gifted may be a questionable practice, in general, and for certain individuals, such as the culturally different, the practice may be indefensible. The following five suggestions may lessen the severity of this problem, however.

1. It is crucial that the most appropriate instrument be selected with regard to the individual's age, learning modality, grade, and cultural heritage. The instrument selected should have been standardized on a population similar in acculturation to that being tested.
2. A positive relationship should exist between the tester and the testee prior to examination. There should be time set aside to establish a working rapport between the examiner and the individual to be tested when unfamiliarity or the lack of a positive relationship is a factor.
3. Because some individuals, such as the culturally different, may be mistrusting of others' motives in the testing situation, it is important that we explain the reasons for testing to the individual when maturity is not a factor.
4. It is important that parents have some understanding of what is taking place in the testing process and that all permissions for testing that need to be secured have indeed been obtained prior to examination.
5. Because of the risks involved in mislabeling any child on the basis of one test score or result, decisions made on identification should, whenever possible, be based on information from more than one source.

Subjective Information Strategy

In the second strategy that can be employed in the identification of gifted learners, emphasis is placed on information of a subjective nature. A program established under such a strategy could include information accumulated from one or several of the following sources.

Sources of Subjective Information

Behavioral or Observational Checklists. The literature of the gifted is inundated with checklists or delineations of behaviors that might serve as indications of giftedness. These checklists assist the observer by calling attention to behavioral manifestations of giftedness that might be present within the context of natural activities rather than in contrived test settings. The Alexander and Muia checklist (1980) is a compilation of many behaviors frequently appearing within the literature (see Exhibit 2-2). In the Alexander and Muia checklist, behaviors have been organized into ten distinct categories entitled ''Positive Performance Criteria.'' The student's behavior is scored for the presence or absence of the specific end products or outputs listed. A total can be derived for each category and compared with scores of other individuals or with established criteria. Renzulli and Hartman (1971), using similar compilation procedures, have produced a behavioral checklist that has been widely used in subjective information gathering. (See Appendix A.)

Exhibit 2-2 The Alexander-Muia Behavioral Checklist

Positive Performance Criteria	Creativity and Creative End Products
1. Ability to communicate ideas and feelings by verbal and nonverbal means	__Has command of a large vocabulary __Uses words fluently and creatively __Dramatizes through use of body language and facial expressions __Is quick to respond __Demonstrates a flair for dramatic or oral presentations __Is eager to relate experiences __Expresses ideas with clarity
2. Ability to interpret ideas and feelings communicated through verbal and nonverbal means	__Is sensitive to the thoughts and ideas of others __Can interpret body language or facial expressions __Displays sympathy or empathy towards others __Appears sensitive to the discrepancy of behavior in others __Appraises quickly and frankly new and unfamiliar people or situations
3. Adaptive behaviors characteristic of cultural group	__Displays a keen sense of humor __Demonstrates "survival" skills by manipulating positive forces and overcoming negative forces in the environment __Is resourceful and can come up quickly with an alternative __Possesses a sense of adventure __Learns from experiences and seldom repeats mistakes __Shows a degree of flexibility when situations call for change __Accepts responsibility for actions
4. Heightened interest in the arts	__Demonstrates an awareness of and appreciation for the environment __Is involved in a variety of hobbies or has a broad range of interests __Appreciates various music and art forms __Reads avidly in a wide area of subjects

Exhibit 2-2 continued

	__Produces creative visual expressions
	__Uses color and form dramatically or uniquely in art
5. Physical capability and adaptability	__Has fewer physical and sensory defects or has compensated adequately for whatever defects are present
	__Is physically robust, stronger and healthier in appearance.
	__Has well-developed psychomotor skills
	__Has received recognition for physical accomplishments
	__Displays a great deal of energy and vitality
6. Emotional/social leadership	__Manifests self-confidence
	__Has a position of leadership within cultural groups
	__In uncontrolled situations, assumes authority naturally
	__Displays emotional maturity
	__Demonstrates social ingenuity
	__Is generally gregarious, outgoing, and friendly
	__Has an individualistic personality that stands out from the group
7. Appropriate application of convergent/divergent processes	__Arrives at a logical conclusion based on given information
	__Sees the plausible yet unique alternatives of a given situation
	__More adept at selecting, organizing, and retrieving information
	__Able to expand information beyond what is given
	__Displays a keen sense of historical time and can sequentially organize information
	__Pays close attention to detail in the analysis process
	__Can transfer learning readily from one situation to the next

Exhibit 2-2 continued

	__Is able to formulate the similarities/differences, the comparison/contrasts, and the causes/effects of objects, ideas, and situations
8. Persistence or commitment to task	__Establishes goals that are realistic although challenging __Demonstrates determination in the fulfillment of goals; tenacity __Is self-disciplined, independent __Displays persistent curiosity __Has a long attention span
9. Energetic response to challenging experiences	__Produces works that have a freshness, vitality, and uniqueness __Often initiates the search for information __Desires to learn rapidly __Creates new ideas, substances, processes, and mechanical devices (inventor) __Is willing to take a risk of failure in new or unfamiliar situations
10. Ability in process-oriented curriculum	__May excel in science and math or other "process-related" curriculum __May require less routine drill when learning new skills __Seems aware of aspects in the environment that go unnoticed by others __Displays some amount of skepticism with new ideas or situations __Asks appropriate, thought-provoking questions __Evaluates carefully based on accurate observation

Source: Reprinted from Gifted Reading Programs: Uncovering the Hidden Potential, *Reading Horizons,* 1980, *20,* 306-309, by Patricia Alexander and Joseph A. Muia by permission of Reading Horizons, Western Michigan University, Kalamazoo, Michigan, © 1980.

Teacher Recommendations. Perhaps the most controversial and yet one of the most frequently used sources of subjective data for gifted programs are teacher recommendations. It was noted, for example, that should teacher recommendations be the principal means of identification, approximately 50 percent of the gifted would go unidentified (Alvino & Wieler, 1979). Gear (1975) has stated that teacher recommendations can become more effective and efficient sources of subjective data with training.

Parent Nominations. Within some school programs, the opinions of parents are solicited in the identification process. Such nominations may consist of merely submitting the name of the learner as a potential candidate for the gifted program or may request more elaborate information regarding the behaviors the parent(s) feels the learner appropriately displays that facilitated the nomination.

Peer Nominations. There is increasing support in the literature (Bernal, 1978; Bernal & Reyna, 1975; Renzulli & Smith, 1977) for the inclusion of peer nominations in the identification process. These nominations seem to prove especially helpful in the location of gifted students from subdominant cultural groups.

Self-Nominations. Gifted learners can aid in the identification process by evaluating their own abilities and capabilities in whatever field they may feel is appropriate. Such self-nomination should be an encouraged procedure at upper educational levels.

Advantages of the Subjective Information Strategy

Among the advantages of this subjective information procedure for gifted identification, consideration should be given to the following factors: personal awareness, breadth of information, situational appropriateness, and cultural appropriateness.

Personal Awareness. While test data generally draw their information in an impersonal, objective way, subjective information is drawn directly from the behaviors of individuals operating within their normal environment. Such information is generally collected, as well, by someone who has had previous personal contact with the person being observed or considered.

Breadth of Information. If we consider giftedness as consisting of three interrelated dimensions (see Figure 1-5) of inputs, cognitive or intellectual structure, and outputs, then it is the third area of outputs from which information for the gifted identification is drawn. In most objective measures, only convergent-thought products are evaluated. In addition, most of these convergent productions are of school-related information. One advantage of the subjective information strategy is that it allows for evaluation of products from more divergent-thought areas and of behaviors not directly related to the school experience.

Situational Appropriateness. Subjective information has the advantage of being accumulated from the behaviors of individuals who can be observed and evaluated in a variety of situations and roles, over extended periods of time. These factors may lessen the effects of temporary physical or emotional difficulties that could threaten the validity of objective test data.

Cultural Appropriateness. Subjective data collected by members of the same cultural group have the distinct advantage of describing the individual's behaviors within cultural context by someone generally capable of evaluating the appropriateness of behaviors with regard to that culture. Because behavior patterns, value systems, and language do differ to some extent from culture to culture, it is important to obtain information from sources sensitive to such differences. Bernal (1974), Renzulli & Smith (1977), and Gay (1978) among others have mentioned this need for soliciting information from individuals with the knowledge or the cultural sensitivity to make judgments about others of varying cultural backgrounds.

Disadvantages of Subjective Information Strategy

Even with these seeming advantages, there are several limitations of the subjective information strategy that need to be addressed. These limitations include the areas of accuracy, consistency, justifiability, and effort.

Accuracy. Probably the biggest question that can be leveled at the subjective information strategy is whether such information is, indeed, accurate. As pointed out previously, the inaccuracy of teacher recommendations is legendary, and even with suitable training such recommendations can still be considered questionable. Not only are many gifted students overlooked by nomination recommendation procedures, but many nongifted students are recommended possibly for such reasons as their appearance or deportment.

Consistency. It is almost impossible to ensure that the judgments made by individuals as part of the gifted identification procedure will be consistent from student to student, class to class, or year to year, even when these judgments are made on the basis of specified criteria. Behavioral checklists may eliminate some of the difficulty in this matter, but even their application cannot ensure consistency of judgment.

Justifiability. When the time comes to support the decisions made about the inclusion or exclusion of individuals in gifted programs, it may be difficult to justify decisions made solely on the basis of subjective data. If appropriate and accurate objective instruments are not available for the particular individual or group being evaluated, however, then the use of subjective information may not be justifiable but warranted.

Effort. It would seem that the amount of effort required to decide what type of subjective information to collect, who should supply such information, how such information should be analyzed, and who should make the final decisions may be more extensive than the effort expended in the objective information strategy. Further research is required to determine if this is, indeed, an accurate assumption.

Comprehensive-Information Strategy

In essence, the comprehensive-information strategy allows the judgments made in the identification process to be based on data gathered from a variety of sources, both objective and subjective in nature. While the disadvantages of both the objective and subjective information strategies will need to be considered as a consequence of this combination, the weaknesses of one approach may be offset by the advantages of the other. The comprehensive information strategy may take several forms, which will be briefly described. These forms include an equivalent, weighted, or alternative-measure procedure. An example of the comprehensive-information strategy is provided in Figure 2-2.

Figure 2-2 A Model for the Identification Process of Gifted Learners from Dominant and Subdominant Cultural Groups

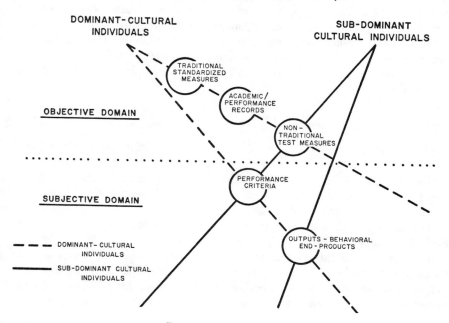

Equivalent Form

In the equivalent form of the comprehensive-information strategy, all individuals who take part in the identification process are subjected to the same subjective and objective measures. The results of these measures are collected and analyzed in the same way for all those evaluated. Decisions on who will or will not participate in a gifted program are then made.

Weighted Form

All individuals who undergo assessment in the comprehensive-information, weighted-form strategy will be evaluated by the same subjective and objective measures. However, particular measures and portions of measures receive different emphasis or weight in the decision-making process. For example, for some subdominant cultural individuals the subjective information obtained from behavioral checklists may receive more numerical emphasis than the results of any objective, standardized instrument. It should be determined before evaluation how much numerical emphasis should be placed on the various types of information collected and under what conditions different scoring procedures should be evoked.

Baldwin (1978) has developed a widely used weighted matrix (see Exhibit 2-3). The score ranges for each weighting are determined by subtracting the median score for the population from the upper limits and then dividing by four. For example, in the exhibit the upper limit of an administered achievement test was the 95th percentile with the median at the 75th percentile. When the difference of 20 is divided by 4, the point spread for each weighting becomes 5. The procedure is continued for each of the assessment items. Students' performances are then plotted, and the number of checks for each column is multipled by the weights and then totaled.

Alternative-Measure Form

In the alternative-measure form of the comprehensive-information strategy, two choices can be made in terms of providing differing procedures for specific segments of the school population. When a diverse segment of the population exists, the choice may be made to forego one aspect of the identification process for that particular segment only. A second choice would be to substitute a more appropriate and perhaps less traditional measure for one that is being administered to the general population (see Figure 2-2).

As is evident from this illustration, the alternative-measure form strategy shifts the emphasis for subdominant cultural individuals from standardized test scores to evaluation of such performance criteria as those described in the Alexander-Muia Behavioral Checklist. The various end products of these performance criteria

Exhibit 2-3 Baldwin Identification Matrix

Baldwin Identification Matrix (BIM)

ADAPTED FOR USE BY: _____

DATE _____

STUDENT _____ | SCHOOL _____

AGE _____ GRADE _____ SEX _____ | SCHOOL DISTRICT: _____

ASSESSMENT ITEMS	SCORES					
	5	4	3	2	1	B·NA
1. Standardized Intelligence Test	140+	130-139	120-129 ✓	110-119	100-109	
2. Achievement Test Composite Score	95%ile	90-94%ile	85-89%ile ✓	80-84%ile	75-79%ile	
3. Achievement Test-Reading Score	Stan 9 ✓	Stan 8	Stan 7	Stan 6	Stan 5	
4. Achievement Test-Math Score	95%ile	90-94%ile	85-89%ile ✓	80-94%ile	75-79%ile	
5. Learning Scale Score	32 ✓	28-31	24-27	20-23	16-19	
6. Motivational Scale Score	36 ✓	32-35	28-31	24-27	16-23	
7. Creativity Scale Score	40 ✓	36-35	32-35	28-31	20-27	
8. Leadership Scale Score	40	36-39 ✓	32-35	28-31	20-27	
9. Various Teacher Recommendations	Superior	Very Good ✓	Good	Average	Below Average	
10. Psychomotor Ability		✓				
11. Peer Nominations		✓				
COLUMN TALLY OF CHECKS	4	4	3	0	0	
WEIGHT	x 5	x 4	x 3	x 2	x 1	
ADD ACROSS	20 +	16 +	9 +	0 +	0 =	
TOTAL SCORE	45					

© 1977

Source: Reprinted from *Educational Planning for the Gifted* by A. Baldwin, G. Gear, and L. Lucito (Eds.) by permission of The Council for Exceptional Children, Reston, Virginia, © 1978.

presented in the checklist can be used as a standard for identifying the gifted learner.

This approach has the benefit of not subjecting individuals to certain tests or measures that provide no useful or accurate information relevant to gifted identification.

BEHAVIORS OF TYPICAL AND ATYPICAL GIFTED

Important in the selection of any definition is the understanding of behaviors characteristic of the trait being evaluated. Giftedness, as Witty (1951) indicated, appears in many different forms in every cultural group at every level of society. Therefore, if schools are to provide educational programs that meet the needs of its gifted learners, then it will be essential that a definition of giftedness not only include those individuals who represent the dominant or mainstream culture but also include those who are economically, physically, emotionally, socially, or culturally different from the mainstream. Consequently, there are many behavioral characteristics that should be considered in the identification of typical and atypical gifted learners.

Behaviors of Typical Gifted

There have been numerous studies conducted that have identified the characteristics of gifted children. Terman's (1925) early research provided important insights into gifted learners. The findings of his studies showed that gifted learners were stronger and physically healthier than average learners, had a wide range of interests, and were very good in the areas of problem solving, organizing, and abstract thinking. In addition, Terman's research also indicated that gifted learners had more gifted siblings as well as fathers who had a higher occupational status. Since Terman's early studies, other researchers have confirmed the findings reported above (Bradley & Earp, 1970; Witty, 1951; Isaacs, 1971; Lucito, 1963; Barbe, 1965).

Following Terman's early research, there have been additional studies conducted by him and others that have expanded the list of behavioral manifestations of giftedness. For example, attributed to the gifted are good memories, curiosity, and excellent leadership abilities (Kirk, 1962; Terman, 1954). The gifted have also been found to possess superior intellectual capability and unusual creative abilities in such areas as mathematics, music, science, mechanics, and writing (Fliegler & Bish, 1959; Schermann, 1966; Torrance, 1962, 1965, 1970).

The similarities in behaviors among gifted learners are the basis for the many checklists that are present in the literature and that are frequently employed as a source of subjective identification data.

Although Terman's work has provided much of the foundation for behavioral analysis of the gifted, his labors have not been without their critics. Indeed, it can be argued that the methodology employed by Terman in his studies may have resulted in a population too culturally and economically restricted for valid comparison. Any serious analysis of gifted behaviors conducted in the future will need to survey, more adequately, the characteristics of the culturally and economically diverse as well.

In addition, the behaviors displayed by gifted learners must not always be of a positive nature. The uniqueness of the gifted can also produce difficulties in their adjustment to certain individuals and situations in their immediate surroundings, especially when values and perceptions of the gifted are brought into conflict. Seagoe (1974) has identified concomitant problems that may be associated with the gifted (see Table 2-3).

Table 2-3 Characteristics of the Gifted and Concomitant Problems

Characteristics	Concomitant Problems
Keen power of observation; naive receptivity; sense of the significant; willingness to examine the unusual	Possible gullibility
Power of abstraction, conceptualization, synthesis; interest in inductive learning and problem solving; pleasure in intellectual activity	Occasional resistance to direction; rejection or remission of detail
Interest in cause-effect relations, ability to see relationships; interest in applying concepts; love of truth	Difficulty in accepting the illogical
Liking for structure and order; liking for consistency, as in value systems, number systems, clocks, calendars	Invention of own systems, sometimes conflicting
Retentiveness	Dislike for routine and drill; need for early mastery of foundation skills
Verbal proficiency; large vocabulary; facility in expression; interest in reading; breadth of information in advanced areas	Need for specialized reading vocabulary early; parent resistance to reading; escape into verbalism
Questioning attitude, intellectual curiosity, inquisitive mind; intrinsic motivation	Lack of early home or school stimulation
Power of critical thinking; skepticism, evaluative testing; self-criticism and self-checking	Critical attitude toward others; discouragement from self-criticism

Table 2-3 continued

Creativeness and inventiveness; liking for new ways of doing things; interest in creating, brainstorming, freewheeling	Rejection of the known; need to invent for oneself
Power of concentration; intense attention that excludes all else; long attention span	Resistance to interruption
Persistent, goal-directed behavior	Stubbornness
Sensitivity, intuitiveness, empathy for others; need for emotional support and a sympathetic attitude	Need for success and recognition; sensitivity to criticism; vulnerability to peer group rejection
High energy, alertness, eagerness; periods of intense voluntary effort preceding invention	Frustration with inactivity and absence of progress
Independence in work and study; preference for individualized work; self-reliance; need for freedom of movement and action	Parent and peer group pressures and nonconformity; problems of rejection and rebellion
Versatility and virtuosity; diversity of interests and abilities; many hobbies; proficiency in art forms such as music and drawing	Lack of homogeneity in group work; need for flexibility and individualization; need for help in exploring and developing interests; need to build basic competencies in major interests
Friendliness and outgoingness	Need for peer group relations in many types of groups; problems in developing social leadership

Source: Reprinted from Some Learning Characteristics of Gifted Children by May V. Seagoe, in R. Martinson (Ed.), *The Identification of the Gifted and Talented,* by permission of the Office of Ventura County Superintendent of Schools, Ventura, California, © 1974.

Behaviors of Atypical Gifted

In the preceding section, the characteristics of those gifted individuals whose cultural, physical, and economic backgrounds more closely approximate the norm were considered. However, the diversity in gifted populations is as great as the diversity of the general population from which these learners come. In much of what we do in gifted education, we collapse gifted subjects into a homogeneous group and ignore the factor of diversification. Working under this assumption of homogeneity, we choose testing instruments, select materials, and plan curriculums that eliminate or overlook the abilities and needs of the more atypical gifted learners. Therefore, to provide a more global view of the gifted, what will need to be considered are the following groups of atypical gifted learners: (1) culturally different gifted, (2) handicapped gifted learners, and (3) gifted underachievers.

Culturally Different Gifted

Giftedness is not nor ever has been the exclusive property of white, middle-class America. Yet, through generations educational programs serving the gifted have been composed, almost exclusively, of such individuals. Some educators have voiced the need to broaden the cultural base of gifted programming, although their actions have not paralleled their words. Consequently, the potential of many gifted learners from diverse backgrounds has been overlooked in our schools and in our society. In this text the term "culturally different" will be given a broad scope not contingent on a single factor such as socioeconomic class, national origin, race, or language but applied to the person who, according to Bernal (1976), behaves in group-identifiable ways. From time to time this same group of individuals will be referred to in this book as the subdominant cultural. The purpose for altering this accepted terminology is to highlight the fact that the "problem" for the culturally diverse does not lie in the differences in behaviors they display but in the fact that these behaviors are not similar to or widely accepted by the dominant or controlling cultural group.

There are at least three apparent causes for this neglect of the culturally different in gifted programming. First, the discovery of the culturally different is hindered by the traditional definition of giftedness, which favors the traits often found in white, middle-class students. Second, standardized tests that are often used to assess giftedness tend to be culturally biased and consequently overlook the culturally different's potential. Finally, the culturally different very often must function in an atmosphere that treats them as disadvantaged or inferior, as well as, different—an attitude that is accentuated by society, peers, test administrators, and, sometimes, teachers. Anastasi (1976) uniquely described this dilemma by stating that:

> Objectively there are only cultural differences between any two cultures or subcultures. Each culture fosters and encourages the development of behavior that is adapted to its values and demands. When an individual must adjust to and compete within a culture or subculture other than that in which he was reared, then cultural difference is likely to become cultural disadvantage. (p. 287)

In view of the factors mentioned and the imminent threat of the loss of the culturally different's potential, a need exists for more adequate assessment methods, a broader definition of giftedness, and an understanding of the culturally different and their specific needs, with the end result being the development of appropriate, effective educational programs.

Traditionally, educators have assessed individuals as gifted on the basis of an unusually high IQ score on such instruments as the *Stanford-Binet* or *Wechsler*

Intelligence Scales. In addition, characteristics such as love of and frequent engagement in reading, high verbal ability, long attention span, and a preference for complex tasks (Boothby & Lacoste, 1977) have also been associated with gifted learners. Since the qualities described above serve as important indicators of success in school, there is little doubt that they are highly predictive of scholastic achievement. However, when these characteristics are used as a yardstick for determining giftedness, the result is an oversight of a large segment of the culturally different gifted population. The behavioral traits most often used to assess giftedness are typical of the white middle class raised in a cultural environment where education is highly valued.

Such traits are not always common to the culturally different, who, with their economic, cultural or educational experiences, do not always seek to emulate the dominant culture. Also suggested throughout this text, the standardized tests that are frequently used to determine giftedness require proficiency in reading, language development, and, often, test-taking skills. This situation tends to favor the middle-class individual and tends to penalize the culturally different who may not hold scholastic achievement as a priority or whose linguistic and cultural experiences are dissimilar to those presented in the tests.

Recently there have been attempts to broaden the definition of giftedness in order to include the culturally different gifted, who have for so long been overlooked. Newly expanded definitions of giftedness include such traits as a well-developed sense of humor, a high level of curiosity, unusual tenacity, an above-average level of intuitiveness, and sensitivity to thought (Boothby & Lacoste, 1977). The current definition of the U.S. Office of Education has assisted somewhat in the identification of culturally different gifted learners by its inclusion of traits such as productive and creative thinking, leadership ability, aptitude in the visual and performing arts, and superior psychomotor skills. However, these traits can be helpful in the identification of the culturally different only if they are evaluated within a cultural context. Characteristics of giftedness that have previously been confined to the dominant culture, such as convergent productive abilities, divergent thinking, and superior memory (Guilford, 1959), are now receiving attention and gradual acceptance for culturally diverse groups as well. These broadened descriptors of giftedness allow for a more accurate characterization of the culturally different gifted learner than was possible with the more traditional behavioral traits. This is primarily the case because the culturally different tend to place their values on humor, survival skills, leadership, entertainment, expression through art, or well-developed athletic abilities.

These findings have been supported in part by Martinson (1974) and Mercer and Lewis (1978). Basically what these researchers reported was that among inner-city children of low socioeconomic status, there were many who possessed these formerly overlooked and previously unacknowledged traits of giftedness.

The interesting and encouraging fact resulting from these broadened definitions of giftedness is the trend toward an evaluation of the learner's behaviors within the context of the individual's own culture. Up to this point it has only been the dominant-cultural individual who has enjoyed the benefits of this culture-sensitive evaluation. If this trend continues, the chances are greatly improved that the behaviors of the culturally different will be fairly assessed and will eventually serve as more adequate indicators of their potential giftedness.

Gifted Handicapped

The term "subdominant cultural" was defined in a previous section as representing those individuals who differ in group-identifiable ways from the dominant group primarily on the basis of cultural experiences. There are other subdominant groups as well whose life experiences, and subsequently their outputs, vary markedly from the dominant group as a result of physical/sensorimotor uniqueness. In addition, the problem of the neglect of the culturally different gifted learner, previously discussed, seems even more accentuated in the case of the handicapped gifted learner. This statement can be supported by the fact that while much has been written about the handicapped, the area of the gifted handicapped learner has been relatively untouched.

With this lack of adequate information on the intellectual potential of the handicapped, misconceptions have continued to predominate. One prevailing myth that is embedded within the perceptions of the handicapped is the idea that individuals who are learning disabled, who have physical or sensory handicaps, or who are emotionally disturbed have some abnormality that completely affects their mental operations. Maker (1977), however, has attempted to dispel some of the myths surrounding handicapped learners. Her extensive treatment of the gifted handicapped learner points out that while the handicapped, like the culturally diverse, are in many ways different from typical or dominant learners, they too, possess behaviors indicative of giftedness.

In addition to the insufficient research in the area of the gifted handicapped, there are three other reasons why this atypical gifted population has been overlooked: (1) the emphasis on traditional assessment measures, (2) the difficulty in evaluating the behaviors of the handicapped, and (3) the past and present educational programs for the handicapped.

As has been repeatedly described throughout this chapter, the more traditional measures of giftedness require proficient verbal or motor abilities. Consequently, they were and continue to be highly inadequate in assessing the potential of some handicapped learners whose abilities to respond are somehow impaired by verbal or sensorimotor difficulties. Recently some of these traditional instruments have been modified or other instruments developed for use with special populations such as the handicapped. These new or modified assessment tools, which will be discussed later, provide a partial solution to this testing dilemma, but an even more submerged problem must be considered. As schematically presented in Figure 1-5, the outputs of any intellectual structure will relate to the experience or inputs of that system. Likewise, how situations will be perceived or interpreted will be, in part, a reflection of those experiences. Questions or items on many of these traditional instruments used in the identification of high potential levels require individuals to perceive the situation from the perspective of the typical learner and disregard other perceptional viewpoints.

It would appear that judging the behaviors of the handicapped as indicators of giftedness would be a difficult task. However, when this evaluation is conducted by measuring the behaviors of these atypical learners against the yardstick of typical learner behaviors, accurate evaluation becomes improbable if not impossible. What should be considered is the handicapped individual's demonstrated strengths and needs and how the behaviors reflect these strengths or abilities. Furthermore, as we might weigh certain aspects of performance more heavily for the culturally different learner to compensate for assessment imbalance, so, too, we can weigh the behaviors of the handicapped learner. If program developers adhere to the narrower view of giftedness as dependent on performance, on measures of IQ, or on achievement, then the chances are greatly reduced that the gifted program will include individuals from the ranks of the handicapped.

The third, and probably the most important, reason for our lack of identification of potential of handicapped gifted learners centers on the educational programs provided for them. Programs first developed for the physically and emotionally handicapped largely involved placement in special schools or special classes. Often the focus of these programs was on the specific disability far more than on the specific abilities of the individuals. Furthermore, in these "special" programs that were frequently housed in some out-of-the-way location the handicapped learner was restricted to interaction with other similarly handicapped individuals. However, with the enactment of recent handicapped/exceptional student legislation (most notably Public Law 94-142), there has been a move to structure programs for these students on educational strengths as well as needs and to conduct such programs in the least restrictive environment. In many instances, this least restrictive atmosphere has offered the handicapped the opportunity to interact with many other types of learners and to participate in a variety of educational experiences.

While the identification of and planning for the handicapped gifted is by no means an easy task, it is one that can be better accomplished through (1) the early identification and nurturance of handicapped learners, (2) a change in society's perceptions of the handicapped, and (3) the continued improvement in the educational treatment of these learners.

Societal views on the handicapped have progressed through several stages. Initially, the handicapped were hidden away from public view and looked on with disgust and disgrace, and many handicapped infants who did not have the benefits of modern medical technology died soon after birth. As the chances of their survival improved and their numbers increased, and as their rights were championed by individuals and groups, there was more of a thrust to locate the handicapped and provide necessary treatment for their disabilities. It was through the educational system that these identification and intervention programs functioned. What needs to be considered now is a program that expands the earlier notion of intervention. To intervene in the situation should no longer be viewed as enough for the handicapped learner. There must also be a striving to nurture the strengths and potentials of these individuals. Those handicapped individuals who display high levels of potentials must be allowed to see themselves in a positive light and should be made to see that they have much to contribute to the society. A restricted educational environment for the gifted handicapped will likely result in restricted growth. Conversely, the more enriching the experiences we can provide, the better able these individuals may be to grow to potential.

As just discussed, the handicapped are often perceived as helpless individuals who will be noncontributing members of society and who need our pity. Combine this with the well-known educational principle that learners often attain the levels of performance others assume they are capable of and you have the ingredients for a major problem for the gifted handicapped. Gifted handicapped learners may succumb to the prevalent belief that there is not much they can be expected to do and thus they attempt little. Society and educational system function as a continuous source of negative reinforcement in such a case.

There is another pattern of behavior that may develop in this atmosphere of low expectations for the handicapped gifted. As Maker (1977) noted, the gifted handicapped may also establish goals for themselves that are unrealistically high for any learner, handicapped or not, in conflict with the unrealistically low goals set by others around them. The negative reinforcement in this type of situation comes from the individuals themselves, who cannot fulfill their own expectations and seemingly provide reinforcement for the misconceptions of others.

What appears needed under both situations described is the clearer understanding of potential and strengths of the gifted handicapped learner. With such an understanding, the society and the individual can begin to develop more adequate and attainable goals. These realistic but enriching objectives will provide the necessary stimulation for the gifted handicapped learners and will counteract the low expectancies of the society.

One of the persistent difficulties that exists in programs for the gifted handicapped is the continued emphasis on the learners' weaknesses rather than on the learners' strengths. This is not to suggest that the disability be ignored or left untreated. What is being said, however, is that treating the disability is not enough and should not become the main objective of the student's educational program. That main objective should be optimal growth.

A program that also provides the gifted handicapped with the opportunity to explore their areas of strength can only serve to increase their self concept and their trust in those who instruct them. Essential, however, in a program designed to work with strengths is the understanding that the outcomes for the gifted handicapped in using such abilities or strengths will be different than those of typical gifted learners. The results of these individuals' efforts will be based on their own perceptions of their experiences and their personal interaction with the world. Consequently, the outputs, as in the case of the blind poet or the hearing-impaired artist, will certainly be unique and different, but nonetheless consistent with that individual's experiences and cognitive development. Where would our civilization be without the contributions of our Helen Kellers, Beethovens, and Franklin Roosevelts?

Gifted Underachievers

A most perplexing group of atypical gifted learners are those commonly referred to in the literature as gifted underachievers. These individuals appear to attain anonymity within the educational system. Generally, a comparison demonstrates a serious descrepancy between expected level of potential and actual classroom performance for these individuals. However, difficulty with such a narrow view of the gifted underachiever is twofold. First, the identification of an individual as a gifted underachiever may rely on an insufficient initial assessment of giftedness. Second, this term "underachiever" is frequently applied only to the gap between intellectual potential, as measured by an IQ or achievement measure, and actual academic performance, disregarding other forms of achievement gaps.

Logically and simply, the first question that must be considered when encountering a marked discrepancy between assumed potential and demonstrated ability is whether or not the level of potential was adequately assessed at the outset. This should not be as potent a consideration in those programs that do not rely on single measures or tests as indicators of giftedness but look, instead, for patterns of evidence. As an illustration, one limitation of some group and individual assessment instruments is the emphasis they place on language proficiency. Consequently, a student who reads early and reads avidly may score extremely high on such measures and yet not possess other behaviors indicative of giftedness.

Assuming the identification process was, indeed, adequate, still another shortcoming of the traditional view of the gifted underachiever must be considered. As was mentioned, the term "underachiever" is often affixed to a student because of a gap between the assessed level of potential and actual performance within the classroom. What is overlooked by this viewpoint are the gaps that may also exist between in and out of school behaviors, present and past school performance, and academic and nonacademic productions. Both achievement and underachievement exist within and outside the school setting and pertain to divergent, creative, as well as traditionally academic areas.

In essence, underachievement encompasses more than a discrepancy between academic abilities and in-class performance. Therefore, there exists both in and out of school comparisons of behavior that may provide great insights as to why the individual appears to be underachieving. One method of evaluation that may prove useful with the gifted underachiever is "situational assessment" in which the learners are evaluated in educational and noneducational settings. For example, in the "situational assessment" of noneducational settings, the learners should be evaluated in terms of their family relationships. In his synthesis of the research on the gifted underachiever, Gallagher (1975) noted that these individuals can often be characterized as having family relationships that were not positive experiences. Because of their poor relationships with parents or the inability to identify with family members, these individuals often turn to their peers for recognition and become a part of a social group that rejects school and even society. Their school behavior can also be characterized by their refusal to take part in classroom activities, as well as their low aspirations, negative self-concept, and narrow range of interests.

Again, it is important to know more about an individual beyond specific test scores and grade-point averages. One population of underachievers that frequently goes undetected is the culturally different who may find their abilities overlooked and unappreciated and prefer to drop out rather than muddle through. This serves to illustrate the point of program/curriculum suitability.

When underachievement exists, one cause may be the lack of stimulation in the present curriculum. There may be a mismatch between student interests and needs and school programming. When a program is developed with the strengths and needs of the gifted learner in mind, then this situation is less likely to occur.

However, as demonstrated in the synthesis of the literature, the main cause of the underachievement may rest outside the realm of the classroom. In such instances, the gifted program can provide what motivation and understanding possible while seeking assistance and guidance from those who can lend such support.

In summary, the idea of the gifted underachiever must first be looked at more broadly. The gap between achievement and potential can be displayed in many more ways than between test score and grades. Underachievement encompasses gaps between in and out of school performance, past and present performance, and academic and nonacademic productions as well.

Where underachievement is suspected, several questions should then be considered:

- Was the level of potential appropriately assessed for the learner?

- Does the principal source of the difficulties seem to lie within the control of the school program?

• Does the main cause of the underachievement appear to exist outside the realm of the classroom?

When we begin to have some answers to these questions there can be actions taken to adjust the present situation in some way that will provide the necessary compensation, support, or motivation to the gifted underachieving learner.

NONTRADITIONAL ASSESSMENT DEVICES

Assessing the Culturally Different Gifted

The literature abounds with references to the inefficiency and ineffectiveness of standardized instruments to identify the culturally different gifted. For example, Klineburg (1935), Davis, Gardner, and Gardner (1941), Hoffman (1962), Black (1963), Pascales and Jakubovie (1971), and Sullivan (1973), to mention only a few, have heralded the deficiencies of IQ tests and other standardized measures in locating the potential and inherent abilities among the culturally different. However, these standardized instruments continued to be employed for such a purpose without the inclusion of other relevant information.

The problems related to the dependence on traditional standardized devices in the assessment of potential among subdominant cultural populations seem to revolve around several key issues that have been discussed within this chapter. These issues were (1) the experiential knowledge required by those instruments; (2) the standard English linguistic competency demanded by such measures; (3) the reliability of those tests, normed on middle-class white populations, for diverse populations; and (4) the nature of the testing process as a potential source of conflict.

Are there less traditional instruments and procedures that, for the culturally different, can provide more reliable and valid assessment of potential? This is the question that will be surveyed in this section. Several nontraditional assessment devices will be presented, and their focus, advantages, and possible disadvantages will be discussed.

The attempts to devise assessment tools that would at least partially rectify the limitations of standardized measures in locating potential among the culturally different have resulted in the development of "culture-fair" instruments. The label *culture-fair* is attached to these devices to highlight the conscious efforts of their developers to bridge the cultural barrier in testing in some way. It must be clarified from the outset, however, that no instrument is totally culture-free or culture-fair, although some may be less culturally biased than others.

An overview of culture-fair measures seems to suggest their breakdown along two continuums. The first continuum, which was discussed earlier in this chapter, is the common dichotomy of objective-subjective (i.e., scoring specificity vs. scorer interpretation). The second continuum, which is unique to culture-fair instruments, is that of culture-free to culture-bound. Culture-free measures attempt to remove any element of cultural influence in the test construction, while culture-bound measures are developed to favor specific cultural groups. The approximate plotting of various culture-fair measures along these two continuums is demonstrated in Figure 2-3. The listings that appear within this figure are not exhaustive but do include the more frequently referred to instruments.

The two culture-bound tests presented have both been biased in favor of black populations. The *Abbreviated Binet for the Disadvantaged (ABDA)* (Bruch, 1971) was developed from the *Stanford-Binet*, which was administered to and then biased in favor of black populations. The *Black Intelligence Tests of Cultural*

Figure 2-3 Plotting Culture-Fair Measures on Objective/Subjective and Culture-Free/Bound Continuums

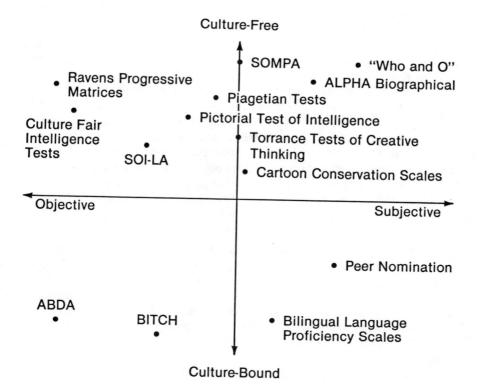

Homogeneity (BITCH) (Williams, 1972a, 1972b) was a more creative attempt to produce a culturally bound device. The *BITCH* not only incorporates the cultural strengths of the blacks but also includes vocabulary items only from that culture.

For Spanish-surname populations, the *System of Multicultural Pluralistic Assessment (SOMPA)* and *Cartoon Conservation Scales* and various bilingual language proficiency scales have been suggested (Bernal, 1976; DeAvila & Havassy, 1975). The *SOMPA* (Mercer & Lewis, 1978) is composed of three models—medical system, social system, and pluralistic model—and can generally be described as a form of weighted case-study approach. While the *SOMPA* does evaluate individuals thoroughly and within their own cultural framework, it requires specific training and involves lengthy sessions for administration. These are practical considerations that must be investigated by program developers.

For certain cultural populations, such as Native Americans and Asian Americans, the availability of culturally sensitive or culturally appropriate instruments is even more limited. One measure, the *Structure of the Intellect-Learning Abilities Test (SOI-LA)*, developed by Meeker and Meeker (1976) has been used in the assessment of gifted potential among Navajos. Because it deemphasizes verbal abilities and emphasizes figural abilities, the *SOI-LA* is applicable with other cultural groups as well.

Two other assessment tools that have broad applicability among culturally diverse populations are the *Torrance Tests of Creative Thinking* (Torrance, 1974) and the *Raven's Progressive Matrices* (Raven, 1956). As in the *SOI-LA,* these instruments place less emphasis on the verbal and more emphasis on the figural abilities of the individual. The *Raven's Progressive Matrices,* however, measures convergent-thought productions and requires less verbalization by the testee than the *Torrance Tests of Creative Thinking,* which assess divergent-thought production abilities. Other points of contrast between these two tools include the fact that the *Raven's Progressive Matrices* is more objectively scored and requires more specialized training for its administration than does the *Torrance Tests of Creative Thinking.* This degree of subjectivity that operates in the scoring of the latter test implies that it is not free from examiner bias, a problem exaggerated when a cultural mismatch exists between the tester and testee.

Other broad categories of devices that can be applied in the assessment of giftedness among the culturally diverse are the behavioral checklists and parent, peer, and teacher referrals previously discussed in the section on subjective information strategy. These subjective methods of assessing giftedness among the culturally different include interviews or rating scales such as the "who" and "O" inventories described by Hilliard (1976) and the more prominent and widely used *Alpha Biographical Inventory* developed by Taylor and Ellison (1968). This inventory is completed by parents, peers, teachers, and any siblings of the individuals, as well as by the individuals themselves.

Assessing the Gifted Handicapped

Since the development of assessment devices for measuring potential, difficulties have existed in evaluating the capabilities of handicapped learners. The problem with the use of traditional instruments for assessing the handicapped can be viewed from two perspectives. First, traditional tests often need major modifications before use with the handicapped, especially those who have physical disabilities. Often these modifications required the deletion of some types of test items or alterations in the administration procedures. Second, most traditional tests have been standardized on typical learners, with few tests using a representative group of handicapped learners as their standardization sample. Therefore, the interpretation of the scores obtained by handicapped learners cannot be accurately interpreted, especially by comparing their scores to those of typical learners, on whom the test was standardized.

Even though there are limitations in assessing the handicapped, there are some testing instruments that are more appropriate than others for determining the potential of these learners.

For the hearing-impaired learner, there are several tests that can be utilized for assessment purposes. The *Nebraska Test of Learning Aptitude* (Hiskey, 1966) measures a wide variety of intellectual abilities. This test is particularly useful because it was standardized on hearing-impaired individuals from ages 3 to 16.

The performance tests of the *Wechsler Intelligence Scales* have also been used for deaf learners. Other tests that are applicable for hearing-impaired learners are the *Arthur Adaptation of the Leiter International Performance Scale* (Arthur, 1950) and the *Raven's Progressive Matrices*.

In testing blind or partially sighted learners, adaptations of the *Stanford-Binet* and *Wechsler Intelligence Scales* have been made. The *Hayes-Binet* is a modification of the *Stanford-Binet,* and uses items that do not require sight. The *Wechsler Intelligence Scales* have been adapted for use for the blind or partially sighted by using the verbal and omitting the performance tests. In addition to the adaptations made to traditionally used measures, there also is the *Haptic Intelligence Tests for the Adult Blind.* This is a nonverbal test (requiring only verbal directions) that involves the use of the tactile sense.

For use with handicapped learners with severe motor disorders, a number of testing instruments have been used. *The Columbia Mental Maturity Scale* (Burgemeister, Blum, & Lorge, 1972), which was designed for the cerebral palsied individual, assesses discrimination and classification abilities and requires the use of the learner's visual perceptual abilities. The *Leiter International Performance Scale* and *The Porteus Mazes* have also been adapted for use with cerebral palsied individuals (Anastasi, 1976). The *Raven's Progressive Matrices,* mentioned earlier in this chapter, is also suitable for the orthopedically handicapped.

A test that has also shown promise with the handicapped is the *Pictorial Test of Intelligence* (French, 1964). This test assesses the general intellectual level of normal and handicapped learners. It requires no verbal responses and permits the accumulation of fairly reliable and valid data.

PROCEDURES AND PARTICIPANTS: WHO MAKES THE DECISION?

The major decisions that are a part of the procedures for the identification of gifted should be the results of a cooperative effort rather than the proclamation of a single individual. This cooperative effort might best be achieved through the organization of a placement committee.

Ideally, the composition of the placement committee should encompass one member from each of the relevant areas of concern discussed in the needs assessment section. Generally, that would involve a representative from the community, school personnel (teacher and administrator), and, possibly, support services. At the more practical end of the spectrum, the placement committee will vary according to the particular institution considered and should consist of an administrator, the individual or individuals heading the placement committee, and, whenever applicable, the personnel making a student referral.

As the committee membership may vary, so too may its responsibilities vary. At the more conservative end of the responsibilities continuum the duty of the placement committee would be to review the cases of those individuals who meet the established criteria for identification and to recommend their inclusion in or exclusion from the gifted program. In some instances, the placement committee may be given the initial task of devising a suitable identification procedure to satisfy the previously developed definition. As part of this task, measures of identification would need to be carefully evaluated in regard to the school population to be assessed, their compliance with any existing guidelines, their accessibility, their administratability, their affordability, and related factors. Should this latter duty be included in the job description of the placement committee, it is strongly suggested that the committee's recommended identification procedures be submitted to a large representative body for their approval. When the students have undergone the approved assessment procedures, it then becomes the function of the placement committee to select and place gifted learners into a suitable program.

The identification of participants who comply with the established criteria may be an easier matter for the placement committee when the information to be analyzed is of an objective nature. The more information that must be considered and the more diverse the sources and types of data employed, the more involved the job of placement may be. Even within the framework of objective information, however, the selection committee may need to judge the individual's suitability for placement. For example, a student may not quite attain the specific cut-off score on the individual IQ test but may possess an extremely high grade-point average.

In order to circumvent some of the common problems that arise in the selection and placement of students into gifted programs, three additional procedural responsibilities should be considered within the realm of the placement or selection committee. These procedural duties include (1) continuous placement/evaluation, (2) student profiling, and (3) periodic review.

Continuous Placement/Evaluation

The major responsibility of the placement committee within the process will be to review student records, to determine which of the students demonstrate the appropriate gifted behaviors, and to determine which program or type of differentiated instruction will best meet the learner's needs. In addition, the committee should review information, such as records, reports, and referrals, about those individuals who have been previously placed in gifted programs and are identified as gifted to determine the extent to which those students' needs are being met by the recommended program, course of study, or instructional procedure.

In order to accomplish the first objective of this strategy, the placement committee may employ the following procedures:

- Determine what data are presently available for student review and what data provide useful and appropriate information.

- Decide what additional information may be needed for each student and how this information could be obtained. Some potential sources of student data are shown in Table 2-4.

- Determine once data have been collected whether the individual, at that point, displays appropriate behaviors to warrant identification as gifted.

- Develop recommendations for each individual identified as gifted based on knowledge of that individual's apparent strengths and weaknesses. Such recommendations are appropriate whether the student will be mainstreamed for instruction or placed in a form of exclusive grouping.

- Mark for later reconsideration the names of those individuals not selected by the committee but whom the committee felt demonstrated some of the appropriate gifted behaviors, as described in the "periodic review" section.

As was indicated, the second objective of the committee in this phase is the evaluation of students who have already been identified as gifted. The major thrust of the committee in carrying out this objective should be the determination of

Table 2-4 Sources of Placement Information

Information	Resource
Family background/home environment	1. Parent interview (e.g., *SOMPA)* 2. Cumulative school record 3. Observation of child in home environment
Physical development	1. Observe the learner for physical handicaps 2. Cumulative school record 3. Vision and hearing screening 4. Information from peers
Interests and hobbies	1. Observation 2. Administer an interest inventory 3. Informally interview the child
Past and present school performance	1. Achievement test scores 2. Cumulative school record 3. Observation of learning situation
Present skill development	1. Informal teacher assessment 2. Test results
Attitude toward school, self, and others	1. Observe the learner 2. Attitude measures 3. Sociogram 4. Anecdotal records
Leadership, creativity, and psychomotor abilities	1. Observation 2. Peer information 3. Parent interview 4. Teacher recommendation 5. Anecdotal record 6. Interest inventory 7. Tests of creativity 8. Cumulative records
Intellectual abilities	1. Results of individual and/or group intelligence tests 2. Behavioral checklists 3. Peer/parent/teacher nomination

whether the instructional program in which the individual is functioning is presently meeting the psychological, social, emotional, and educational needs of the learner or whether a modification or alternative placement is justified.

Student Profiling

There will be repeated instances in the selection process when an individual is referred to the placement committee as a potential candidate for the gifted program but will not ultimately satisfy established criteria. It is important in these instances that the time spent by the placement committee should not seem wasted and that the information accumulated on each individual learner, whether that individual is chosen for the gifted program or not, should not go unused. When ascertaining the individual's suitability for program placement, therefore, it would seem wise to share the knowledge gained about the learner's potential areas of strength or weakness with others who can apply this knowledge in positive ways. For example, the placement committee might provide the student's teacher with feedback as to the learner's capabilities, with some recommendations as to how his or her needs might be met in the classroom. In addition, the committee may feel, after reviewing a particular case, that some type of follow-up evaluation may be indicated. In some situations the committee may not possess the specialized skills or knowledge to adequately assess the potential of certain learners such as the handicapped and may require the assistance of specialists.

What is essential in this procedural responsibility is that the information accumulated and synthesized by the placement committee be used. In addition, it is important that this information serve to improve the education of every individual referred, whenever possible.

Periodic Review

Within the duty of periodic review there are two principal objectives for committee members. First, as previously described, there are those instances in which an individual demonstrates some but not all of the appropriate behaviors to be classified as gifted at the time of review. In such cases the placement committee should establish some type of review procedure. During this review process, the committee should reevaluate their earlier recommendations and determine the student's progress in the areas in question in the initial evaluation. Information obtained about the individual's present performance should be used in making a decision as to whether this individual should now be accepted into the gifted program.

The second goal of the placement committee in the area of periodic review involves the evaluation of recommendations made for students selected for the gifted program. In this review, determination is made as to whether the type of placement or instructional strategies appear suitable for the specific learner.

The role of the placement committee, in general, should be viewed as dynamic and ongoing, with its members actively involved in the process of education of the gifted. There are two final points that must be considered before leaving this issue of selection and placement.

First, the more exclusive the gifted program membership, the more critical the decisions of the selection committee. By this is meant that if the benefits of the proposed gifted program can only be received by a relatively small number of students, then it is extremely important that the right students receive such benefits. This format is in contrast to the type of mainstreaming or enrichment program that is less affected by membership numbers or financial restraints. To illustrate, certain gifted programs might involve the selection of the top two percent of the student body for inclusion in a special accelerated course of study. This top two percent was to be identified in September of the school year and maintained without review for an entire academic year. In this particular case, the job of the placement committee would be quite critical.

Second, all learners have the "right to review" by the placement committee. Because the rights of every individual must be safeguarded, there should be a provision in the selection procedure that allows for the "right to review." This right to review could take two forms. In the first place, there may be those students whose cases are not brought to the committee through normal referral channels. Under such circumstances, the student or student's parents may request that such an evaluation be conducted. Similarly, there are those instances when a student has been referred to the placement committee but has not been selected for participation in the gifted program. These individuals as well should be provided with the opportunity to have their cases reanalyzed by the placement committee. Again, this right to review should not be viewed as an affront to the selection committee but rather as a method of ensuring the correctness of the decisions made.

SUMMARY

In this chapter currently employed procedures and alternative strategies for identifying gifted potential have been described in detail. Three types of identification procedures were proposed, and the advantages and disadvantages of each were discussed. The first method uses only objective information compiled from such sources as achievement tests and IQ measures to determine giftedness. By contrast, the second procedure, the subjective information strategy, employs information from such sources as behavioral checklists and peer or teacher nominations. The various instruments and forms pertinent to these two strategies were also discussed in some detail. The third identification approach presented in this chapter was the comprehensive information strategy, which considers both subjective and objective data in the decision-making process. Three ways of initiating the comprehensive approach were outlined.

Also, identification procedures relevant to atypical learners were considered along with techniques and nontraditional devices useful in the assessment of potential among this population. Specifically, the needs of the culturally diverse, the handicapped, and the underachiever were surveyed within the topic of atypical gifted learners.

REFERENCES

Alexander, P., & Muia, J. Gifted reading programs: Uncovering hidden potential. *Reading Horizons,* 1980, *20,* 302-310.

Alvino, J., & Wieler, J. How standardized testing fails to identify the gifted and what teachers can do about it. *Phi Delta Kappan,* 1979, *61,* 106-109.

Anastasi, A. *Psychological testing.* New York: Collier-Macmillan Publishing Co., Inc., 1976.

Arthur, G. *The Arthur adaptation of the Leiter international performance scale.* Chicago: C.H. Stoelting, 1950.

Baldwin, A.Y. The Baldwin identification matrix. In Baldwin, A., Gear, G., & Lucito, L. (Eds.), *Educational planning for the gifted.* Reston, Va.: The Council for Exceptional Children, 1978.

Barbe, W. B. *Psychology and education of the gifted.* New York: Appleton-Century-Crofts, 1965.

Bernal, E. M. *Gifted Mexican-American children: An ethnico-scientific perspective.* Washington, D.C.: Office of Education,1974. (ERIC Document Reproduction Service No. ED 091 411)

Bernal, E. M. Gifted programs for the culturally different. *NASSP Bulletin,* 1976, *60,* 67-76.

Bernal, E. M. The identification of gifted Chicano children. In Baldwin, A., Gear, G., & Lucito, L. (Eds.), *Educational planning for the gifted: Overcoming cultural, geographic, and socio-economic barriers.* Reston, Va.: The Council for Exceptional Children, 1978.

Bernal, E. M., Jr., & Reyna, J. Analysis and identification of giftedness in Mexican-American children: A pilot study. In Boston, B. O., (Ed.), *A resource manual of information on educating the gifted and talented.* Reston, Va.: The Council for Exceptional Children, 1975.

Black, H. *They shall not pass.* New York: W.W. Morrow, 1963.

Boothby, P. R., & Lacoste, R. J. *Unmined gold: Potentially gifted children of the inner city.* U.S. Educational Resources Information Center, 1977. (ERIC Document Reproduction Service No. ED 154 076)

Bradley, R. C., & Earp, E. Children with original & novel ideas: The creative. In Bradley, R. C. (Ed.), *The education of exceptional children.* Wolfe City, Tex.: The University Press, 1970.

Bruch, C. B. Modification of procedures for the identification of the disadvantaged gifted. *The Gifted Child Quarterly,* 1971, *15,* 267-272.

Burgemeister, B. B., Blum, L. H., & Lorge, I. *Columbia mental maturity scale* (3rd ed.). New York: Harcourt Brace Jovanovich, 1972.

Cattell, R. B. Theory of fluid and crystalized intelligence: A critical experiment. *Journal of Educational Psychology,* 1963, *54,* 1-22.

Davis, A., Gardner, B. B., & Gardner, M. R. *Deep south.* Chicago: University of Chicago Press, 1941.

DeAvila, E. A., & Havassy, B. Piagetian alternatives to I.Q.: Mexican American study. In Hobbs, N. (Ed.), *Issues in the classification of exceptional children*. San Francisco: Jossey-Bass, 1975.

Fliegler, L. A., & Bish, C. E. Summary of research on the academically talented student. *Review of Educational Research*, 1959, *29*, 408-450.

French, J. L. *Pictorial test of intelligence*. Boston: Houghton Mifflin, 1964.

Gallagher, J. J. *Teaching the gifted child* (2nd ed.). Boston: Allyn & Bacon, 1975.

Gay, J. E. A proposed plan for identifying black gifted children. *The Gifted Child Quarterly*, 1978, *22*, 353-360.

Gear, G. H. *Effects of the training program, identification of the potentially gifted, on teachers' accuracy in the identification of intellectually gifted children*. Unpublished doctoral dissertation, University of Connecticut, 1975.

Guilford, J. P. Three faces of intellect. *American Psychologist*, 1959, *14*, 469-479.

Hilliard, A. G. *Alternatives to IQ testing: An approach to the identification of gifted minority children*. San Francisco State University, California, 1976. (ERIC ED 148-038. Virginia: ERIC Document Reproduction Service)

Hiskey, M. *Hiskey-Nebraska test of learning aptitude*. Lincoln, Neb.: Union College Press, 1966.

Hoffman, D. *The tyranny of testing*. New York: Crowell-Collier, 1962.

Isaacs, A. F. Biblical research IV: Perspectives on the problems of the gifted, and possible solutions as revealed in the RentaTeach. *Gifted Child Quarterly*, 1971, *14*, 175-194.

Kirk, S. A. *Educating exceptional children*. Boston: Houghton Mifflin, 1962.

Klineburg, O. *Race differences*. New York: Harper & Row, 1935.

Lucito, L. Gifted children, In L. Dunn (Ed.), *Exceptional children in the schools*. New York: Holt, Rinehart, & Winston, 1963.

Maker, J. C. *Providing programs for the gifted handicapped*. The Council for Exceptional Children, 1977.

Martinson, A. *The identification of the gifted and talented*. Ventura, Calif.: Office of the Ventura County Superintendent of Schools, *10*, 1974.

Meeker, M., & Meeker, R. *Structure of the intellect-learning abilities test*. El Segundo, Calif.: SOI Institute, 1976.

Mercer, J. R., & Lewis, J. F. Using the System of Multicultural Pluralistic Assessment (SOMPA) to identify the gifted minority child. In A. Baldwin, G. Gear, & L. Lucito (Eds.), *Educational planning for the gifted: Overcoming cultural, geographic, and socioeconomic barriers*. Reston, Va.: The Council for Exceptional Children, 1978.

Newland, T. E. Psychological assessment of exceptional children and youth. In Cruickshank, W. (Ed.), *Psychology of exceptional children and youth*. Englewood Cliffs, N.J.: Prentice-Hall, 1971.

Pascales, P., & Jakubovie, S. *The impossible dream: A culture free test*. Available from ERIC Document Reproductive Service (ERRS), Bethesda, MD: Microfiche ED054-217, 1971.

Raven, J. C. *Guide to the standard progressive matrices: Sets A B C D and E*. London: H. K. Lewis, 1956.

Renzulli, J., & Hartman, R. Scale for rating behavioral characteristics of superior students. *Exceptional Children*, 1971, *38*, 243-248.

Renzulli, J. S., & Smith, L. H. Two approaches to identification of gifted students. *Exceptional Children*, 1977, *43*, 512-518.

Salvia, L., & Ysseldyke, J. *Assessment in special and remedial education*. Boston: Houghton Mifflin, 1978.

Schermann, A. A research institute's approach to giftedness. In I. E. P. Wellenberg (Chrm.), *Special education: Strategies for educational progress.* Papers presented at the Meeting of the Council of Exceptional Children, Toronto, Canada, April, 1966.

Seagoe, M. Some learning characteristics of gifted children. In R. Martinson (Ed.), *The identification of the gifted and talented.* Ventura, Calif.: Office of Ventura County Superintendent of Schools, 1974.

Sullivan, A. R. The identification of gifted and talented black students: A hidden exceptionality. *Journal of Special Education,* 1973, *7,* 373-379.

Taylor, C. W., & Ellison, R. E. *Alpha Biographical Inventory.* Salt Lake City: Institute for Behavioral Research in Creativity, 1968.

Terman, L. M. *Mental and physical traits of a thousand gifted children.* Stanford, Calif.: Stanford University Press, 1925.

Terman, L. M. The discovery and encouragement of exceptional talent. *American Psychologist,* 1954, *9,* 221-230.

Torrance, E. P. *Guiding creative talent.* Englewood Cliffs, N.J.: Prentice-Hall, 1962.

Torrance, E. P. *Gifted children in the classroom.* New York: Macmillan, 1965.

Torrance, E. P. *Encouraging creativity in the classroom.* Dubuque, Iowa: William C. Brown, 1970.

Torrance, E. P. *Torrance Tests of Creative Thinking: Norms-technical manual.* Lexington, Mass.: Personnel Press, 1966. (Revised, 1974).

Williams, R. L. *The BITCH-100: A culture specific test.* ERIC Document 070799. Bethesda, Md.: ERIC Document Reproduction Service, LEASCO Information Products, 1972 a.

Williams, R. L. *The BITCH test (Black Intelligence Test of Cultural Homogeneity).* St. Louis: Williams and Associates, 1972 b.

Witty, P. (Ed.). *The gifted child.* Boston: D.C. Heath, 1951.

Chapter 3

Needs Assessment: Clarifying Program Focus

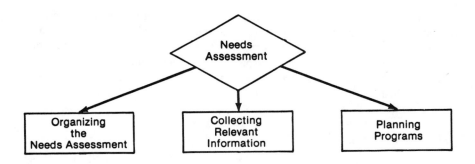

Just as a traveler would use a road map to find the most logical way to reach his destination, so, too, educators desiring to develop a program for gifted learners would follow a logical and well-thought-out plan. Such a plan in educational programming for the gifted should involve a careful delineation of the objectives or goals to be accomplished by that program. These objectives can be compared, in a rather simplistic fashion, to the markers and road signs along the highway that provide information on how far we have come in our undertaking and how much more may lie ahead before our destination can be reached. However, even before these objectives can be written accurately and with relevance to the theoretical foundation and to the intended population, it is necessary to consider factors that may seriously affect program development and the context in which this program will ultimately function. This chapter, therefore, will be concerned with developing a rationale and methodology for conducting a needs assessment prior to objective writing and will consider the importance of viewing program planning from the various levels or contexts in which it will operate.

NEEDS ASSESSMENT

There are many interprogram and intraprogram factors in operation that will have impact on the effectiveness of educational experiences we plan for the gifted learner. It is important, therefore, to determine what these factors may be and what positive or negative impact they may have on gifted programming. This information may be amassed, in part, by conducting a needs assessment.

The needs assessment not only provides information as to what presently exists in terms of the school program but also examines the present curriculum's goals and gives insight as to the relevant socioeconomic, geographic, educational, and cultural characteristics of the program environment.

Organizing the Needs Assessment

If conducted and organized efficiently, the needs assessment can provide invaluable information for program planning and goal development. Consideration of several factors is essential, however, for an effective needs assessment and should be incorporated into its organizational phase. These factors include (1) the areas that should be included in the needs assessment, (2) the method of information collection that should be employed, and (3) the individuals selected to conduct the needs assessment.

The Areas to be Assessed

As demonstrated in Figure 3-1, the relevant physical, geographical, cultural, socioeconomic, and educational characteristics of the school district, the community, the individual school's curriculum, the general population and personnel, and the projected or existing gifted population should undergo assessment (Wiles & Bondi, 1979). All of these areas appear to have a direct or indirect effect on the goals and objectives of gifted programming. Assessment allows careful analysis of these areas to determine the positive contributions that might be expected and the apparent weaknesses that may need to be compensated for in the program design.

The Method of Information Collection

Prior to the initiation of the needs assessment, it will be useful to organize the method of collecting the data so as to provide the maximum return. Careful planning should help ensure that all essential data are collected for employment in the gifted program's development and, in addition, that once collected this information will be in a form that is usable rather than overwhelming and understandable rather than vague. What may facilitate more simplified, systematized, and organized data collection is some type of needs assessment form that considers the area from which this information is drawn, what the perceived strength or resulting need may be, and the way this situation may be or should be reflected in the gifted program (see Exhibit 3-1).

Another method for data collection and an example of the process used in collecting such data are presented in Figure 3-2.

Figure 3-1 Needs Assessment Model

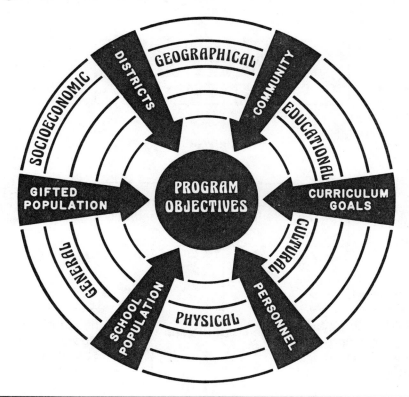

Exhibit 3-1 Needs Assessment Form

NEEDS ASSESSMENT
INFORMATION FORM

Area of concern _____
Perceived situation_____
_____

Possible effect on education _____
_____

Resulting need for gifted programming _____
_____

Name_____ Date_____

Figure 3-2 Needs Assessment Model

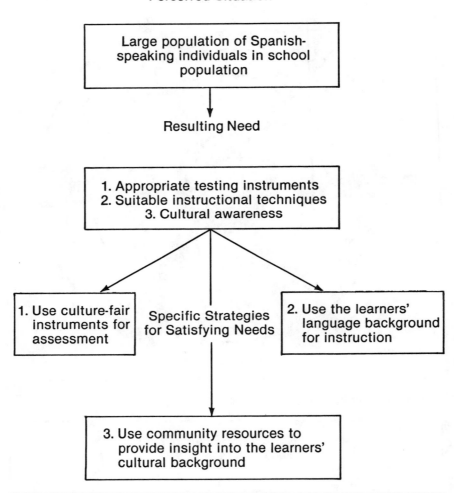

Perceived Situation

Large population of Spanish-
speaking individuals in school
population

Resulting Need

1. Appropriate testing instruments
2. Suitable instructional techniques
3. Cultural awareness

1. Use culture-fair
instruments for
assessment

Specific Strategies
for Satisfying Needs

2. Use the learners'
language background
for instruction

3. Use community resources to
provide insight into the learners'
cultural background

Who Performs the Needs Assessment

As briefly outlined, the information to be collected, analyzed, and synthesized in an effective needs assessment must, by necessity, come from the diversity of sources. It is essential, therefore, that individuals rooted within these various areas engage in the assessment process. The committee selected to conduct the needs assessment should be comprised of parents, community leaders, teachers, administrators, and students who have the knowledge, skills, and motivations to partici-pate in the project and contribute directly to the gifted program. Under certain situations the need may arise to divide the committee into smaller groups to work on different areas of the assessment. Should this occur, each subcommittee may select a chairperson whose job it would be to oversee the movement of the group toward its goal. A team leader should also be chosen to guide the work of the entire needs assessment committee, establish deadlines, review information, and present findings. It is also quite important that before the first piece of data is contributed that the committee members be made adequately aware of their purposes. By comprehending the importance and application of their labors, the committee members will be better equipped to conduct the business for which they were brought together.

AREAS OF ASSESSMENT

What may facilitate the job of the assessment committee is to consider, at the outset, types of situations within the specific areas that may be sources of valuable information.

Examining the Relevant Characteristics of the School District

Some of the major questions that should be asked in the initial stages of gifted program development are:

- What interest has been demonstrated within the school district towards gifted program establishment?

- What programs for the gifted, successful or unsuccessful, have operated within the school district, and what factors may have contributed to their success or lack of success?

- What financial support exists in the school district for educational programs for the gifted learner?

- What types of facilities can be found within the school district that may be employed in the gifted program?

Because no special program can successfully operate over any extended period of time without approval or support of school officials, the questions posed above deserve more detailed analysis.

First, it is important to identify the school district's philosophy toward the handling of and programming for children with different needs. This philosophy may be expressed in policy statements or program guidelines issued by school officials and in the outward support that has been afforded special programs for special students, whether gifted or not. Determining what programs exist in the schools gives the gifted program developers some insight into the school district's attitude toward providing special courses for students as well as their willingness to modify scheduling or provide for special class arrangements. This type of information will also prove important in substantiating the decision on gifted program format made by program developers. No special program can function independent of the school district, and, therefore, it is important to assess the attitudes and beliefs of school officials toward gifted program development. A strong positive attitude will certainly work to the benefit of program development. However, should a negative or apathetic attitude apparently exist, much work and time should be allotted to demonstrating the rationale for and importance of educational programs for gifted learners to those officials at the district level.

In many instances, an initial investigation of gifted programs successfully or unsuccessfully attempted within the school district or even within nearby districts may keep the gifted program developers from having to reinvent the wheel, so to speak. By reviewing the organizational format of such established programs, strengths, and/or possible shortcomings of the programs could be ascertained. Steps can be taken, thereafter, to incorporate suitable aspects of existing programs that proved advantageous while taking precautions to side-step the situations that might lead to problems. It must be cautioned that in the evaluation of preexisting programs, strengths and weaknesses must be carefully considered in the context in which they occurred. Situations differ from school to school. Therefore, strengths in one context may appear as weaknesses in another, or vice versa. Not only the model programs in the school district but also even less successful programs can serve as sources of information for program developers. Should no specific programs for the gifted exist within a school district, it may prove useful to examine the organizational framework of other programs developed for special learners.

While explicit and implicit support of a verbal or written nature from school officials is valuable to the success of the gifted programming, the importance of financial support from the school district should not be overlooked either. Most program initiations will require some amount of financial support, and it would prove useful to assess the budgetary commitments made to program development. In this tightly controlled expenditure period, a commitment of monetary support for gifted programming can probably be interpreted as a serious commitment. While the specific allotments for gifted programming may not exist, the categories for expenditures that do exist may be applicable to some cost incurred in gifted program development.

Generally speaking, facilities available in school districts can be classified under the headings of building, supplies, and personnel. With tighter controls being placed on school districts, the supplies, personnel, and space for new programs are at a premium. While the type of facilities needed for the gifted program will depend largely on the type of program designed, a thorough evaluation of the school facilities will lend some direction and assist the program developer in being more realistic about the choice of gifted programs.

Also, the success or failure of the gifted program can depend largely on the staff who will be responsible for working with the gifted learners. Consequently, acquiring as much information as possible about the school staff will assist the program developer in a variety of ways. Particularly helpful will be information about the kinds of resource people located in the district and the kinds of students they usually work with in their programs. In many school districts, specifically trained teachers are hired to act as resource personnel and provide classroom teachers with assistance in dealing with children with special needs. Teachers with these special skills and experiences can assist program developers in locating gifted children with special needs or handicaps as well as provide some direction in program planning for meeting their needs.

In addition, the identification of any teachers or individuals at the district level who have had experiences working with children with differing needs, especially the gifted child, is important information for gifted program developers. Because many teachers will not have the experience of working with the gifted learner in a special programming context, the knowledge gained by individuals with such experiences should be tapped.

Finally, in assessing the situation at the district level it is essential that program organizers orient themselves to the special services that operate at this level. Compiling a list of names, numbers, and services performed is a labor that will greatly benefit gifted programming by functioning as an easily accessible information source. For example, (1) is there a school psychologist available for testing of students in the district; (2) what instruments has this individual applied in the identification of high potential students; (3) are there counseling services available, and how may these services be applied in the gifted program?

Examining the Relevant Characteristics of the Community

In addition to considering the strengths and weaknesses that may exist at the district (or county) level, it is essential to assess the important characteristics of the community and to determine how these relevant characteristics can assist program developers in choosing the appropriate assessment and instructional strategies for the learners.

Very often in education we hear that a program is designed to meet the individual needs of the students. However, on close inspection, the program may at best take into consideration only the students' academic needs and omit other important aspects such as the cultural or socioeconomic characteristics of the environment that may have contributed to the academic situation.

Demographic Information

One of the first steps in the needs assessment that should occur at the community level is the accumulation of demographic data on the population to be served by the gifted program. Such information as to the race, age, family size, and major occupations of adult members of the surrounding community will be extremely helpful in providing an overall understanding of the context in which the gifted program will ultimately function. The presentation of the information should be in easy to comprehend, visually understandable, condensed form (see Exhibit 3-2 and Figure 3-3). At the district or county levels of program development, much of the necessary demographic data may be readily available from census information. For the school level of program initiation, the type of information necessary for demographic charting may be condensed from data accumulated in permanent school records.

Economic Characteristics

In addition to the information on average income levels represented in a brief demographic survey (as shown in Exhibit 3-2 and Figure 3-3), there are several

---

Exhibit 3-2 Presentation of Demographic Data

Express as percentage

Race   Asian American ＿＿＿ Black ＿＿＿ Spanish surname ＿＿＿
Native American ＿＿＿ White ＿＿＿ Other ＿＿＿

Age   (head of household) 65 or over ＿＿＿ 45-64 ＿＿＿ 25-44 ＿＿＿
15-24 ＿＿＿

Income   (based on occupation of head of household)
over $50,000 ＿＿＿ $40-50,000 ＿＿＿ $30-39,000 ＿＿＿
$20-29,000 ＿＿＿ $10-19,000 ＿＿＿ under $10,000 ＿＿＿

Years of Education (head of household) over 16 ＿＿＿ 14-16 ＿＿＿
12-14 ＿＿＿ 9-12 ＿＿＿ under 8 ＿＿＿

Number of Children (at home)
over 7 ＿＿＿ 5-6 ＿＿＿ 3-4 ＿＿＿ 1-2 ＿＿＿ none ＿＿＿

Location of Residence
urban ＿＿＿ suburban ＿＿＿ rural ＿＿＿ other ＿＿＿

Type of Residence
single family residence ＿＿＿ apartment ＿＿＿ other ＿＿＿

Figure 3-3 Graphic Representation of Demographic Data

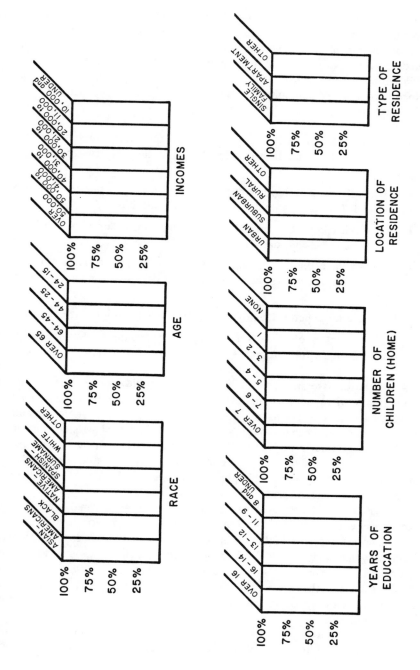

pertinent areas that should be pursued relevant to economic situations within the community as part of the needs assessment. For example, data relevant to the appropriate organization of educational programs for the gifted should consider the predominant types of employment supported by the community.

What this may provide is insights into the key source or sources of economic support within the community. From this base of knowledge, many other questions may be posed, including:

- Is there employment diversity within the community, or is the economic stability of the community closely aligned to the prosperity of a few industries?
- What is the relationship between labor and industry within the community, and what factors may contribute to this relationship?
- How stable is the work force? Is there a large transient or migrant work force that needs to be considered?
- How can the economic growth of the area be described? Is there increased industrialization, or has there been a recent decrease in major employment sources?
- Is there a large percentage of unemployed adults within this community?
- What percentage of adults is receiving public assistance within the area to be served by the gifted program?

As the needs assessment at the district level should produce some listing of supporting services, so, too, should the needs assessment at the community level provide such a listing. The names, numbers, and key personnel of organizations at the community level capable of providing verbal or financial assistance should be accumulated. Contacts made throughout this needs assessment should not be lost to future use within any phase of educational planning. Often, one of the big frustrations in such planning is simply knowing *who* to ask. A carefully developed contact list may lessen this.

No matter in what physical part of the world we are located, new learning experiences exist around us. For some areas there are large farms that provide the sustenance and experiences that are important in our daily lives. In another part of the country there may be a steel mill that provides these materials and experiences. If program developers labor under the assumption that an effective gifted program should be based on the experiences of the individual learner, then knowledge about the geographic design of the community plays an important role in the program development.

Certainly, children living in rural areas will not have all the same types of experiences as children who live in cities; yet they will have many experiences unique to their geographic surroundings. Many of the situations faced by these diverse populations even within the same geographic area will be different and, consequently, deserve important consideration in program organization. For example, the well-publicized environmental problems of urban/suburban Los Angeles are greater, and may deserve more emphasis in gifted programming, than the environmental problems of a predominantly rural community in Virginia. However, within that rural Virginia community, the needs, experiences, and problems of those individuals living near a textile factory or paper mill may also deserve some consideration within the gifted program.

Educational Characteristics

A demographic survey of the community from which the gifted program arises provides an estimation of the educational levels within that community. Additional analysis of educational characteristics of the community population should include other categories, such as:

- the operation of educational institutions within the community—colleges, community colleges, universities, special schools, and vocational and private institutions

- the presence of libraries, museums, and other potential sources of educational experiences

- the existence of special programs or activities with relevance to the gifted learner

- the availability of knowledgeable individuals who could serve as advisors, consultants, or evaluators or assume other direct roles in program development.

Pulling together these facts about the existing educational situation within the community setting can provide the program developers with certain insights into the educational values as well as educational levels of its residents.

Cultural Heritage

At the community level of assessment there are two aspects of heritage or tradition that should come under analysis. First, each community has its own cultural traditions that make it unique from all others. The wealth of history and culture within the community, as well as the extent to which and the manners in which this heritage is displayed, should be evaluated and incorporated into program goals.

Also within each community there exist individuals who come from different cultural backgrounds, and there are many wonderful and beautiful cultural traditions that enable individuals to learn more about each other. Furthermore, there are numerous ways actual information about cultural heritages can be effectively used in the gifted program.

The multicultural aspects of the community provide a means of assisting learners in acquiring an understanding of other learners, thereby assisting each learner to focus on his own identity, posing and looking for the answer to the question of "Who am I?" In areas where there are large concentrations of individuals of diverse cultural backgrounds, not only should the personal and educational needs of these individuals become a specific part of program development but also their knowledge and experience should provide learning opportunities for others. By accumulating data about cultural groups that exist in the surrounding community, we develop an awareness of these cultures. As we begin to incorporate the knowledge gained from the needs assessment, we demonstrate an acceptance of, and appreciation for, the cultural diversity that may abound. It would appear that the optimal growth of a learner through gifted programming necessitates this awareness, acceptance, and appreciation for whatever cultural heritage the learner brings to the learning situation.

Examining the Relevant Characteristics of the School Curriculum

Because the gifted program will need to operate within the framework of the current school curriculum, it will be advantageous if not essential for the program developers to gather information about the present school curriculum that will enable them to develop a gifted program that complements the present curriculum and operates harmoniously within the total school philosophy. Therefore, the first step in this aspect of the process is the identification of the overall school philosophy and goals. If the school is adhering to the overall philosophical belief, then these beliefs will be reflected in such areas as the types of instructional strategies and materials used or the types of grouping and class structure arrangements. Other areas that will reflect the school's overall philosophical beliefs will be the types of assessment procedures used to place children in special instructional groups or programs. In addition, the overall methods of evaluating both the school program and students will give some indication of the school curriculum and its relationship to the school philosophy.

Key elements that should undergo scrutiny at the curriculum level of assessment include:

- What are the scope and sequence of the present school curriculum?
- What special materials, equipment, and strategies are being applied within the classroom setting?

- What educational programs are in operation outside the context of the regular classroom?
- How are students vertically and horizontally grouped for instruction?
- What is the physical environment of the school itself?
- What is the decision-making process within the educational institution?

The trend in the recent literature on gifted programming appears to indicate a move toward providing the differentiated instruction the gifted learner requires within the classroom setting (a fact that will frequently appear throughout this book). Should this, indeed, be the case, then it is even more imperative that program developers have some concept of what is being covered throughout the grades and what generally is being studied at each level. Unless completely removed or segregated for instruction for the entire period of education, the gifted learner at some point must come into contact with the regular curricular program. How to provide the gifted learner with needed instruction while still maintaining, to some degree, the integrity of the curriculum content is a topic discussed at length in Chapter 5.

When any special program is initiated, there is sometimes an urge to purchase new equipment and materials or to attempt innovative teaching strategies. Such an urge is not bad, although such purchases or innovations should be pursued only with an awareness of what materials, equipment, or strategies may already be available. New is not always better. Therefore, some assessment of workable and available materials and equipment is clearly called for, and a look at teaching strategies that have applicability to the gifted learner should be considered. There may be classes in which the teacher is meeting the needs of high potential students and from which information can be synthesized, or there may be another class in which the teacher appears to have a knack in reaching culturally different students. However, if the procedures and materials employed by the entire school are not equitable for children from diverse cultures, it will be essential to develop alternate strategies for these culturally diverse individuals within the gifted program.

As alluded to previously, the gifted program has much to gain from an assessment of other alternative programs, and vice versa. The trials, tribulations, and triumphs of existing programs within the school setting can furnish valuable information. For example, much can be learned about administrative procedures, referral processes, and areas of possible difficulty. In addition, programs that also mandate testing as a part of the identification process could serve as a source of information on test release forms and on methods of reporting test data, for example. Operating instructional programs can also serve as illustrations of such things as housing difficulties, unanticipated paper work, and sources of volunteer aides. These existing programs also reflect the attitude and philosophy of the school on providing for individual differences, often more realistically than that school's theoretical statements of beliefs.

Probably no other factor demonstrates the true philosophy of a school or school system more vividly than how that school or school system chooses to organize its population of learners. Is the student population homogeneously or heterogeneously grouped? Is this a graded or nongraded curricular situation? Are students tracked according to various criteria? Is there flexibility in the group setting, allowing students to move about within the curriculum according to their interests and needs as well as abilities? Certainly, in settings where learners' educational experiences are dictated on the basis of verbal test scores the experiences will be controlled by such factors as the student's language system, language competence, test conditions, and test content, to name only a few, and may not be guided by that student's specific strengths, needs, interests, and motivations. How students are grouped for regular instruction may have some bearing on how the administration may suggest gifted classes be grouped or how the classes should be scheduled.

Quite frequently we overlook the physical plant of the school as one aspect of the total school curriculum. Although other components may weigh more heavily in this process, the structural environmental facets of the educational institution will have some bearing on the programs for gifted learners. Is the school open-spaced or the more traditional closed-space structure? Are special classes held physically apart from regular classrooms or integrated in space? Is there sufficient area in which to conduct separate gifted classes?

How are major decisions made within the school, and what kind of effect will this chain-of-command have on the development of the gifted program? Should the principal play a key role from the outset of program conceptualization or only after committee groundwork has been laid? Do parents and students, as well as teachers, have input into the decision-making process?

In relation to this aspect of needs assessment, it may prove invaluable for those interested in initiating curriculum modifications for gifted students to start with some formal assessment of parents, students, teachers, and administrators. Such an assessment may take the form of a Likert-type questionnaire, which would demonstrate the favorable or unfavorable attitude of those surveyed toward these curriculum modifications and the corresponding needs of gifted learners (see Exhibit 3-3).

This assessment of parent, teacher, student, and administration opinions can also take the form of a discrepancy model (see Exhibit 3-4). In a discrepancy model, the individual judges the existing situation against the desired situation, thus allowing for an obvious comparison of the ideal to the existent.

By conducting an assessment of the opinions of those directly or indirectly associated with the education of the gifted and, consequently, affected by attempts to modify gifted programming, three critical goals are met. First, quantifiable data may be amassed that supports or substantiates the claims made by program

Exhibit 3-3 Gifted Opinionnaire

SA = Strongly agree
A = Agree
U = Undecided
D = Disagree
SD = Strongly disagree

Please circle the letter(s) that correspond to your opinion on the related question. Be sure to mark what you actually believe and not what you may think you should believe.

1. The gifted will learn regardless of instruction.   SA A U D SD
2. The gifted are often bored in regular classes.   SA A U D SD
3. Better programs for the gifted are needed.   SA A U D SD
4. Classroom teachers are adequately prepared   SA A U D SD
   to instruct the gifted.
5. The gifted should help plan their own   SA A U D SD
   educational experiences.
6. Too much attention is given the gifted.   SA A U D SD
7. The gifted are easily identified.   SA A U D SD
8. There are gifted in all cultural groups.   SA A U D SD
9. The gifted should get all they need in   SA A U D SD
   the regular classroom.
10. Classroom teachers should be responsible   SA A U D SD
    for providing adequate instruction for
    the gifted.

---

initiators regarding the desirability of and need for more comprehensive education for gifted learners. Second, should no support or interest be expressed in these opinionnaires, the program developers may either abandon any further attempts at change, pursue their beliefs in spite of the relevant data, or rethink their position in light of this and other pertinent information.

A third consequence of this needs assessment that should not be overlooked is that it serves as a vehicle for involvement. This means that from the earliest phases of program development, the opinions and reactions of many segments of the school community are actively sought and purposely considered as part of the decision-making process. These various groups begin to view the gifted program that unfolds as a product of diverse interactions rather than as the ''baby'' of a few. However, for any program to survive, it requires a strong base of continued support, and the assessment procedures outlined here are but one means of actively soliciting such support.

Exhibit 3-4 Discrepancy Model

1. Almost never, or never
2. Seldom
3. Sometimes
4. Often
5. Very frequently or always

These questions should be answered as they pertain to your particular school or school district.

Is	Item	Should Be
1 2 3 4 5	Teachers are provided with information about the gifted.	1 2 3 4 5
1 2 3 4 5	Regular classrooms are responsible for educating the gifted.	1 2 3 4 5
1 2 3 4 5	Parents have a role in gifted education.	1 2 3 4 5
1 2 3 4 5	Gifted education is a priority of the school (or school system).	1 2 3 4 5
1 2 3 4 5	The needs of the gifted are being met.	1 2 3 4 5
1 2 3 4 5	There is careful formulation of identification procedures.	1 2 3 4 5
1 2 3 4 5	Teachers are adequately prepared to teach the gifted.	1 2 3 4 5
1 2 3 4 5	Suitable instruction is available for the gifted.	1 2 3 4 5
1 2 3 4 5	When materials are needed to work with the gifted, they are available.	1 2 3 4 5
1 2 3 4 5	The administration shows concern for the gifted.	1 2 3 4 5

In summary, if the gifted learner must function within the context of the regular school curriculum for any portion of the school year, it is vital for the developers of gifted programming to construct some link to that preexisting curriculum. If not, a barrier rather than a bridge to the regular curriculum may arise from the noble endeavors of the architects of educational programs for the gifted.

Examining the Relevant Characteristics of the School Personnel

When assessing the relevant features of the personnel, whether at the district or school level, three areas of importance must come under consideration. These three areas are competencies, capacities, and concerns. Although each segment should be analyzed and weighed separately, the ideal personnel to be associated with the education of the gifted should be adequate in all three categories. The components of competencies, capacities, and concerns will now be analyzed individually, with attention paid to the various relevant criteria within each.

Competencies

Those criteria labeled under the heading of competencies will relate to *demonstrated* abilities with direct relevance to the education of the gifted. Among pertinent criteria that desire consideration within this area are the following.

Certification in Gifted Education. Such certification is available throughout the country through several institutions of higher education.

Coursework in Gifted Education. An individual, although lacking specific certification in gifted education, may have completed courses relevant to the gifted at either the preservice or inservice level of career.

Instruction of the Gifted. Not to be overlooked as a competency would be an individual's role as instructor within a gifted program. While the two previous criteria represent demonstrated abilities at the theoretical level, this criterion views one's actual performance with the gifted. It must be cautioned that how well the individual functioned should warrant as much consideration as the simple fact of having such an experience.

Descriptive or Research Studies Regarding the Gifted. Personnel should be viewed as a potential source of knowledge in the quest for comprehensive education of the gifted. Knowledge can be accumulated in any of several ways. While actual experiences with the gifted may receive more weight in the assessment process, those of a vicarious nature should not be ignored. Those who have knowledge to contribute in the development of comprehensive education for the gifted should be encouraged to do so.

Capacities

Within this area of relevant characteristics, the personnel are evaluated not for direct experiences with the gifted but for demonstrated abilities that could have applications in the gifted program. These capacities fall into the broad classifications of teaching proficiency, administrative abilities, community and/or cultural awareness, and communication skills.

Teaching Proficiency. There are those among the school personnel who appear to have the ability to interact positively with students. These teachers are often held in high esteem by the students as well as by their colleagues. This teaching proficiency deserves recognition within the assessment process.

Administrative Abilities. Not all critical roles or positions within the gifted program will be filled by those whose experiences lie within the teaching arena. Often, the success of the program will rest on the effective organization and administration of that program. Therefore, when assessing the available personnel, program initiators must be sensitive to those individuals who exhibit proficiency within the administrative arena.

Community and/or Cultural Awareness. One fact that has been and will be continually mentioned in this text is that the gifted program cannot operate within a vacuum. The program must reach out and connect with the surrounding community. Frequently, among the school personnel there are those individuals who have the cultural sensitivity and community awareness necessary to establish the link to the surrounding populace (Hass, 1974).

Communication Skills. The development and survival of the gifted program will revolve around the ability to communicate what is occurring to others within and outside the school setting. Keeping those who are not immediately involved in program development in the dark, so to speak, can only result in their apparent disenchantment or disinterest in the process. Consequently, it is not only important to share occurrences with others but to structure these communications to obtain the most favorable results. This could best be achieved if those with special skills in communication apply these skills in gifted programming.

Concerns

While the areas of competencies and capacities deal with demonstrated behaviors (the latter with direct relevance to the gifted learner and the former with potential application to the gifted), the area entitled "concerns" encompasses the attitudes, interests, and motivations of the school personnel. Because of the more nebulous characteristics associated with this classification, the identification of appropriate behaviors becomes more difficult. Yet, the willingness of individuals to perform tasks important to program development, the interest in the gifted expressed by these individuals, and their motivations to achieve better programming for the gifted are the sparks that ensure the success of the gifted program.

Why Assess Personnel?

The topic of the assessment of relevant characteristics of the personnel should not be put aside without some analysis of the purpose behind this evaluation. The reasons for careful consideration of the personnel are threefold.

1. *It profiles the areas of potential personnel strengths and weaknesses as they pertain to gifted programming.* This is probably the most obvious and important advantage of conducting an assessment of the personnel. What it

creates is a profile of the areas of potential strength and probable weakness, including the presence or absence of experiences with the gifted learner, the expressed adequacy or inadequacy of the personnel, and their demonstrated interests and concerns as they relate to the gifted.

2. *It may indicate sources of support or conflict.* As the needs assessment may pinpoint sources of strength and weakness among the personnel, so, too, does this activity function as a source of other information as well. What this information provides is an indication of bastions of support that might exist among the personnel or the apparent lack of such support. For example, if the discrepancy evaluation produces a high, favorable rating among classroom teachers while displaying a low, unfavorable rating for administrators, it can be speculated that these classroom teachers might provide added support to program initiation efforts. The administrators surveyed, however, may require much convincing.

3. *It identifies the personnel who may play key roles in gifted program development.* It would be wasteful to accumulate information about the school personnel unless maximum benefit can be realized from its use. Therefore, as we become aware of available personnel who have the experiences, capacities, and concerns to make positive contributions in the education of the gifted it seems imperative to make use of these individuals' abilities. For example, should one individual in the school system have certification in gifted education, it would seem ridiculous *not* to make full use of that individual's talents and knowledge.

Examining the Relevant Characteristics of the School Population

Before full implementation of programming for gifted learners can be realized, it is necessary to consider the characteristics of the school population from which these gifted learners will be chosen. Although the information obtained on the school population will, in many respects, closely resemble that obtained in the needs assessment of the community, additional information such as the sex ratio of the school, enrollment size, and projected trends should also be obtained. This information will be helpful in more accurate estimations of the kinds of services and facilities that will be needed to ensure adequate gifted programming. In addition, while information on the stability of the school population as well as on the racial, religious, and cultural characteristics should correlate closely with that obtained in the community assessment, the average grade levels completed, the dropout trends for that particular school, and the scores on tests administered across grade levels should also be closely evaluated.

In summary, the needs assessment of the school population is primarily conducted to give the program developers an overall understanding of the students enrolled. Such data are crucial in order not only to understand the students' physical and cultural makeup but also to obtain a general idea of the students' pattern of achievement in the school.

Examining the Relevant Characteristics of the Gifted Population

If previous gifted programs have operated within the school or school district, program developers or coordinators, as the case may be, should include an analysis of existing or preexisting gifted populations. From this analysis, decisions can be made regarding the apparent effectiveness of identification procedures in locating a diversity of gifted learners, of instructional strategies suitable for these individuals, and of the program format, to mention a few. When a gifted population is already in existence, the question must be raised as to whether this population matches the philosophy of the program now or if modifications are required. If the profile of the population appears satisfactory, then questions regarding the relevance of the program to this population could then be considered.

One method of providing a match between population and program could begin with the feelings, beliefs, and views of gifted learners themselves. By sitting down with the gifted in our schools and by encouraging an open discussion of relevant issues, we can accumulate more accurate information than might be gained solely from inference or speculation. Round table discussions and attitudinal ratings, for example, could be employed in this process.

Summary of the Assessment Process

The needs assessment phase in comprehensive educational planning for the gifted should be seen as a vital component of program development. Although the labors of information collection and synthesis may appear overwhelming at first, their efficient planning and execution serves many purposes. Not the least of these purposes is the fact that what can be achieved is a precise and vivid display of the immediate context in which the proposed gifted program must operate. The knowledge gained by an effectively done needs assessment can provide program initiators with a basis for identifying strengths and weaknesses within relevant areas; with a sense of the favorable or unfavorable attitudes of students, parents, teachers, and administrators toward considered modifications in the existing curriculum; and with a link to individuals within the various areas of concern from the outset of the program's conceptualization who can play a vital role in that program's success or failure. In essence, all the rigorous investigation undertaken in the initial phase of organization furnishes a strong basis on which appropriate decisions can be made. Without such a basis much time and energy may need to be invested in unraveling or undoing those actions taken without adequate forethought. It should not be concluded, however, that steps taken following a needs assessment cannot also be inappropriate. What should be concluded is that inappropriate steps can and should be minimized through the needs assessment process. Questions that may be used as a guide for conducting the needs assessment are provided in Exhibit 3-5.

Exhibit 3-5 Pertinent Questions in Conducting the Needs
Assessment

Examining the Relevant Characteristics of the School District

- What is the school district's philosophy toward providing differentiated instruction for children with special needs?

- What types of special programs or courses already exist in the school district?

- Is the school district flexible in its approach to scheduling and/or providing special class or course arrangements?

- What are the strengths and weaknesses of other gifted programs presently operating within the school district?

- Are there other gifted programs, outside of the school district, that could provide useful information?

- Is the school district willing to provide a budget for the type of gifted program being proposed?

- How are other gifted programs, existing in the school district, being funded?

- What types of resource teachers operate within the school district?

- Are there any buildings or rooms that can be used for the gifted program?

- Are supplies available within the school district that can be obtained without purchasing?

Examining the Relevant Characteristics of the Community

- What are the important demographic data describing the community to be serviced by the gifted program?

- What percent of the population is unemployed?

Exhibit 3-5 continued

- What percent of the population within the service area is on public assistance?

- What major type(s) of employment is(are) characteristic of your community?
  Professional
  Semiprofessional and business
  Skilled workers
  Semiskilled
  Unskilled

- What is the status of the population living in the city?
  Transient population
  College community
  Military population
  Stable population

- What major occupations or industries are located in the community that would be important resources in the development of the gifted program?

- What individuals in the community could be an invaluable resource to your program?

- What clubs, organizations, and agencies are available to call on for assistance?

- What are the most pressing concerns facing the community?
  Local government
  Land
  Energy
  Other

- What are the long-range projections for your community?
  Controlled growth
  Rapid expansion

- Are there local educational institutions that could provide support services for the gifted program?
  Community colleges
  Colleges
  Universities
  Special schools
  Vocational and private schools

Exhibit 3-5 continued

- What are the educational resources existing in the community?
  Libraries
  Museums
  Other

- Are there other special programs or activities being conducted in the community that could provide assistance to the proposed gifted program?

- What are the names of individuals who can provide assistance in the development and implementation of the gifted program?
  Advisors
  Consultants
  Evaluators

- What are the cultural characteristics of the community to be serviced by the gifted program?

Examining the Relevant Characteristics of the School Curriculum

- What is the overall school philosophy?

- Are the types of instructional strategies and materials used consistent with the school's philosophy and goals?

- What are the school's methods of evaluation of programs? students?

- What is the decision-making structure operating within the school?

- What methods are used for assessment and placement of pupils into programs?

- What are the school's present grouping and/or class structure arrangements?
  Homogeneous or heterogeneous
  Graded or nongraded
  Structured or open environment
  Other

- How will the gifted program operate within the scope and sequence of the entire curriculum?

Exhibit 3-5 continued

Examining the Relevant Characteristics of the School Personnel

- What are the school personnel's attitudes toward providing programs for gifted learners?
- Are there any personnel that have special qualifications for working with the gifted?
  Previously taught the gifted
  Coursework in gifted education
  Certification in gifted education
- Are there any personnel who have demonstrated particular skills or abilities essential for the success of a gifted program?
  Teaching proficiency
  Administrative abilities
  Community/cultural awareness skills
  Communication skills

Examining the Relevant Characteristics of the School Population

- What is the racial/sex/religious makeup of the school?
- What were enrollment size and trends over past five years?
- What are the dropout trends?
- What is the stability of school population?
- What are the test score averages across grade levels?

Examining the Relevant Characteristics of the Gifted Population

- How effective were previous attempts to identify gifted learners?
- What are the perceptions of gifted learners presently enrolled in other programs about the structure of their education?
- What have the gifted learners who are to be served by this program expressed as their concerns and points of view about the proposed gifted program?
- What are the physical, psychological, social, and emotional needs of the gifted learners to be served by the proposed program?

LEVELS OF PROGRAM PLANNING

In the previous section it was shown that throughout the needs assessment there will be a systematic and detailed analysis of the immediate context into which a gifted program will be placed. As was stressed, no gifted program can exist in isolation and, therefore, such an analysis is mandatory if one is to understand the local framework in which the conceived improvements in gifted education must somehow function. This framework just alluded to does not exist only at the local level of education, however, but encompasses the actions, trends, issues, and policies at the national and state levels, as well (Wiles & Bondi 1979). Consequently, the entire scheme into which the desired program must mesh should be scrutinized and patterns of actions discerned in much the same way as one would scrutinize a puzzle into which a particular piece must fit. It will be the purpose of this section, therefore, to consider these levels of program planning, to pose various questions about them for which the answers may furnish useful information, and to provide an overview of the patterns of policy making that may arise across these levels.

If we view these levels in gifted education as the framework for program planning, then it is important to consider two qualities of that framework: consistency and flexibility. *Consistency* refers to the limits or bounds that have been established at each level in regard to program implementations. These limits or constraints are often labeled as the guidelines for program development. *Flexibility,* on the other hand, refers to the options possible within these established guidelines. Theoretically, these two aspects, although seemingly contradictory, must function simultaneously at and across each program stage, whether it be at the national, state, district, school, or individual level.

As suggested by Figure 3-4, these qualities of consistency and flexibility operate directionally. Moving downward through these stages of program planning from national to individual levels, the thrust moves from more theoretical concerns such as policy statements to more learner-relevant activities such as developing specific curricular objectives. At the national level, for example, while directing or overseeing gifted education, it is necessary to develop guidelines that provide leeway for state and local program planners who must meet the specific needs of their particular gifted populations. Similarly, as states write guidelines for their educational institutions, they, too, must allow adequate flexibility within those guidelines for those levels (district, school, and individual) that must apply them to gifted learners.

From the more learner-specific levels, conversely, the major concern for program initiators is that what they choose to do for the gifted student will be consistent with the actions suggested by those planning stages above. To demonstrate this directionality, the specific curricular decisions made regarding a single gifted learner should be consistent with policies established at the school level.

Figure 3-4 Levels of Program Planning

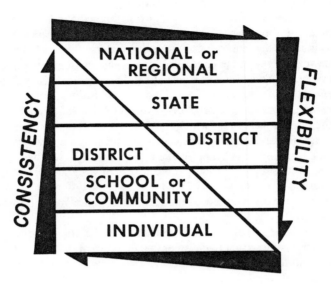

School gifted programs, in turn, should be established within the guidelines provided by the district level, and so on.

Therefore, these two planning aspects of consistency and flexibility will interact to some degree at each program level, although the thrust or emphasis will differ according to the major concerns at each level. Only at the district stage does this interaction between flexibility and consistency approach a balance. This would suggest that program developers at the district level must be as concerned with creating policies that satisfy the guidelines coming down from the state level as they are with providing guidelines that permit schools the leeway they require to meet the needs of their specific gifted populations. However, at each stage of program planning these aspects of consistency and flexibility should be applied to all institutions and individuals on an equal basis. The flow of information throughout this planning process should be continuous. Whenever needs are expressed or conflicts arise, there should be careful analysis of the situation. Accommodations can be made in the framework or consensus can be reached within the situational level, and this need or conflict can be reflected in actions that arise at other levels. For example, problems that appear within the context of the classroom, if of sufficient universality, may eventually be reflected in changes that occur at the national stage of policy development.

It would also be useful to consider several of the details of operations at each of these program levels, in addition to the broader overview just presented, and to relate these operations to actions taken at the school/individual stages.

National

At the national level of program planning, there is a more immediate concern for the types of gifted legislation enacted by Congress than for other planning levels. Specifically relevant to actions taken at these other stages, however, is how this federal legislation relates to the selection of students for particular programs and the implementation of those programs themselves. This issue will be discussed in greater depth in Chapter 8.

In addition to and often connected with federal legislation, there is funding that is made available to various agencies from the federal government for the implementation of gifted programs. Generally, federal monies are allotted first to the states for providing services to their respective institutions and jurisdictions. The states, therefore, disseminate a portion of their funds to the localities and institutions that satisfy the criteria established for education of the gifted. Localities, in turn, allot funds to specific areas in accordance with budgetary and policy guidelines.

Besides being a disseminator of finances, this national segment in gifted education serves as a disseminator of information as well. Individuals working at the federal level of program planning collect data, commission reports and studies, evaluate programs, establish guidelines, and synthesize, publish, and distribute massive amounts of information. The federal government also operates the Office of the Talented and Gifted, along with numerous leadership conferences, experimental programs, and consulting services.

For organizers of gifted programs at other levels of planning, the knowledge from the national agencies can be of invaluable assistance in developing more effective programs based on the latest trends and information available.

Although not directly affiliated with the federal government, there are several nonprofit support organizations operating at the national and regional levels of planning. These organizations may hold conferences, publish journals or magazines, and provide speakers—services that may prove useful to those interested in gifted education. Examples of organizations are the Council for Exceptional Children (CEC) and the National Association for Gifted Children.

State

On a smaller scale than the national level, the states perform the similar functions of developing program guidelines consistent with those of the federal government, providing services, and disseminating funds and information to localities. However, their responsibilities do not end here. In addition, the states are responsible for correctly interpreting the federal law as it affects them, as well as assisting local program developers in the interpretation of federal policies and guidelines. State consultants are sometimes available to provide inservices or to clarify questions that arise in the program's development.

Another function that is often carried out by the states is the provision of opportunities for staffs of gifted programs to meet and share ideas. This is usually done through state conferences and meetings. State personnel often take an active role in these meetings. Sometimes conferences are sponsored by nongovernment organizations dedicated to providing quality instruction for the gifted.

Many states have also established an advisory council made up of members from the state, district, and local levels. While the committee's role may vary somewhat, its primary purposes are generally to: (1) advise state agencies about the progress of gifted education, (2) provide input into developing a state plan of action, (3) evaluate actions already taken on behalf of the gifted learner, and (4) function as liaison among the different levels.

District

The pivotal point in program planning is the district level of gifted education development. It is at this stage that the interaction between flexibility and consistency is markedly apparent and probably most demanding. Receiving information directly from the local institutions, district organizers must be sensitive to the expressed needs of school personnel regarding their gifted populations. Simultaneously, these district program planners must adhere to federal and state guidelines on gifted education, as well as their own educational philosophy. Providing the most comprehensive gifted programming possible requires district planners to perform a tenuous balancing act among the variables of constraints, needs, and beliefs. Factors that may alleviate some of the difficulty at this level are the solicitation of counsel from supporting agencies or other available sources and the encouragement of input directly from institutions and individuals under the district's jurisdiction.

School

At the school level the major consideration for program developers becomes the effective organization of a curriculum for the gifted that can function harmoniously within the existing school context and still satisfy the specific needs of the gifted population. Farther removed from the theoretical mandates of establishing guidelines for other institutions, schools must manipulate policy into some practical plan of action. One prerequisite to program planning, as demonstrated in the needs assessment, is the clarification of the school's philosophical position. The closer to the institution's overall philosophy the philosophy of the gifted program is, the more harmoniously it can blend into the existing curriculum. Certainly, the success of implemented gifted programs will be greatly influenced by their flexibility for combining with the school curriculum at large.

It becomes vital for school personnel concerned with gifted program implementation to approach the task well informed and well motivated. These individuals must communicate their feelings and ideas about gifted education to many persons in and out of the school context. It is frequently at this stage in program planning that many questions such as the following are asked: Why do we need special programs for the gifted? Gifted students can learn on their own—why do we need to change things? What do you mean by "gifted" anyway? These are difficult questions that require justification. We cannot expect school personnel, parents, and students to wholeheartedly support any program which they do not adequately understand. It is, therefore, necessary to provide this understanding in the best way possible.

This process of communication just described, however, should be reciprocal. Program planners at the school level should ask questions and should seek advice whenever appropriate. Furthermore, school level planners should involve the community, students, and school personnel in their efforts from the outset. The broader the base of involvement and commitment, the greater the probability of program survival.

Individual

All the intensive and effective planning conducted at the other levels of program planning will prove fruitless if positive change and educational growth does not take place for the individual gifted learner. On the one hand, the knowledge, support, and guidance provided through effective gifted educational planning can assist in effective and efficient decision making with regard to the gifted learner. On the other hand, the effect of what we do with that gifted learner, positive or negative, should serve as a catalyst for change in policy whenever it appears that what is occurring in actuality deviates from what is suggested in theory.

What must be remembered at this level of program planning is that from the top-down in processing there is the need to adapt policies and theories to specific learners, while from the bottom-up the knowledge of effects and results of suggested procedures on gifted learners should be employed in policy and theory modification. What this demands is not only a working knowledge of the theories and policies behind gifted education but also an understanding of the strengths and weaknesses of the gifted learner. Indeed, comprehensive education for the gifted is a two-way process of communication.

What has been presented here is but a skeleton of the complete structure that operates in gifted program planning throughout all levels of education. Other questions and concerns that might be raised in the decision-making process are summarized in Exhibit 3-6. It would be wise for program developers to pose such questions at the outset of planning for the gifted learner when their answers could prove the most valuable.

Exhibit 3-6 Pertinent Questions for the Levels of Program Planning

National

- Are there federal laws that must be considered in program planning?
- What types of federal funding are available for gifted program development?
- What information is available at the national level?
  Research studies and reports for the edification of program developers?
  Literature useful in public relations endeavors?
- Are experimental programs sponsored at the federal level that could serve as program models?
- What national meetings and conferences on gifted education are being conducted that might suit the program's particular needs?
- Are there training or leadership sessions on gifted education operating at the national level?
- Does the federal government furnish consultants to other levels of planning?
- What offices at the federal level are responsible for gifted education, and what are the names of contact persons within these offices?

State

- Has there been a state plan for gifted education developed?
  Does this plan take the form of mandates or guidelines?
  Does the state plan include an interpretation of federal laws and guidelines?
- How does the state disseminate funds for gifted education?

Exhibit 3-6 continued

- What services does the state make available in regards to gifted education?

    Is training provided by the state?

    Does the state hold conferences on the gifted?

    Are speakers and consultants made available through the state?

- Is an advisory council or task force on gifted education operating in the state?

- How does the state evaluate gifted programs?

- What model gifted programs, if any, are functioning in the state?

- What government or nongovernment gifted organizations exist at the state level?

- Who are the contact persons at the state level in charge of gifted programming?

- Does the state publish information for professionals and nonprofessionals about the gifted or gifted education?

District

- Has the district allowed for gifted programming within its budget?

- Have any inservices been planned for personnel in the area of gifted education?

- Does the district publish newsletters or brochures that could be of use in disseminating information about the gifted?

- What types of programs does the district provide for other special student groups?

- What special staff members at the district level, such as guidance counselors or school psychologists, can be used as resources for the gifted program?

- How are important curricular decisions made at the district level?

- Has the district prepared guidelines on gifted education?

- Who, if anyone, is responsible for gifted education at the district level?

Exhibit 3-6 continued

School/Community

- Are there any personnel with training or experience in gifted education?

- Does the school have a clearly stated philosophy of education?

- Does the present curriculum make any provisions for the gifted learner?

- What physical modifications would be necessary to house a gifted program?

- What staff members have expressed commitment to education of the gifted?

- Are there grade level or department chairpersons that should be involved in the decision-making process?

SUMMARY

In this chapter the planning of comprehensive gifted education was surveyed in two ways. First, procedures were suggested that would allow initiators of gifted programming to accurately and thoroughly assess the immediate environment in which the proposed program would eventually operate. Referred to as the needs assessment, this process involved the evaluation of the existing situation to ascertain the areas of apparent strength or weakness relevant to the education of the gifted. Those areas involved in the needs assessment included not only the school district and community but also the curriculum, personnel, student body, and gifted population. Each of these areas was subsequently evaluated from geographic, cultural, physical, general, educational, and socioeconomic perspectives, and their pertinent characteristics were determined.

Second, the gifted program was considered from a vertical direction of organization. The questions and information presented in this section pertained to how the proposed program would mesh into the entire educational scheme. What is proposed at the district level, for example, must carefully consider the policies and programs implemented at the state and national levels of education.

The principal point to be made by this chapter is that no gifted program can function in isolation. Consequently, those who prepare programs for the gifted must consider educational occurrences at the immediate level of operation as well as those occurrences across these various educational levels. This consideration must involve the accumulation of relevant and accurate information through some type of assessment procedure. Relevant information that can be acquired and synthesized through the assessment process should lead to the establishment of program objectives based on determined needs rather than unfounded speculation. Furthermore, this pertinent data can serve as the foundation for future evaluation of the newly implemented gifted program.

REFERENCES

Hass, G. Who should plan the curriculum. In G. Hass, J. Bondi, & J. Wiles (Eds.), *Curriculum planning: A new approach.* Boston: Allyn & Bacon, 1974.

Wiles, J., & Bondi, J. *Curriculum development: A guide to practice.* Columbus, Ohio: Charles E. Merrill, 1979.

Chapter 4

Establishing Program Goals and Objectives

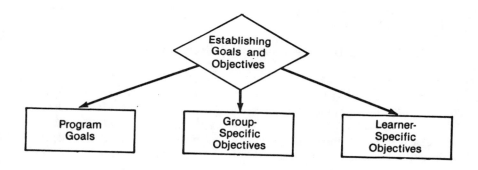

Through an in-depth analysis of factors affecting educational experiences for the gifted provided by a needs assessment, program planners have been furnished with a blueprint of concerns and situations to be addressed by the gifted program. It is these needs that are eventually transformed into the goals and objectives of the gifted program. While the needs assessment poses the questions to be answered, the goals become their tentative solutions and the objectives become the methodology applied to arrive at such solutions. In general, goals provide the sense of direction to be taken within program development and the objectives provide the means of transporting theory into practice.

Within this chapter, the goals and objectives for educational programming for the gifted learner will be distinguished, discussed, and detailed. To begin, the interpretation of these terms will be clarified and the goal areas presented. The procedures for objective formulation will be outlined, followed by an analysis of the levels of objectives, with illustrations of each offered. The overall purpose of this chapter, therefore, will be to move the gifted educational process from general statements of program intent to specific and realizable ends deeply rooted in an understanding of the strengths and needs of the individual gifted learner.

UNIT-SPECIFIC OR PROGRAM GOALS

Often in the literature the terms "goals" and "objectives" appear to be used interchangeably. However, a more accurate interpretation of these terms will be necessary as program development moves into the stage of specifying general and specific aims. Goals for gifted programs can be defined as the general or broad statement of intent or direction. These goals are unit specific in nature, implying that their base of reference will be the entire gifted population-at-large as knowledge of this population pertains to the instructional institution or unit under consideration. These unit-specific or program goals should arise directly from the information amassed in the needs assessment and should indicate, in writing, the priorities of the established program (see Figure 4-1). This knowledge accumulated within the needs assessment can generally be focused into three relevant areas: (1) giftedness and the learning process, (2) the influence of society, and (3) knowledge and content.

Areas Influencing the Development of Program Goals

The acquisition of data in the needs assessment provides program planners with an understanding of the perceived strengths and needs of the environment in which the gifted program must function. Once these perceived needs have been collected the next step in the process will be to focus and organize this information into interrelated areas. The three areas of focus to be discussed include (1) those aspects of the needs assessment that relate to the gifted learner and the individualized and internalized process of learning that takes place, (2) those involving the interaction between the learner and the surrounding context, and (3) those describing the interaction between the gifted learner and the content to be learned. Being organized in this manner, the needs assessment enables program planners to draw a comparison between the perceived needs and the theoretical framework that underlies what is already known about giftedness and the learning process, the influence of society, and knowledge of the gifted learner.

Figure 4-1 The Process of Goal Development

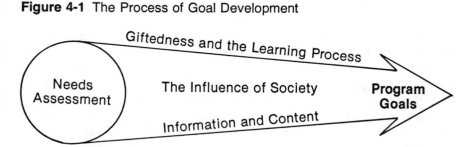

Gifted Learners

One of the primary sources used in selecting the overall aims of the gifted program is the gifted learners themselves. In the goal development process, taking into consideration what is presently known about learning and human development and information about gifted learners and their needs, interests, and abilities will ensure the development of relevant and realistic goals for these learners.

A generally accepted fact is that all students learn differently. Consequently, in order to ensure the uniqueness of the individual, the overall aims of the gifted program should provide for diversity in learning. This can be accomplished by carefully studying different learning theories and recognizing the influence these theories have on the development of the gifted program. The cognitive, behaviorist, and social learning theories, for example, have provided great understanding about students and how they learn. The cognitive theorists, such as Bruner (1960), have focused attention on the structure of knowledge and the acquisition and understanding of general principles. The behavioral theorists have stressed the influence of the environment in shaping an individual's behavior, and the social learning theorists have argued that learning takes place in, and is dependent on, the social atmosphere, which includes, school, family, peers, and societal influences.

Research on human growth and development has also provided important insights into the learner. As humans we are constantly changing; thus, as developmental theorists indicate, we proceed through a series of fixed stages. For example, Piaget's theory (Flavell, 1963), described in Chapter 1, includes four stages of development, starting with the sensorimotor period and ending with the formal operations stage, which exemplifies more advanced cognitive development. Havighurst (1953), another developmental theorist, presents a series of developmental tasks in the psychological, biological, and cultural areas. In addition, theorists Erickson (1968) and Kohlberg (1964) provide insights into the emotional and moral development of the individual.

Certainly the goals of the gifted program are not mutually exclusive; thus, what is designed for the gifted learner will also be beneficial to other students as well. However, research that has attempted to focus more on the gifted has identified characteristics of these learners that would be essential to consider in the formulation of program goals. For example, while the development of divergent-thinking skills should be taught to all learners, the cultivation of these skills is crucial for gifted learners because of their consistent demonstration of unique conceptualization and problem-solving skills. Likewise, because gifted children are highly aware of their unique abilities and the strain this sometimes places on their relationships with other peers, it is essential that the design of the gifted program take into consideration for these learners the development of self-awareness and self-realization skills.

The literature also abounds with numerous references to the special talents and interests of the gifted learner. It is essential, then, in order to assist gifted learners in developing their potential abilities that outlets be provided in the curriculum for them to demonstrate their unique talents and to pursue special areas of interest.

From such information about the learning process that is presented here, and much more, program planners can begin to match or compare their perceived needs with the knowledge about the learning process that is available. This comparison should give rise to many questions or concerns that can ultimately be framed into program goals. Some examples of these questions are:

- Does our thinking about the gifted program provide for a diversity of learning styles?

- What influence will theories of human growth and development have on the sequence of presentation of subject matter?

- How can we best ensure that learners will enter into learning at their appropriate level of development?

- How can the curriculum foster the social, moral, and emotional development of the learners?

- Is our thinking about the gifted curriculum such that we will be able to provide opportunities for gifted learners to display their unique talents and abilities?

Influence of Society

Society, the values of society, and information about the changing nature of society is a second area from which the overall aims of the gifted program will be formulated. One premise that has been frequently referred to in this text is the fact that the gifted program cannot exist in isolation but must fit within and be complementary to the overall school program. Likewise, the gifted program must be influenced by society and the future of society. It may not be enough that school and school programs provide opportunities for learners to grow consistent with their needs. The very nature of education, itself, assumes that learning will involve experiences that will enable students to realize their role in society and the role they will play as citizens in solving problems facing our nation and the world. It is essential then that the gifted curriculum not only prepare learners for living in today's world but also prepare learners for their role in the future.

Alvin Toffler describes the impact of our rapidly changing society in his classic work *Future Shock*. All around us there are various media that influence our beliefs, values, and goals. The danger with such rapid changes in society is, and will continue to be, an inability to cope with those changes. Stress and anxiety constantly invade our emotional stability, and daily societal concerns such as energy, crime, drugs, environmental control, and political unrest all influence our development. It is essential then that program planners accept the fact that part of their responsibility to gifted learners will be to involve them in understanding the problems facing society, to assist and guide them in clarifying and developing their own values, and to prepare them to meet the challenge that our rapidly changing society provides.

A second important aspect that must be considered is the development of the gifted learners' acceptance and appreciation of their cultural heritage as well as the cultural backgrounds of others. Gifted learners live in a pluralistic society that abounds with the tradition and heritage of many peoples. Curriculum planners must directly involve the gifted in educational experiences that can lead them to a better understanding of their own needs and desires, as well as those of others.

In essence, what we must advocate and build among learners is pluralistic appreciation and the abiding sense of dignity and worth of all peoples. The questions that may be considered in selecting goals from society are:

- What types of problem-solving skills should be considered in planning the gifted program?

- What are the current social and political problems at the international, national, and local levels that may influence the design of our program?

- In what ways can we assist gifted learners in reaching an understanding of themselves and appreciation for others who are different from them or their culture?

Information and Content

One of the concerns of those who embark on the journey of program development arises over the material to be taught or the knowledge that should be imparted to the learner. Gifted program planners will very often be working within an already existing curriculum in which the subject areas to a great extent will be determined. However, program planners should become aware of various types of information and how they relate to subject matter areas designed for the gifted. In addition, it is essential at this stage that curriculum planners work closely with subject matter specialists in order to accurately identify the aspects of knowledge for a particular subject that will be most relevant and provide the student with the most utility.

Because "information" is an often-used but little-explained term, it is useful to have a clearer understanding of its meaning. Several educators have attempted to take this abstract concept and organize it into more comprehensible units. Orlosky and Smith (1978), for example, identified various types of knowledge, some form of which they felt occurred in all subjects. These types were:

- *facts*—statements describing some act or anything that requires little inference and is directly observable.

- *laws and lawlike principles*—laws are claims that there exists some regularity in the external events occurring in the natural world; lawlike principles have the potentiality of becoming laws.

- *concepts*—categories for objects and events that express them as equivalent, thereby reducing the complexity of the environment.

- *rules*—norms that govern an individual's behavior in relationship to what should be done and how.

- *values*—a particular type of concept that involves a person's feelings but implies some type of verification (e.g., John is a good mechanic).

- *attitudes*—expressions of feelings or desires about some person, place, or object (e.g., poor little Michael was held back in school).

Bloom's *Taxonomy* (1956) is perhaps the best-known system of classifying cognitive behaviors. Bloom's *Taxonomy* encompasses the dimensions of:

- *knowledge*—the remembering of previously learned materials.

- *comprehension*—the grasping of the meaning of information.

- *application*—the use of information in a concrete situation.

- *analysis*—the breaking down of information into its components.

- *synthesis*—the bringing together of the fragments of information into a whole product.

- *evaluation*—the valuing or judging of information according to established or defined criteria.

The purpose of the presentation of examples of information categorization is to demonstrate a key fact in the learning process. The organization of information for any learner, and possibly even more so for the gifted learner, must be viewed more broadly than the communication and reiteration of factual knowledge. An awareness of these various knowledge hierarchies should be an awareness of the more complex and less obvious components of information that should find their way into the curriculum of the gifted program. Using the understanding of how these forms of knowledge relate to subject areas will assist program planners in not only choosing relevant program goals but also influencing the choice of materials and strategies for teaching.

Furthermore, as a result of the advances in science and technology, the mass-media communication, and social and political changes that are taking place daily, it is impossible to think that any gifted program, no matter how well structured or intense, would be able to impart all the knowledge associated with any area of study. Program planners must begin to work in terms of assisting the gifted learner to develop the modes of thinking that will enable these students to see relationships among various pieces of knowledge, to develop the organizations and structures to assist them in understanding their world, and to assist them in dealing more efficiently with new information with which they are continuously bombarded.

It would appear that broadly determining the content area to be incorporated or investigated is not sufficient in gifted programming. Program organizers must also be acutely aware of the fact that there are many ways of imparting this content, which may involve differing processes or different strategies of varying degrees of complexity. Gifted learners should be exposed to information in its many forms if they are to develop their own abilities to the fullest. The gifted program, therefore, should be seen not only as an opportunity to impart knowledge to gifted learners but also as a vehicle for teaching these individuals how to seek out knowledge on their own. The ultimate goal of the gifted program should be to produce learners capable of self-instruction and motivated enough to seek out and apply knowledge appropriately.

With this ultimate goal in mind, there are several questions that curriculum organizers should reflect on when developing the content component of the gifted program:

- How can the gifted curriculum be organized to enable learners to acquire general rules, principles, and concepts that relate to their areas of study?

- In what way will the curriculum be organized so as to enable gifted learners to personally develop an organizational structure for dealing with knowledge?

- What role will both the teachers and students play in the acquisition of knowledge? How will this role influence the classroom organization?

Constructing Program Goals

The entire process of developing objectives and goals for the gifted program should be looked upon as many faceted. The various dimensions of goal and objective development—content, behaviors, levels—are integrated and interrelated within the educational scheme for gifted learners.

As demonstrated in Figure 4-2, each of the desired behaviors or outputs of the gifted program should be considered in relation to the various content areas into which the curriculum is organized. The particular behaviors listed in this partial model of the goals and objectives development process are outputs adapted from the

Figure 4-2 Model of the Goals and Objectives Development Process (Unit-Specific Level)

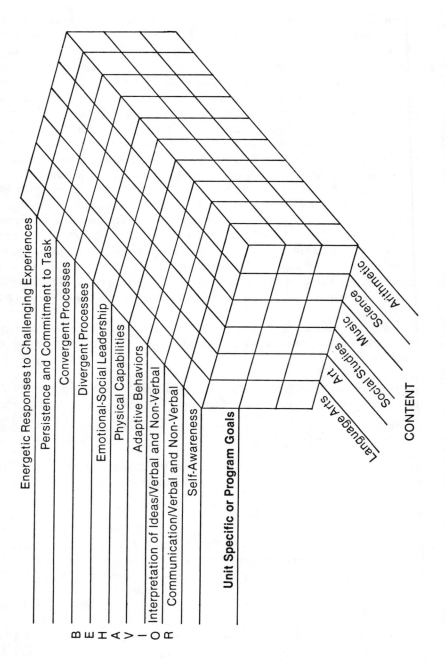

CONTENT

Language Arts
Art
Social Studies
Music
Science
Arithmetic

B E H A V I O R

Energetic Responses to Challenging Experiences
Persistence and Commitment to Task
Convergent Processes
Divergent Processes
Emotional-Social Leadership
Physical Capabilities
Adaptive Behaviors
Interpretation of Ideas/Verbal and Non-Verbal
Communication/Verbal and Non-Verbal
Self-Awareness

Unit Specific or Program Goals

Alexander-Muia Behavioral Checklist presented in Chapter 2. Mentioned previously in the discussion of the positive performance criteria, these behaviors represent those identified in the literature as being most characteristic of gifted learners. The final behaviors presented in the objectives and goals of a specific program may be altered to suit the particular needs of that program, however. What this model displays is an overview of the facets of goal and objective development that are operating throughout this important phase of comprehensive educational planning for the gifted.

As previously noted, the development of goals and objectives for the gifted program proceeds from the more general goal statements suitable for an entire institutional population to specific objectives molded to the individual learner. In this portion of the chapter, the concern will be for the first level of development—the selection of the overall aims or goals of the gifted program. Because these goals pertain directly to the instructional unit under consideration, they will be identified as unit-specific or program goals.

While much attention is directed to the construction of objectives in education, less information is afforded the questions of how to select, organize, and write unit-specific goals. The selection of unit-specific goals should revolve around the desired ends of the gifted program. These desired ends arise from the careful evaluation of the existing situation in the needs assessment and a comparison of the ideal educational environment. The desired goals that will emerge need not be only those elements that are perceived as lacking in the present environment but also those strengths of the existing general educational curriculum that should be reinforced in the gifted program. Goals are areas of interest or concern that can eventually be translated into many behaviors or outputs and adapted for several content areas. While the aims of gifted programs will differ according to the needs of the particular gifted learners and the area in which the gifted program is located, some commonality may exist in the goal development. Researchers of the American Association of Curriculum Development (AACD) (Wiles & Bondi, 1979) have developed ten major goals that may have applicability in gifted programming:

1. self-conceptualization (self-esteem)
2. understanding others
3. basic skills
4. interest and capability for continuous learning
5. responsibility as member of society
6. mental and physical health
7. creativity
8. informed participation in the economic world of production and consumption
9. use of accumulated knowledge to understand the world
10. coping with change

The goal areas presented by the AACD are obviously broadly stated concerns in the education of the gifted. It is important then that the goals selected for the gifted program have the potential to be translated into objectives that can be evaluated in some way. Consequently, one of the criteria in unit-specific goal construction is not only that these goals relate to the strengths and weaknesses of the surrounding educational environment but also that objectives for instruction can be logically developed from these aims. A determination of this factor can be accomplished by an analysis of the activities associated with the various aims and a breakdown of these activities into the specific skills, knowledge, and understanding that are essential to acquire those aims. Those goals that cannot be analyzed in such a way may have questionable validity for the program and may raise many questions during the evaluation stage. When considering a potential unit-specific goal, therefore, program organizers must determine the desirability of the aim as well as its workability and possibility of evaluation.

The wording of the unit-specific goals must convey the direction or area of concern and provide a springboard for more group- or learner-specific objectives. To display this idea, a series of goals and objectives will be carried throughout the chapter, moving progressively from general to specific statements (see Table 4-1).

Table 4-1 Examples of Unit-Specific Goals

Areas of Concern	Unit-Specific Goals
Creative expression	The gifted program should provide learners with opportunities to develop their divergent production abilities in various forms including written and oral expression and within the visual and performing arts.
Higher level thinking (problem-solving)	The curriculum of the gifted program should encompass activities in which learners can apply their problem-solving skills in creative and functional ways.
Human relationships (leadership)	Gifted learners will have educational experiences in which they can develop skills in leadership, cooperation, and personal problem solving.
Communication (interpretation of ideas and feelings)	Gifted learners will be exposed to activities designed to develop skills in expressive and receptive language, nonverbal communication, and skills in the interpretation of ideas and feelings of themselves and others.

THE GROUP-SPECIFIC OBJECTIVES LEVEL

Once the areas of concern have been delineated for the entire instructional unit under consideration, whether that unit is a school, school district, or state, these goals must be transformed into more specific statements of intent. These revised goal statements are developed around a group of learners often within a particular segment of the curriculum. Identified as group-specific objectives, and unlike the more general unit-specific goals that precede them, these statements must provide some of the "how-to" information for implementation and evaluation. In Figure 4-3, this level is added to the model of goal and objective development introduced earlier. However, while objectives continue to be applied widely in most educational programs, they remain one of the most controversial techniques in education. Before discussing the construction of group-specific objectives within the gifted program, it is essential to address the various concerns that surround the use of objectives in general.

Objectives—Help or Hindrance?

Questions and issues surrounding the employment of objectives in gifted educational programming can be classified into the advantages and problems associated with their implementation and construction. Those who advocate the use of objectives within the curriculum process point to several benefits that can be reaped from their application. These benefits will be discussed under the topics of accountability, evaluation, differentiation of instruction, and organization.

Accountability

With education repeatedly facing social pressures that demand that it be more accountable for its actions, there continues to be a need for program planners to substantiate claims that it is adequately providing for gifted learners. Although objectives alone cannot stand as evidence of effective educational organization for the gifted, they do indicate that program initiators have given considerable forethought to the needs of the gifted population. Furthermore, they take those needs and presents them as achievable outcomes that can be reviewed and discussed by the public.

Evaluation

Related to the issue of accountability is the area of evaluation. Because the implementation of objectives does reconstruct conceptual goals into a series of more concrete ends, these ends can readily function as the basis for evaluation of program effectiveness. Also, with the increased competition for funds at the national, state, and district level, it is important that program planners demonstrate the effectiveness of the gifted program in terms of desired pupil outcomes.

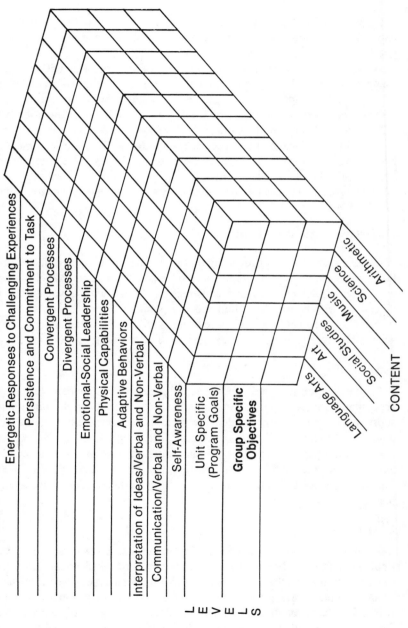

Figure 4-3 Model of the Goals and Objectives Development Process (Group-Specific Level)

The advantage of objectives as tools for evaluation is not limited solely to the determination of program effectiveness, however. Carefully developed learner-specific objectives can also provide a means to assess the performance of gifted learners in relation to the predicted outcome. Under certain conditions objectives also offer the gifted learner an opportunity for self-evaluation.

Differentiation of Instruction

One of the largest obstacles in the path of the gifted program is the erroneous perception of many individuals both in and out of educational circles that the gifted can learn without special or differentiated instruction. Through the careful construction of objectives, program developers should have the material to demonstrate how their aims for the gifted learner will, indeed, differ from the aims for learners within the general educational curriculum. This evidence of differentiation of instruction is especially potent at the learner-specific level of programming, discussed later in the chapter, in which objectives are molded to the needs of a particular gifted learner.

Organization

For some instructors involved in the actual implementation of curriculum, objectives serve as a guide or framework for instruction. These objectives organize the gifted program into an instructional plan that can be more easily understood and followed. When the individual needs of the gifted learner must be met, objectives permit the instructor to be continually aware of the program goals for the specific gifted learner.

Objectives, however, are not without several apparent concerns that should be brought to the attention of gifted program organizers. One of the strongest complaints leveled at objectives is the statement that some aspects of growth and learning are not measurable and cannot be addressed adequately by objectives. Certainly, in the gifted program attention must be paid to growth within the affective domain as well as within the better measured areas of cognitive and psychomotor development. While the use of attitude, interest, and self-concept scales and inventories may provide some method of evaluation within the domain of feelings, attitudes, and interests, this concern cannot be completely eliminated. However, objectives should not be perceived as the only evidence of growth but as only one important technique within the gifted educational process that provides an indication of goal attainment. Later within this chapter a variation of the more traditional instructional objective, the expressive objective, will be introduced to address this concern.

A second issue that is frequently raised in regard to objective writing is that these objectives fractionalize learning into small, isolated pieces of instruction. As with the previously stated concern, this is also a legitimate issue in gifted programming.

Yet, unlike the previous, theoretical problem, this concern can be greatly alleviated by the attention of program planners and gifted instructors to two ideas voiced throughout this book. First, objectives should be logical progressions built on a careful analysis of needs and strengths of the gifted population and developed from deliberately established program goals (see Figure 4-4). With this awareness of the overall aim in mind, instructors have lessened the risk of producing objectives for gifted learners that have little regard for the concepts and principles of knowledge and growth from which they should proceed.

In addition, objectives should be developed by those individuals who have a broad view and understanding of the process of education, in general, and the instruction of the gifted, specifically. If the individual composing objectives cannot see beyond the objective being written to the system and exceptional population to which it will be applied, then the education that might ensue from this narrow or limited perspective cannot reflect a full understanding of the field of knowledge to which it relates.

Not only must the objectives created for the gifted program be relevant, but they must also possess the qualities of flexibility and functionality. As noted, objectives should be envisioned as guides in the educational process. They are, in essence, the minimum of what should be accomplished rather than the maximum. While objectives are the framework of what might be pursued in the course of an educational program, planners must make allowances for random and incidental learning, open-ended discussions, and creative endeavors that arise within the

---

Figure 4-4 The Process of Program Goal and Group-Specific Objectives Development

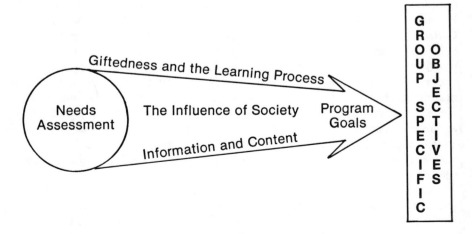

classroom interactions. All learning experiences cannot be planned for within the gifted program, and many of those experiences that spontaneously emerge have as much value in terms of student growth. Those preparing objectives must be aware of the need for flexibility within the planned instructional program and must construct objectives accordingly. This degree of flexibility pertains especially to group-specific objectives, which are structured around a varied population of individuals and which attempt to mold overall learning experiences. Teachers must be able to reevaluate and modify their objectives as the need arises.

Another issue that concerns education in relation to objective writing is the utility or functionality of the learning that is specified in objectives. While an effort must be made to link learning at the various levels of goal and objective development, it is as important that instructors of the gifted establish a bridge between the learning within the classroom and the knowledge necessary in the real world. The gifted learners, themselves, must be helped to see the utility of the knowledge included within the group-specific objectives. The functional quality of the learning experiences can be assisted, in part, by the appropriate selection of activities that place that knowledge in a familiar and motivational context for the gifted. Incorporating the interests and behaviors specific to the age and experiences of the learners will further ensure the suitability and applicability of the conceived instructional situations. If the learner is given frequent opportunities for input into the objective writing process, along with the input of school and community personnel, a more relevant context for the objectives may result.

Instructional and Expressive Objectives—Alternatives

Just as alternatives exist for most other aspects within the educational process, so, too, do alternatives exist in the form of objectives that may be written to guide the gifted program. These two variations in objective development are instructional or behavioral objectives and expressive objectives.

Instructional Objectives

When one mentions "objectives," the form envisioned is most frequently that of the behavioral or instructional objectives. These objectives are constructed from three rather specific procedures identified by Mager (1962) as follows:

First, the terminal behavior must be identified by name, specifying the kind of behavior that will be accepted as evidence that the learner has achieved the objectives. The terminal behavior should be explicit enough to explain what the student will be doing to demonstrate the established criteria. Program planners should be aware that objectives should be written using words that are measurable (see Table 4-2). Vague terminology that cannot be as readily evaluated should not be employed. To illustrate, words such as "know" or "understand" do not clearly

Table 4-2 Terminology and Components in Behavioral Objectives

	Acceptable Terminology	Unacceptable Terminology
External Condition	*After* a class discussion *Following* the presentation of *Given a story* *During* a group discussion *Using* reference materials	To learn To enjoy
Terminal Behavior	Will be able to recite Will be able to list Will be able to identify Will be able to construct Will be able to choose Will be able to write Will be able to differentiate	Will appreciate Will enjoy Will believe Will understand
Acceptable Performance Criteria	That which gives an indication as to what the learner must do to demonstrate acceptable performance of the task	

specify a behavior that can be evaluated as do words such as "list," "write," or "recite."

> Terminal Behavior: The student will be able to describe and construct a city of the future.

Second, the desired behavior should be defined further by describing the important conditions under which the behavior will be expected to occur. In specifying the conditions, objective writers describe the exact circumstances that will exist prior to or during the student's performance. Stating the condition clarifies the objective for the instructors and learners alike. The appropriate terminology that should be used in stating the external condition is indicated in Table 4-2. The description of an appropriate condition is added to the previously introduced example.

> Condition   After discussing the various problems facing American cities.
>
> Terminal Behavior   The student will be able to describe a city of the future.

Third, the criteria of acceptable performance should be specified by describing how well the learner must perform to be considered acceptable.

In meeting this part of the behavioral objective, planners must concern themselves with establishing the specific acceptable behavior resulting from the successful completion of the task. The performance criteria are added to the other two components of the behavioral objective, producing a complete instructional objective.

Condition	After discussing the various problems facing American cities.
Terminal Behavior	The student will be able to describe a city of the future.
Performance Criteria	Addressing and presenting solutions to at least three of these major problems.

One concern that arises in the specification of the performance behavior is the level of performance accepted as an indication that the student has acquired the desired objective. The performance criteria should be established by the teacher, with input from learners. Performance criteria should be realistic, and attainment of the established criteria should actually indicate that the learner has achieved the desired outcome.

To ensure that performance criteria are realistic and appropriate for gifted learners, objectives can be developed using what Baldwin (1978) refers to as evaluative behaviors. Evaluative behaviors are basically alternative performance criteria appropriately selected on the basis of the learners' strengths or weaknesses and provide learners with a variety of ways in which they can demonstrate the accomplishment of the objective. Providing different types of evaluative behaviors will assist in meeting the needs of a diverse gifted population. In addition, generating multiple evaluative behaviors enables learners, with the guidance of the teacher, to select those behaviors that focus on their strengths. In essence, developing alternate activities for the students to show mastery of skills and concepts reinforces the notion that knowledge can be used in many ways.

Expressive Objectives

Many of the concerns discussed earlier in this chapter have direct bearing on the more traditional instructional objectives just described. One attempt to provide an alternative strategy in the construction of objectives for gifted programs was developed by Eisner (1969). Termed "expressive objectives," this type of objective enables both the teacher and student to proceed in directions that are of interest and importance to the learner. Unlike the instructional type, these objectives do not specify what behavior the learner will demonstrate after taking part in a particular learning activity. Eisner, in describing expressive objectives, indicates that:

> The expressive objective is intended to serve as a theme around which skills and understandings learned earlier can be brought to bear, but through which those skills and understandings can be expanded, elaborated and made idiosyncratic. . . . In the expressive context the teacher hopes to provide a situation in which meanings become personalized and in which the children produce products, both theoretical and qualitative, that are as diverse as themselves. (p. 16)

In the context of utilizing expressive objectives, learners are not given the criteria by which they are to demonstrate a particular behavior; rather, the learners' products are evaluated using a constructive approach with input from both the teacher and the learners.

The principal advantage of the expressive objectives is that they provide educators with a different and refreshingly new approach to objective construction that can be embraced by many who would otherwise reject the employment of objectives for reasons such as those previously described. The gifted learner is also given a more direct role in the evaluation process as a result of expressive objectives in which students' products are critiqued according to creativity, uniqueness, and approach. Students along with the teacher learn to critically evaluate their own work, identifying the qualities that exemplify the products' strengths and identifying those areas that will need development for future projects of this type. In addition, the outcomes of expressive objectives are evaluated on an individual basis. What this means is that a student's performance need not be considered in relation to the performance of all other gifted students within the same instructional group but are measured according to that student's own particular strengths and needs. In addition, because this form of objective writing can lead to the production of literally hundreds of objectives, it furnishes instructors of the gifted with added flexibility.

However, this alternative approach to the construction of objectives within the gifted program is not without its limitations. Since expressive objectives are not as stringently composed as the behavioral objectives, they may not provide as much instructional direction as the situation requires. As alluded to earlier, the major distinction between instructional and expressive objectives is that the latter do not specify the exact learning outcome that results after the learner has been involved in the learning experience. Yet, while expressive objectives do not use specific performance criteria, neither do they use vague terminology. The following are examples of expressive objectives:

- The student will be able to interpret the meaning of *The Call of the Wild*.

- The student will be able to develop a painting modeling the art form of a great artist.

- The student will be able to sculpture a form utilizing clay.

- The student will be able to discuss the important economic problems facing the community.

Expressive objectives should not be used as substitutes for instructional objectives but rather as an alternate way of generalizing and expanding skills and concepts acquired as a result of successful performance of other instructional objectives. Gifted programs should include both instructional and expressive type objectives, with each type being designed for subject areas or units of study within subject areas that are deemed appropriate by the teachers and learners. Certainly there are skills associated with some subject areas the attainment of which are crucial to the development of further skills. For example, the precise demonstration of basic reading skills is essential before the student can successfully proceed to more complex skills. These foundation skills, as they might be referred to, may best be taught through the acquisition of specific instructional objectives. These instructional objectives on which a gifted educational program is based may then be supplemented and enriched by the use of expressive objectives. Thus, the gifted learner is not just evaluated according to carefully determined behavioral criteria but also is given the opportunity to proceed independently without prerequisite guidelines or criteria within certain areas of the curriculum content.

Eisner (1969) clarifies the use of both instructional and expressive objectives when he states that:

> Instructional objectives embody the codes and the skills that culture has to provide and which make inquiry possible. Expressive objectives designate those circumstances in which the codes and the skills acquired in instructional contexts can be used and elaborated; through their expansion and reconstruction culture remains vital. (p. 18)

Examples of Group-Specific Objectives

With a clearer understanding of the issues and concerns related to the implementation and development of objectives within the gifted program and with knowledge of the forms that objectives can assume, we can redirect attention to the group-specific objectives previously detailed. In organizing the group-specific objectives for the curriculum to be developed, the program goals previously outlined should be considered first, in relation to an area of that curriculum. Then,

Table 4-3 Examples of Developed Curriculum Goals and Objectives

Area of Concern	Unit-Specific Goals	Group-Specific/Learner-Specific Objectives
Creative expression	The gifted program should provide learners with opportunities to develop their divergent production abilities in various forms, including written and oral expression and within the visual and performing arts.	Content Area: American Literature After studying early American writers, students will choose a writer of interest and produce a work in a similar style of writing. The student will read about Emily Dickinson and produce several poems in the personal style of Dickinson, the information and product to be shared with classmates.
Higher level thinking (problem-solving)	The curriculum of the gifted program should encompass activities in which learners can apply their problem-solving skills in creative and functional ways.	Content Area: Science After completing a science unit on the national energy crisis, students will be able to identify implications of a short energy supply and provide several solutions to the problems presented. The student will develop a TV commercial depicting the problems faced by the public as a result of the energy crisis and ways people can lessen these problems.

Human relationships
(leadership)

Gifted learners will have educational experiences in which they can develop skills in leadership, cooperation, and personal problem solving.

Content Area: Social Studies

After completing a social science unit on young leaders in America, students will demonstrate their understanding of characteristics or attributes of leadership. The students will compare themselves to a young leader, past or present.

Communication
(interpretation of
ideas and feelings)

Gifted learners will be exposed to activities designed to develop skills in expressive and receptive language, nonverbal communication, and skills in the interpretation of ideas and feelings of themselves and others.

Content Area: Fine Arts

During a lesson on the use of color students will be able to discuss the relationship between mood and color.

The student will produce an abstract watercolor that displays a particular mood.

several methods of performance criteria or behavioral manifestation should be provided. These criteria are still stated in terms suitable for a group of gifted learners and not in terms of a specific individual. Therefore, the inclusion of several alternatives or evaluative behaviors, as they are called by Baldwin, should offer some leeway or flexibility within the group-organized gifted curriculum (see Table 4-3).

THE LEARNER-SPECIFIC OBJECTIVES LEVEL

When the learner-specific level is finally reached within the process of developing goals and objectives to guide the gifted program's curriculum, the group-specific objectives previously discussed must be transformed or modified to meet the needs of the individual. The concerns and issues expressed about objectives written at the group-specific level also apply at the learner-specific level. The difference between these stages of objective development is that those constructed for a group of gifted learners must now be individualized to incorporate the particular needs, interests, and strengths of each learner. Certain objectives established at the group-specific level may even be totally eliminated in certain instances and others added, depending on the special behaviors of the learner involved and the outcomes desired. At this level of objective construction, student input into the established aims should be maximized as well.

As is demonstrated in Figure 4-5, the process of focusing the desired, general aim of the gifted program into an achievable group-related objective now flows

---

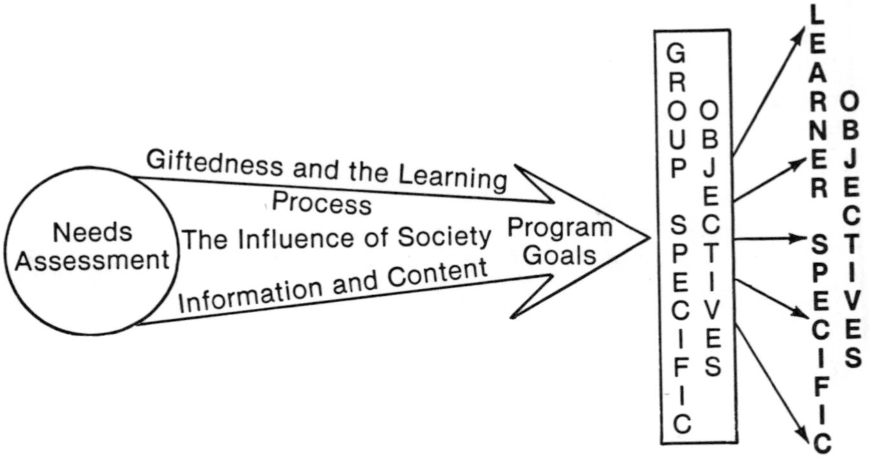

Figure 4-5 An Overview of the Goal and Objective Development Process

outward. One objective designated as an important end product for gifted learners can ultimately be achieved in any number of ways suitable to the strengths, learning modality, and experiences of the individual gifted learner. These learner-specific objectives then form the basis of a special instructional plan built around the gifted students' strengths and needs.

Developing the Specific Learner Instructional Plan (SLIP)

The question that might logically occur to program initiators once the learner-specific objectives have been decided on is—now what should be done? In this section of the chapter we will present a method by which learner-specific objectives are molded into an organized and individualized instruction program for gifted learners. This viable program, which can be utilized at the learner-specific level of program development (see Figure 4-6), is referred to as the *Specific Learner Instructional Plan (SLIP)* (see Exhibit 4-1).

The idea of utilizing a written plan of instruction for an individual learner is not a new educational concept. The passage of Public Law 94-142, the Education for All Handicapped Children Act, in 1975 has had a significant impact on the provision of specific educational programs for certain segments of the exceptional learner population. Thus, focusing on the specialized needs of exceptional learners through individualized instructional plans has clear precedent in the educational community. If we have recognized, and appropriately so, the necessity of a specific plan of action for certain groups of exceptional learners, it would seem fitting that we also provide our exceptionally able learners with a carefully, individually designed and administered program.

By employing a written plan, such as the *SLIP*, teachers of the gifted can translate the words of group- and learner-specific objectives into actual practice. The attention to such details as committee approval, appropriate learning strategies, and materials helps to provide a more systematic, organized approach to individual instruction of the gifted.

The development of the *SLIP* can best be achieved with the assistance of individuals representing various dimensions of the learner's education. It is recommended that this committee be composed of the learner, the teacher of the gifted, the parents of the gifted child, and an administration representative. The primary purpose of using the input of these various individuals in the *SLIP* is to ensure that the program outlined for the gifted learner has the stamp of approval from those who have the knowledge, commitment, and interest in the student's education.

The *SLIP* has a number of important features that make it beneficial to program planners. First, information concerning the perceived strengths, needs, and interests of the learner along with the means of assessment is summarized. These data provide insights into the level at which the learner is functioning within certain

Figure 4-6 Complete Model of Goal and Objective Development Process

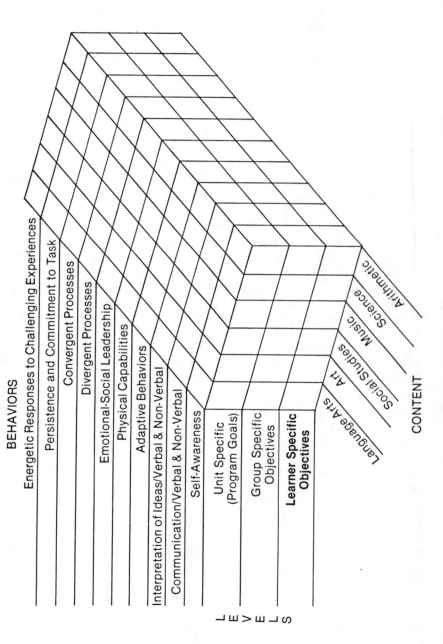

Exhibit 4-1 Specific Learner Instructional Plan *(SLIP)*

Student _____ Date _____
School _____ Age _____
Address _____ Birthdate _____
_____ Responsible _____
_____ Teacher _____

Program Form Recommended _____

Administrator _____
Teacher _____
Parent(s) _____
Student _____
Other(s) _____

Date Started	Unit Specific Objectives	Learner-Specific Objectives	Learning Strategies	Materials Needed	Person Responsible	Evaluation	Date Completed

Exhibit 4-1 continued

Student_____   Date_____

PERCEIVED STRENGTHS	MODE OF ASSESSMENT
PERCEIVED NEEDS	MODE OF ASSESSMENT
INTERESTS AND HOBBIES	

areas of the curriculum and into interests that could serve as springboards within the educational process.

Once group-specific objectives have been identified, both the teacher and the learner can cooperatively develop the specific objectives that will assist the learner in achieving the desired educational outcomes in a way best suited to that individual's present level of functioning and learning style. The *SLIP*, thus, becomes a cooperative venture between the teacher and the learner.

Probably one of the most important sections of the *SLIP* is the evaluation component. This component should consist of three types of evaluation: (1) the teacher's evaluation of the learner, (2) the learner's self-evaluation, and (3) the teacher's self-evaluation.

The teacher's evaluation of the learner is conducted to ascertain the extent to which the student has accomplished the instructional objectives according to the prespecified criteria. However, in the use of expressive objectives, evaluation will be a cooperative effort by both the learner and teacher.

If the evaluation of an instructional objective indicates that the learner has not attained the specified objective, the teacher must work through the process of reevaluating the suitability of the objective itself, the strategies used to teach the objective, and the materials used as the medium for learning. This process of reevaluation should also occur if students have difficulty in the experiences set forth in expressive-type objectives.

One objective of any educational program should be to develop the learners' ability to evaluate their own work, examining it critically but constructively, yet at the same time being able to recognize and appreciate a product's value. With specific objectives, learners can, with the assistance and guidance of their teacher, examine their work in relationship to the designated criteria.

Finally, through the *SLIP*, teachers of the gifted are given the opportunity, if not the mandate, to examine their own role in the educational process. This evaluation should not be viewed as a need to "place blame" for unachieved aims. Instead, the teacher-evaluation component, as with the entire evaluation aspect of the *SLIP*, must be seen as a positive experience through which the teacher becomes more attuned to strategies and techniques that produce gains and growth in the gifted learner. Again, it must be emphasized that the overall evaluation component of the *SLIP* is a necessary undertaking that considers the needs and growth of the gifted learner in relation to established objectives. Furthermore, this evaluation should become an opportunity for the individuals most directly concerned with the gifted learner's educational experiences—the teacher and the gifted learner—to work together toward the goal of improved programming for the gifted population.

SUMMARY

The purpose of this chapter was to show the logical progression involved in developing specific learner objectives. The first step in developing specific objectives is to identify the overall goals or aims of the gifted program. These goals represent the philosophical beliefs about gifted education. The goals of the program are selected from a number of areas that reflect the learner's academic, social, emotional, and physical development. In addition, goals are not the thoughts of one person but rather the thoughts and beliefs of all those who will be in some way involved with the gifted program.

The second phase of objective development is the development of group goals designed specifically for various types of gifted learners. These group goals are developed from, and are a reflection of, the overall goals of the program.

The third and final phase of objective development is the creation of specific classroom learner objectives. Based on the group goals, these specific objectives outline specific learner tasks and specify the performance criteria needed for successful completion of the tasks. Expressive objectives that are open ended in the performance criteria were also discussed.

REFERENCES

Baldwin, A. Curriculum and methods—what is the difference? In A. Baldwin, G. Gear, & L. Lucito (Eds.), *Educational planning for the gifted*. Reston, Va.: The Council for Exceptional Children, 1978.

Bloom, B. S. (Ed.). *Taxonomy of educational objectives: The classification of educational goals—Handbook I, cognitive domain*. New York: David McKay, 1956.

Brunner, J. S. *The process of education*. Cambridge, Mass.: Harvard University Press, 1960.

Eisner, E. Instructional and expressive educational objectives: Their formulation and use in curriculum. In J. Popham, E. Eisner, H. Sullivan, & L. Tyler, (Eds.), *Instructional objectives—AERA monograph series on curriculum evaluation*. Chicago: Rand McNally, 1969.

Erickson, E. H. *Identity: Youth and crisis*. New York: Norton, 1968.

Flavell, J. H. *The developmental psychology of Jean Piaget*. New York: D. Van Nostrand Company, 1963.

Havighurst, R. J. *Human development and education*. New York: Longmans, Green, 1953.

Kohlberg, L. Development of moral character and moral ideology. In M. L. Hoffman & L. W. Hoffman (Eds.), *Review of child development research* (Vol. 1). New York: Russell Sage Foundation, 1964.

Mager, R. *Preparing instructional objectives*. Palo Alto, Calif.: Fearon Publishers, 1962.

Orlosky, D. E., & Smith, B. O. The curriculum and types of knowledge. In D. E. Orlosky & B. O. Smith (Eds.), *Curriculum development, issues and insights*. Chicago: Rand McNally, 1978.

Wiles, J., & Bondi, J. *Curriculum development: A guide to practice*. Columbus, Ohio: Charles E. Merrill, 1979.

Chapter 5

Determining the Program Format

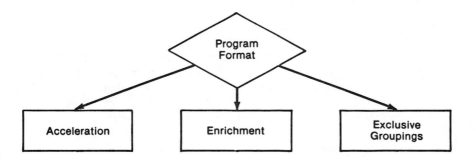

It is not surprising that a particular destination a traveler selects can be reached by any number of routes as indicated on a chart or road map. Before the trip actually begins, the traveler must carefully consider all plausible alternatives in relation to a tentative itinerary and then must select the most desirable route available. Throughout this book, we have attempted to draw an analogy between the individual embarking on a physical journey and the school or school district undertaking the task of developing comprehensive education for the gifted learner. We can expand our analogy even further to show that, as more than one direction exists for the individual embarking on a physical journey, so, too, do alternatives exist for those undertaking the task of establishing a program of gifted education. These alternatives or directions open to planners in gifted education are the types of program formats from which they may choose—alternatives in format that must be carefully considered, analyzed, and scrutinized before any additional distance is covered.

Therefore, it is the intent of this chapter to develop guidelines for the consideration of formats for gifted programming. Common classifications of these formats will be presented, and the advantages, disadvantages, and implications of each will be discussed. Finally, methods of format organization or arrangement will be reviewed to provide program developers with a blueprint or chart to follow in the course of format selection.

PRINCIPAL FACTORS AFFECTING THE STRUCTURING OF GIFTED PROGRAMS

The organization of a program for the gifted will be influenced directly or indirectly by many factors, some more under the developer's control than others. Consideration of some of the more manageable factors throughout the initial stages of program development will ensure not only a more effective program but also one that is more consistent with the overall educational program in operation. The elements that exert influence in the organization of gifted programs appear to fall into two broad categories—theoretical considerations and practical guidelines—both of importance in appropriate format selection.

Theoretical Considerations

Many of the theoretical factors that exert their influence on the establishment of gifted programs require attention in the initial stages of development. These theoretical considerations, as displayed in Figure 5-1, include the philosophical viewpoint established, defined, and refined throughout the early phases of program formulation; the assessed needs that became apparent in the period of needs assessment; and the stated objectives that convert those needs into program goals. These influences, however, do not terminate at the moment of program organization but remain continuous forces throughout the educational process. The interaction of these theoretical considerations with the program structure should be briefly addressed.

Philosophical Viewpoint

A philosophy of education can be defined as a positional statement of the academic and developmental ideals held by an individual or institution in the attainment of educational goals. This philosophy is mirrored in the definition of the term "gifted," which is then framed by the objectives that guide program development. However, even throughout the phase of objective construction the philosophy of gifted education remains little more than a profession of belief. Only in the stage of program structuring does the statement of philosophy take on a more concrete appearance. In essence, as the development process continues, the philosophical perspective blossoms from a held belief to an expressed position to a course of action. With actual program structuring, words become actions (see Figure 5-2).

The philosophical viewpoint of a school becomes even more apparent to gifted program developers through their observation of the way in which educational experiences are structured for all students. Furthermore, gifted program organizers can acquire a better understanding of the acceptability of their program proposals by evaluating the attitude and approaches assumed in the general educational

Figure 5-1 Theoretical and Practical Influences on Gifted Program Format

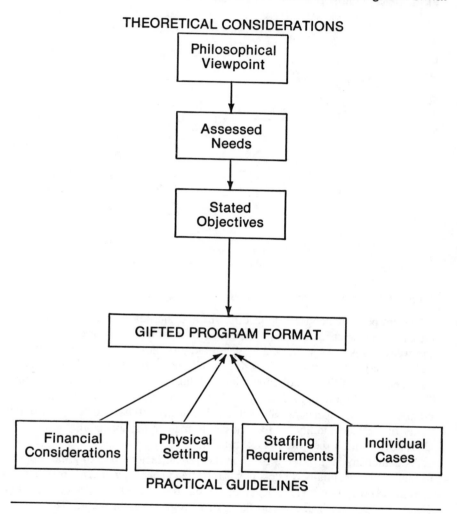

program. Certainly, while the educational philosophy at large may not dictate the structure to be followed in the development of the gifted program, it does exert a major influence. It would seem that the more closely aligned the philosophy of the gifted program is to the school's operational philosophy, the more easily the program can be implemented and the more acceptable it may become to those affected by the program's implementation. For example, if the philosophy of a school or school system is toward mainstreaming of exceptional students, it would be more difficult to justify the exclusive grouping of the gifted.

Figure 5-2 Philosophical Progression

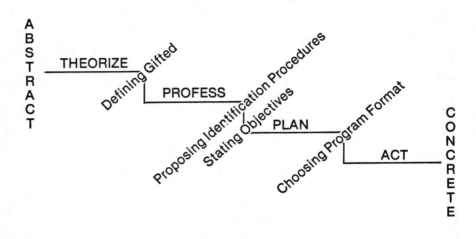

Assessed Needs and Stated Objectives

The purpose of conducting an efficient and thorough needs assessment, as presented in Chapter 3, was to provide organizers with an analysis of the strengths and weaknesses to be addressed by the gifted program. These needs, to be dealt with by the gifted organization, will basically be of two types—those affecting large segments of the school population and those that are more student-specific. Those needs of more mass concern will have a greater, more direct influence on program structure decisions. Student-specific needs will have to be considered in terms of the adaptability of the chosen format or the availability of various alternatives within the gifted organization.

As demonstrated in Figure 5-1, the theoretical factors affecting the program format flow sequentially. Philosophy is reflected in needs, which are then considered in the objectives that are developed. Objectives, like needs, can exert both a direct and indirect influence on the gifted program organization. Those goals pertaining to a broadly stated purpose or established for a large segment of the population should be more influential on the selection of program format. Those objectives that are more learner-specific should also be workable under the chosen program organization. Thus, a degree of flexibility is required within the program format; although the basic framework of the program is maintained, it might be altered to suit particular cases. If the utilized program organization offers several alternatives, one of these may prove more suitable than the others for accomplishments of objectives.

Practical Guidelines

While most literature on gifted education speaks more specifically to those theoretical considerations discussed in the preceding section, little has been written about those factors of a more practical nature that also enter into the process of format selection. Often, a school or school system's idealistic guidelines for the implementation of a gifted program are tempered by the realism of such aspects as:

- financial considerations
- physical setting
- staffing requirements
- individual student cases

Financial Considerations

An important factor that can strongly influence the decision as to the most suitable program for the gifted enrolled in a specific school unit will be the financial investments required for the program's implementation. There are several sources of funding that a school or school district can tap for the development of education for the gifted at the national, state, and local levels. The acquisition of funding is discussed in Chapter 8. Regardless of how appropriations are procured, it is important to understand that the more modifications made to the existing school program to accommodate the gifted student, the more financial investment may be required. To illustrate, the decision to place the gifted in a particular school in homogeneous groups may necessitate additional hiring of personnel to oversee instruction, whereas a decision to conduct an enrichment program within the regular classroom may reduce the expenditures to supplemental materials only. Prior to the formation of any commitment on program organization, therefore, the possible cost of operating such a program is one of the elements that must be reviewed.

Estimated Budget

As part of the financial considerations in the development of practical guides to program success, an estimated budget must be included. The initial step in this process is for program organizers and school officials to reach a decision as to the approximate amount that can be justifiably allotted for program development and operation. This estimated figure can serve as a starting point from which later adjustments or renegotiations can be conducted prior to any final budgetary decision.

Once total expenditures have been estimated, the next step for program planners will be the breakdown of potential funding into line items within the budget. Itemization of the budget permits the allocation of funds into predetermined areas of need in accordance with the assessed importance of each category. A budget form containing frequently included item areas is presented in Exhibit 5-1. This type of budget summary can be useful in outlining the overall costs of the desired gifted program, and it may help pinpoint specific areas of monetary concern. While a cost estimation of the yearly operation of the program will be required before the program begins, a monthly budget sheet may be used to record actual monthly expenditures once the program is in operation. In a newly established gifted program, it will be necessary to estimate the budgetary expenses entirely on speculated needs, or on the basis of expenditures incurred by similar programs. In addition to this monthly monitoring of expenses, a comparison of the actual vs. the estimated cost of the program should be carried out at the end of the year. For example, a visual comparison between estimated and actual expenditures of an after-school gifted program is shown in Exhibit 5-2. Any financial changes required for the following year's operation may be more accurately determined from the expenses actually incurred throughout the year. Line items and their estimated amounts should be scrutinized to identify areas of cost overrun or those areas where estimated amounts significantly exceeded actual expenditures.

In the following sections, areas commonly of financial concern to program developers are presented with some analysis of the scope and importance of these items in the establishment of a workable program budget.

Staffing. The school or school system's staffing requirements for the gifted program will be highly dependent on the program under consideration. As an illustration, if schools initiating gifted programs adopt a philosophy of homogeneous grouping in special classes, it may be necessary to hire an additional staff member. Because the cost of additional personnel may place a large burden on the estimated budget of the program, this category deserves adequate consideration. Often, decisions to hire additional personnel require far more justification and approval than other budget items.

Special Testing. The accurate identification of the gifted child frequently necessitates the conducting of specialized testing. This is especially true in instances in which gifted students will be homogeneously grouped for instruction or those in which special populations are to be assessed. Careful diagnosis of the student considered for a gifted program may encompass not only intellectual development, as measured by individual or group IQ tests, but also may involve analysis of creativity (by means of tests of creative thinking) and social and emotional adjustment (diagnosed through observational checklists, anecdotal records, and sociograms, for example). Consequently, the cost of such testing and test instruments should be included as possible expenditures.

Exhibit 5-1 Example of Annual Estimated Budget Form

Budget Item	1 Estimated Expen-diture	2 Actual Expen-diture	3 Variance	4 Total Variance	5
Staffing					
Curriculum Materials					
Diagnostic Materials					
Field Trips/ Enrichment Activities					
Structural Cost/ Maintenance					
Inservice/ Consultation					
Professional Conferences and Materials					
Transportation					
Miscellaneous					
Total Estimated Budget					
Total Actual Budget					

Curriculum Materials. Curriculum materials, which perhaps represent the most common expenditure in gifted program budgets, include those instructional items adopted as the base of a specific program, as well as any supplemental or enrichment materials purchased. While there is no limit on the number and types of curriculum materials that can be purchased for a gifted program, there is also no one-to-one relationship between the number of materials and the strength of the

Exhibit 5-2 Example of Completed Annual Estimated Budget

Budget Item	1 Estimated Expenditure	2 Actual Expenditure	3 Variance	4 Total Variance	5
Staffing	00 —	00 —	00 —	00 —	
Curriculum Materials	150 —	200 —	<50→	<50→	
Diagnostic Materials	50 —	75 —	<25→	<75→	
Field Trips/ Enrichment Activities	75 —	75 —	00 —	<75→	
Structural Cost/ Maintenance	225 —	150 —	75 —	00 —	
Inservice/ Consultation	100 —	100 —	00 —	00 —	
Professional Conferences and Materials	50 —	75 —	<25→	<25→	
Transportation	00 —	20 —	<20→	45 —	
Miscellaneous	100 —	25 —	75 —	30 —	
Total Estimated Budget	750 —				
Total Actual Budget		720 —			

program. In other words, it is imperative that the students' needs dictate the selection of materials. In addition, it is the appropriate selection and application of materials rather than their quantity that improves the educational program. The budget category of curriculum materials not only should make provisions for commercially manufactured items but also should allot funds for the supplies needed in the creation of teacher-made materials.

Field Trips and Enrichment Activities. Another area that may need to be considered in the establishment of a working budget for any gifted program is the probable expenses incurred from field trips or other supplemental programs and activities. These enrichment activities carefully planned in relation to the established program objectives are often viewed as justifiable expenditures by gifted program developers regardless of the financial restrictions.

Structural Costs and Maintenance. One budgetary item that may not be apparent at the outset of program development is the structural and maintenance costs involved. Structural and maintenance costs are those expenses related to the furnishing, housing, and maintenance of the physical space allotted to the gifted program and include such possible expenditures as desks, chairs, tables, heating, lighting, and structural modifications. Again, the amount of structural and maintenance costs is highly dependent on the type of program selected. For example, if gifted students are placed in an accelerated program, it is less likely that any additional classroom space will be required. Since the student who is accelerated moves to an already existing curricular program at a higher grade level, costs of maintaining a room may not be applicable. However, if gifted students are to be removed from their various classrooms and relocated into a special room or area, additional space and furnishings may be needed.

In-Service and Consultation. Although there may be some overlap in the functions and purposes of in-service and consultation, in-service will be identified as those activities that are designed to stimulate professional growth and awareness by providing working educators with the opportunity to broaden their expertise. In planning in-service programs, most school systems set aside a specific number of days in the school calendar for just this purpose. It may prove useful, therefore, to schedule some in-service time prior to the school term to prepare and acquaint those personnel who are directly and indirectly affected by the program implementation with current practices in the area of gifted education. This may be especially true for school systems in which a new program for the gifted is under consideration.

The underlying costs of an in-service program would possibly involve the fees paid to those from outside the institution who provide their services and expertise. Also to be considered within this budgetary area are the salaries that must be paid to aides or substitutes who take over for teachers during school hours to allow for their participation in such a program.

Consultation, on the other hand, is the involvement of experts who act in an advisory capacity in the ongoing program and evaluation. Consultants, when they are hired specifically to review the program and offer suggestions, need to be carefully chosen and involved in the gifted program as soon as possible from the time of the program's inception. It should be remembered that the costs of both in-service sessions and consultations will vary considerably according to the extent of involvement desired.

Professional Conferences and Materials. In order to assist teachers in continuing their professional growth and development, it may be worthwhile for school personnel to attend or take part in professional conferences that include some discussion of the gifted learner. Inclusion of an allotment for professional conferences to cover at least partial cost of related travel, lodging, and admission fees may serve as an incentive to teachers who might consider attending professional conferences. In turn, educators who participate in or attend these conferences can bring back and share their newly gained knowledge with associates, thus enriching the existing educational system. These conferences are held at local, state, and national levels at locations throughout the United States.

While knowledge about the gifted can be acquired by attendance at conferences, professional growth is also highly dependent on the continuous awareness of what is occurring in the field of gifted education. Consequently, budget considerations should also include resources to maintain a professional library for school personnel as well as parents and community members wishing to know more about the gifted.

Transportation. Another category of expense that may require consideration in certain types of gifted programs is transportation costs. In schools in which a limited gifted program has been established or in which the existing organization cannot accommodate the diverse needs of particular gifted students, transportation of gifted students to schools that can provide adequate instruction will possibly become a line item in the estimated budget. Cooperative programs between educational institutions frequently carry a transportation charge unless students commute before or after regular school hours or unless transportation can be provided on a volunteer basis.

What has been presented in this section on budgetary analysis are various categories as well as expenditures within those categories that deserve the consideration of program developers. While these financial areas do exert influence on gifted program organization, they should not be allowed to control the process of format selection.

Physical Setting

No matter what format or combination of formats is eventually chosen, the gifted program must operate within the immediate school environment and within the larger context of the surrounding community. This direct relationship demands a closer look at the physical setting in which the program will function in order to judge the elements of the surroundings that will be advantageous or disadvantageous to the gifted program or that will suggest the direction such programming should take. It is important to evaluate what is presently available both in the school and in the community that will make the implementation of the gifted program more successful. This evaluation should involve an analysis of material as well as nonmaterial contributions that can be assimilated from the surroundings.

School

One of the first factors that arises as an influence on the program format of gifted education for a specific institution is whether that institution is elementary, middle, secondary, or collegiate. Another element of the school's setting that may play a role in the selection of an appropriate format for gifted programming is the horizontal and vertical organization of the school's curriculum. Whether the educational sequencing of the curriculum is nongraded or graded will generally have some effect on the programs established for the gifted. In a nongraded, continuous-progress school organization, for example, acceleration in the traditional sense of grade skipping would not be applicable, while grade telescoping or rapid pacing through the curriculum are two obviously appropriate forms of acceleration. The horizontal arrangement of the school, on the other hand, or whether classes are self-contained, open, or departmentalized should be evaluated as well to determine their possible effects on the gifted program. As an illustration of this fact, should the classes be departmentalized, it may be necessary to establish a referral committee as part of the identification process as a means of obtaining information from all teachers involved without a duplication of data. Or, in a true open school atmosphere, characterized by a student's freedom of curricular choice, an independent study approach may seem more logical.

Two other factors that should be analyzed with regard to the school's physical setting are the availability of space in the existing school plan, especially if an exclusive grouping format is under consideration, and the type of equipment and materials that are accessible.

Community

It is often too easy to overlook the connection that exists, or should exist, between the community and the gifted program. Within the needs assessment that is conducted in the initial stages of program development, a conscious effort is made to thoroughly research the surrounding community in order to ascertain information that would have direct bearing on the success of the gifted program. Among the data that would provide usable information in the selection of a suitable structure for the gifted is knowledge of the physical characteristics of the community. Certainly, the needs of a rural school system will differ to a certain extent from those of an urban system. Just such factors as population density, distance between schools, and population diversity should be reflected in the chosen program organization. In a district where schools are widespread and student populations are dispersed, the idea of exclusively grouping gifted students may need to be carefully weighed against the costs of transporting students for long distances.

It is also valuable for program initiators to be aware of colleges, persons, or institutions that can serve as arms of the gifted program. Some colleges provide special placements or advanced classes for gifted pre-college-age individuals, for example. This type of information can provide alternatives for gifted program formats.

Staffing Requirements

When selecting the most appropriate format for a gifted educational program, one of the principal considerations for the administrator must be the personnel that would be required to staff the desired program. As was noted briefly under the heading of estimated budget, it can be generalized from the outset that the more specialized the intended program, the more specialized the staff that would be required to maintain that program. The more modifications to an existing educational system that are to be implemented, the more likely it is that changes in the present staffing arrangements will be necessary. Only after a tentative program format has been placed under consideration will it be possible to consider the staffing plan that it is apt to require and the related costs of such staffing.

To demonstrate this situation, we can hypothesize an example in which a school is considering the adoption of special classes for the gifted to be conducted on a full-time basis. As part of this consideration, program developers must analyze what effect this proposed format may have on the present school personnel. Would it necessitate the hiring of extra personnel? What kinds of demands or added responsibilities will it place on the current staff? Certainly it could prove to be an overwhelming task to establish special classes for the gifted when no personnel can be hired to instruct this group or when none of the current staff has the time or inclination to take on the responsibility. An adequate understanding of an institution's professional and paraprofessional staff based on information accumulated in the needs assessment procedure will help program initiators determine what qualifications, abilities, and interests in the field of gifted education are available among present personnel.

The roles, responsibilities, and necessary qualifications of various categories of personnel will be discussed in detail in Chapter 6. However, we should briefly consider the role that can be played by certain school faculty under different program formats. A simplified overview, such as the one presented in Figure 5-3, allows program initiators to visually assess the staffing structure on which the gifted program could possibly be established.

Figure 5-3 Overview of Potential Staff Assignments in Various Gifted Program Formats

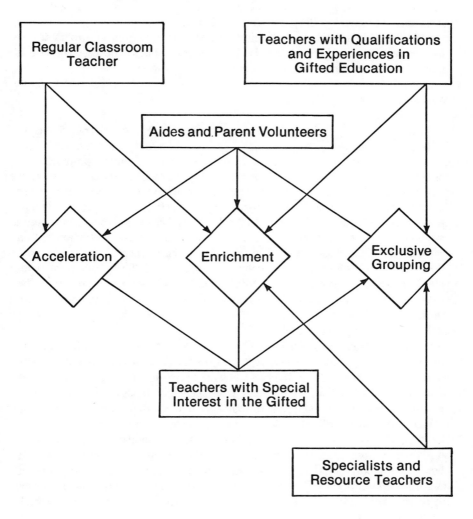

Deficiencies in staff numbers in any program format can be compensated for by the interest and commitment of the personnel. If, for example, a goal of exclusive grouping of gifted learners is established by a school hampered by a small but dedicated faculty who cannot reschedule time for full- or part-time classes during regular school hours, other educational alternatives may be possible. After-school and weekend classes are just two options that could be implemented to satisfy the goal of exclusive grouping for the gifted without creating the need for changes in the regular school-day schedule. These "extra hours" classes would have to be overseen by teachers willing to volunteer their time.

While the determination of the most suitable format for gifted programming does not rest exclusively on expected alterations or additions to the existing staff, it does remain an essential factor in program determination.

Individual Student Cases

No factor is more important in deciding the most appropriate program format to be followed than the particular needs of the individual gifted student. Two assessments of student needs must be made in effective educational programming for the gifted. The first of these assessments should be a general determination of population needs based on an accurate population profile, as discussed in Chapter 3. From the broad analysis of the population to be served by the gifted program, certain priorities can be established that reflect themselves in terms of the chosen program organization. Should a large percentage of the school population be of a culturally different background, for example, an enrichment format may seem more advantageous by providing opportunities that enrich the sociocultural experiences of the subdominant cultural child. Should the gifted population prove to be small in numbers and well distributed among the grade levels, it may prove more financially feasible to use some form of enrichment or a very limited type of exclusive grouping arrangement.

The general assessment of the school population, therefore, leads quite logically to an appropriate program. However, there do arise situations in which deviations from the regular policy for gifted education are necessitated by the characteristics of the individual student. The second assessment that must be undertaken is a careful analysis of individual cases that appear to deviate markedly from the typical profile of the gifted student being served by a school area. Outstanding talents, abilities or disabilities, personalities, or socioeconomic factors may make an alternative format more desirable in a specific instance. No matter how well chosen and appropriate the gifted program may be for the population-at-large, it must also be flexible enough to adjust to the student whose needs cannot be met by the established format. Consider the following illustrations as cases in point.

Case 1

Henry, a culturally different high school junior identified as a gifted learner, was enrolled in his school's enrichment program. Background information on Henry indicated that he appeared to be socially and emotionally well adjusted. Not only did his curricular record show that

Henry applied himself well in academic tasks, notably in the areas of science and math, but also that he was involved in many extracurricular activities in which he assumed leadership roles.

Sessions with Henry and his parents revealed a strong family relationship. His parents were very supportive of Henry's present school activities, as well as his desire to continue his educational career in the field of medicine.

However, because of the cost of a college education, it was determined that Henry's parents would be able to provide him with only some financial assistance beyond possible college scholarships. In addition, Henry's test scores revealed a discrepancy between his verbal and math abilities, with the latter being slightly higher.

Based on a thorough analysis of Henry's case, school personnel recommended that attempts be made to place Henry in the job market as quickly as possible, thus alleviating some of the financial burden to his family. A plan was envisioned whereby Henry would be accelerated to a university program after having completed his high school requirements in three years. Even though Henry was identified as a gifted learner from a subdominant cultural population who could profit immensely from enrichment activities, it was felt that because of his social-emotional development and academic interest and performance he could be successful in this accelerated program.

Even though there was a discrepancy between Henry's verbal and math abilities, university admissions personnel reviewed Henry's academic file, placing more emphasis on school recommendations and past academic performance. After completing high school, Henry was admitted to the university and was immediately administered proficiency examinations in science and math. Since Henry successfully passed these exams he was given credit for these basic courses and was allowed to enroll in more advanced classes.

Case Analysis. A review of this case brings to light some of the important factors that might necessitate the consideration of program alternatives for certain gifted learners. To begin with, Henry was felt to be socially and emotionally, as well as academically, ready for an accelerated program. Although there did appear to be some discrepancy between this student's tested verbal and math abilities, such a discrepancy could be explained by two factors. First, as a culturally different learner, the language and experiences presented in the measures of verbal ability may not be closely related to the language and experiences that are part of Henry's background. Second, Henry's expressed interests tend to lie more in the areas of math and science. Also important to consider in regard to this gap between verbal and math abilities is the fact that the noted discrepancy did not prevent

Henry from performing well at his studies. The decision to place a student like Henry in an accelerated program can only be made after a careful review of the individual involved.

Case 2

Loretta, who is in the fourth grade, has been diagnosed as gifted and talented. An analysis of her background indicates that she is a well-adjusted child who comes from a supportive home environment. Loretta has been playing the piano since she was six years old and has composed several musical pieces. Much of her free time is spent at the piano.

Within the regular classroom setting, observations show that Loretta often completes her work rapidly and carelessly and appears bored with regular studies. Her teacher also commented that when Loretta is not involved in some kind of work she frequently gets into mischief with other students.

One day a week Loretta attends an exclusive grouping program for the gifted. Activities in this program involve the development of divergent and problem-solving skills. Teacher observation of Loretta in this program indicates that she relates well with other students and often assumes a leadership role, initiating discussions and guiding students in new projects. However, it was also noted that while Loretta shows enthusiasm and interest in the activities in this program, this attention is often short-lived. In an attempt to motivate Loretta, her teacher asked her to develop a musical program involving the other gifted students that would eventually be put on for the student body. The teacher observed that Loretta became highly interested in this assignment and without hesitation began to develop a program. Throughout the development of this project, Loretta's teacher noted that she maintained a high level of interest in the project with little evidence of boredom. The teacher reported that Loretta seemed to gain a sense of strength from each new challenge that arose.

Owing to Loretta's developing behavior problem in the regular classroom, a conference was called to determine an appropriate course of action. Based on the marked difference of Loretta's performance and behavior between the gifted and regular class and because of her extremely high potential, it was decided that an alternate approach was needed.

Because of Loretta's love for music and the noted changes in her behavior when involved in her music, it was suggested that Loretta should be placed in a special school for the gifted and talented that held classes for the musically gifted student—an idea strongly supported by Loretta and her parents.

Case Analysis. There are times, as in the case of Loretta, when it will be justified to consider placement of a gifted learner in a special school setting even when no such arrangement exists in the gifted program format of a specific school or school system. Although Loretta's enrollment in a special school setting was not the only alternative available to the placement committee, it can be viewed as a viable alternative for several reasons. First, Loretta exhibited disinterest and boredom with the approach to learning taken within the regular classroom, a situation that led to some apparent discipline problems. This boredom and Loretta's inattention to tasks were alleviated to a certain degree by her participation in special gifted classes. However, even the approach taken within this gifted program acted only as a temporary stimulator unless curriculum was more directly related to Loretta's musical interests.

At this point, attempts could have been made to structure more of Loretta's curriculum in the direction of her intense interest in music. However, due to the availability of a special school where focus on music was possible, this option was selected.

Cost vs. Benefits—Ideal vs. Functional

Throughout this section we have attempted to view the selection of the gifted program format as a dichotomy with theoretical considerations on the one side and practical guidelines on the other. Certainly, such an analysis is extremely oversimplified. This oversimplification, however, does allow us to visualize more readily the factors that will exert influence on whatever choice of program organization is under consideration. This dichotomy between theory and practice can also be understood as a contrast between the ideal and the functional. What must be reached in the determination of an appropriate gifted program organization is a balance between a desired structure and a workable one. As in the establishment of any curricular project, there is likely to be some degree of give and take between these two elements. The question remains as to how much the program ideals must be compromised to satisfy the practical constraints that exist.

In answering this dilemma, program initiators must carefully weight the cost of any deviation from an established goal or ideal against the benefits that this deviation would produce. It must also be remembered that there are many ways to achieve a goal or ideal. Before major compromises are made, these plausible alternatives should be sought. Finally, program initiators should firmly establish their priorities and be able to justify them to others. In that way, the importance of a particular goal, as supported by facts as well as beliefs, can be more accurately weighted against the difficulties of its implementation.

As the process of choosing an appropriate format is underway, it would be helpful, at the very least, to be familiar with the categories of program organizations in operation and certain alternatives within each of these categories that may have applicability.

CATEGORIES OF GIFTED PROGRAM FORMATS: DESCRIPTION, ANALYSIS, AND IMPLICATIONS

Educational programs for the gifted student can generally be classified under three main categories. Although there are numerous variations in gifted programming in operation throughout the American educational system, these variations principally fall within one of the major categories of acceleration, enrichment, or exclusive grouping, with some overlapping and combining of the elements of two or more categories. Within this section, each of these categories will be defined, various common types of each category presented, several advantages and disadvantages of each given, and the implications of these formats analyzed. It should be understood that the terms applied to these categories may have slightly different connotations in the gifted literature, depending on the researchers' application of terminology.

Acceleration

"Acceleration" can be defined as an organizational procedure whereby gifted students are advanced through the curriculum at a more rapid rate than are their peers. This procedure involves providing these students with learning experiences at a pace consistent with their cognitive development. The most common conception of acceleration is the situation in which a child foregoes all or a portion of academic training as well as the accompanying social-emotional experiences at a regular instructional level and is promoted, instead, to a higher level. Such a promotion often involves a one-year advancement from the learner's present placement. However, the student who begins kindergarten at the age of four or the young adult who enters college after completing high school in only three years serves as an alternative example of acceleration in action. In all three instances, the pace of learning is accelerated so that the individual is able to complete the established educational requirements within a shorter time span than is normally the case.

Of all three major formats that can operate in educational programming for the gifted, acceleration presently represents one of the most controversial and one of the least-applied approaches in American school systems. Although acceleration is more readily acceptable as an educational alternative in Canada, it has been largely overlooked by our own educators, perhaps for administrative convenience or for administrative protection from those parents who believe their children should be moved ahead.

However, even in the United States the accelerated approach to gifted education does have its supporters. One of the most notable is Julian Stanley, who since the early 1970s has developed a nationally known math project at Johns Hopkins University. As part of this project, young learners who have demonstrated their mathematical proficiencies are given the opportunity to work through a more advanced mathematics curriculum at an accelerated pace. Stanley is not only a very vocal supporter of accelerated programs for the gifted but also a vocal critic of the more watered-down approaches to gifted education (Stanley, 1976).

While there are certain educational risks inherent in the format of acceleration, schools should be more willing to consider acceleration in individual cases with the same reservations and careful scrutiny that is applied in the consideration of student retention. Some of the risk in the decision to accelerate a student may be alleviated, in part, by a clearer understanding of the advantages and disadvantages associated with such an approach and by adequate and effective diagnosis of a student's strengths and weaknesses.

Advantages

The most obvious benefit that can be ascribed to an acceleration format is that it allows a student the opportunity to work at an appropriate academic level without requiring any major alteration in the existing program. In essence, a match is made between the learner and the curriculum by bringing the student into an already existing and more appropriate situation, rather than by molding the immediate curriculum to bring it up to the level of student need. In this way, acceleration can be viewed as an effective use of instructional time and energies within the gifted program.

Acceleration may also serve as a motivational force in the situation in which students are made to stay in a classroom where the work is markedly below their potential. Since emotional maladjustment could possibly result from a lack of academic challenge, supplying these gifted students with a curriculum not equal to their abilities is probably more harmful than any temporary difficulty associated with an adjustment to a slightly older group—a belief supported by the research of Bish and Fliegler as early as 1959.

Rice and Banks (1974), in a survey of 119 junior high and high school students on the topic of recommended program changes, found that all groups selected acceleration as an appropriate means of providing gifted learners with advanced studies. Most of those surveyed, however, did tend to favor an accelerated approach based on subject-by-subject assessment of abilities.

The issue of productivity also focuses on several advantages to an acceleration format. As a result of acceleration, less time must be devoted to basic training or educational preparation. This frees the individual earlier to enter a career area while at a productive peak and makes further delay in independence unnecessary.

Connected to the issue of productivity are the economic advantages reaped from acceleration. The sooner any professional training can be completed, the sooner an economic contribution in terms of man-years can be made. The school system also profits financially by having to invest less in the education of the gifted student than would otherwise have been the case. Therefore, a positive consequence of acceleration appears to be the significant savings it provides not only to parents and students but also to the school and community.

In addition, monetary and motivational factors aside, the accelerated format of gifted programming is one organizational approach that can be put into operation in any institutional setting.

The ultimate question that must be raised in the consideration of acceleration is this one: why postpone appropriate educational experiences for gifted learners or prolong their academic careers when neither is necessary?

Disadvantages

As is the case with controversial topics, the question of acceleration has several negative aspects that require consideration.

First, while acceleration may provide a means of eliminating possible boredom for certain gifted students, there are other less drastic methods available that can be used to challenge the intellect without the apparent risks involved in acceleration. One of these "risks" frequently referred to among many practitioners is the threat that advanced placement would pose to the learner's social-emotional well-being. This idea of acceleration as damaging to the social-emotional well-being of the gifted child remains a persistent argument against its implementation, even though this position is not upheld in the research (Bish & Fliegler, 1959; Gallagher, 1975; Lehman, 1953; Pressey, 1955). It should be noted, however, that much of the research on the effects of acceleration was conducted in the years just prior to and soon after the launching of Sputnik. More current research in this area can update these findings in light of prevailing attitudes and practices. The risk of acceleration appears less intense when the individual under consideration is highly gifted or in those instances in which the acceleration is more subject-specific.

A final caution should be voiced in relation to the accelerated format of gifted education. When an accelerated format is decided on, there is a chance that the sequence of skills and pattern of learning will be negatively disrupted. As Bish and Fliegler cautioned (1959), pure skipping within the established curriculum sequence may leave gaps in the student's learning that could alter future academic achievements.

Types of Accelerated Formats

Although grade skipping is possibly the most commonly thought of variety of acceleration, there are other forms within this category that deserve mention. Within these forms of acceleration, the focus of the gifted program will rest on the rate of the learners' exposure to educational curriculum. These examples should be viewed as only several of the possible variations within the accelerated approach.

Grade Telescoping. In this type of program the student is rapidly moved through the elementary, junior and senior high school grades. Unlike grade skipping, this approach encompasses the subject matter of the entire school curriculum. The student is given the opportunity to master the curriculum more quickly.

Continuous Progress. This approach is synonymous with nongraded schools. Continuous progress involves subdividing the material into objectives or units and enables the gifted learners to work at their own pace. The curriculum expectations can be viewed as more fluid and less grade-level bound. Therefore, the subject matter that normally requires two years for completion may require only one year for the gifted learner. Variations of this approach may also include independent studies, tutoring, or enrollment in courses of special interest.

Advanced Placement. Advanced placement is the educational advancement of gifted learners as a result of their entrance in the curriculum at a higher stage than is normal. Several examples of how advanced placement can be accomplished include the admission of a learner into a new or different, higher level of education, as when the three-year-old enters kindergarten, or the repositioning of a learner into a higher educational level within the same instructional institution, most often as a result of demonstrated proficiency.

Increased Academic Load. This approach is more applicable to learners in the high school or collegiate setting. Increased academic load focuses on providing gifted learners the opportunity to assume a greater number of academic hours than is normally permitted.

Implications of an Accelerated Approach

Because of the strain that acceleration may place on a gifted student's social and emotional maturity, as well as cognitive development, it is extremely important that the recommended individual be given careful consideration and undergo sufficient diagnosis. An adequate evaluation of the whole student is mandatory in order to eliminate the selection of those students whose social and emotional development have not attained the level needed to ensure a greater degree of success. The diagnostic process in acceleration should parallel as closely as possible the comprehensive information strategy described in Chapter 2, incorporating an analysis of such elements as the quality of work done, maturity (social, emotional), test results, mental ability, conferences with parents and pupils, and teacher recommendation.

Because of the highly individualized evaluation process required by an acceleration format, it is obvious that such an approach should not be adopted on a blanket basis. However, acceleration, as an alternative approach, can, when wisely applied, provide the flexibility required in gifted programming to meet the unique or special needs of particular gifted students. Furthermore, when introduced into a school system where the curriculum is appropriately chosen and properly sequenced, such "guided acceleration," as it is defined by Pressey (1962), will not only eliminate waste in the system but also will "be the cutting edge of efforts toward programs better coordinated and paced for all in the school."

Enrichment

When the curriculum of the regular classroom is supplemented for the gifted student by the inclusion of additional or more in-depth learning experiences, the instructional procedure is referred to as enrichment. Enriched education for the gifted individual or small group is probably the most popular approach in gifted programming being applied in school systems at present. Because of its flexibility, the enrichment format can be undertaken in many ways, including field trips, libraries, lectures, demonstrations, modular scheduling, and small group instruction.

As far back as 1964, Durr identified three basic dimensions of the enrichment approach that could be put into operation in the classroom—horizontal, vertical, and supplementary.

"Horizontal enrichment" is defined as learning experiences that proceed outward from those activities planned for students of average ability in the class. The program is extended within the confines of the present grade level curriculum to meet the needs of the nonaverage student, such as the gifted. Materials or units of study pursued at later grade levels are purposely excluded in horizontal enrichment, and only modifications in the regular grade level offerings are considered (see Figure 5-4).

In contrast, it is vertical enrichment that concentrates on the gifted student by encouraging that individual to move through the normal school learning at a more rapid rate (see Figure 5-5). The gifted student is, therefore, exposed not only to the curriculum that is part of the present grade level but also to experiences relating to the curricular content of later grade levels. A diagram of supplementary enrichment is shown in Figure 5-6.

Renzulli (1977) has presented another view of the enrichment approach to gifted education, which he has entitled the Enrichment Triad Model (see Figure 5-7). Within the model, Renzulli identifies three types of enrichment experiences and activities built around the regular curriculum and environmental experiences. Type I enrichment activities are basically those of an exploratory nature through which learners are exposed to a wide range of topics or areas of investigation that may spark further interests. The focus of type II enrichment, which is identified as group training activities, is to provide gifted learners with the skills necessary to locate, assimilate, and evaluate materials within the curriculum to be pursued. It is the objective of the type III enrichment to afford the learner the opportunity to

Figure 5-4 Horizontal Enrichment

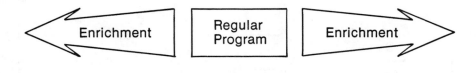

Figure 5-5 Vertical Enrichment

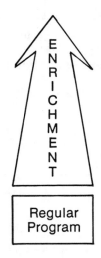

Figure 5-6 Supplementary Enrichment

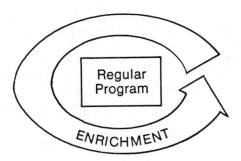

Figure 5-7 The Enrichment Triad Model

Type I
General
Exploratory
Activities

Type II
Group
Training
Activities

Type III
Individual and Small Group
Investigations of
Real
Problems

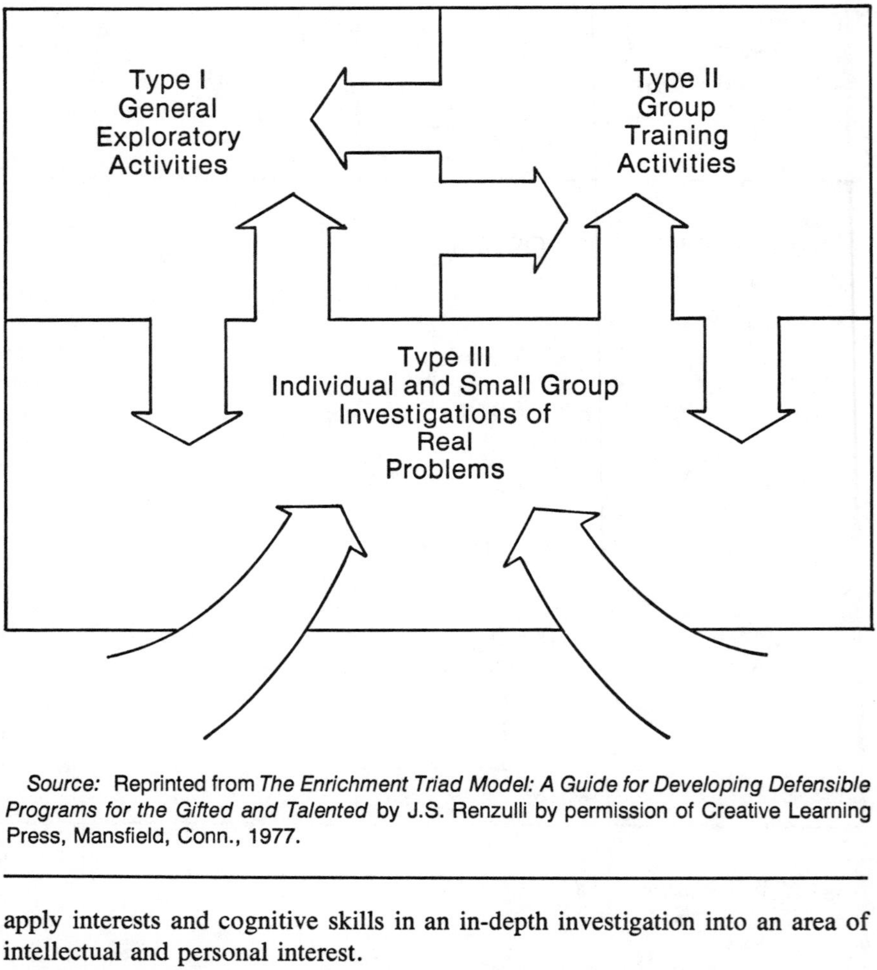

Source: Reprinted from *The Enrichment Triad Model: A Guide for Developing Defensible Programs for the Gifted and Talented* by J.S. Renzulli by permission of Creative Learning Press, Mansfield, Conn., 1977.

apply interests and cognitive skills in an in-depth investigation into an area of intellectual and personal interest.

Enrichment is probably the most widely implemented of all the varieties of program approaches for the gifted. However, even with the wide-scale implementation of such programs, there appears to be a misunderstanding of the role of enrichment and its purpose in gifted education. In essence, a true enrichment program has as its overall purpose the provision of additional educational experiences that supplement or augment regular classroom activities. In this type of program it becomes important for implementors to be aware of the scope and sequence of the curriculum in order to differentiate that curriculum for the gifted learner.

Essentially, then, an effective enrichment program should be qualitatively rather than quantitatively different from the regular school program and should attempt to provide gifted learners with the opportunity to pursue in-depth a wide variety of experiences that are beyond the scope of the regular class.

Advantages

One of the major advantages of implementing an enrichment program is the provision it makes for gifted learners to broaden their educational experiences and the challenge it provides for them to seek out similarities and differences in the topics they study. Involving gifted learners in such activities increases their interest and motivation and will enable them to develop and refine their thinking and problem-solving skills.

A second advantage of an enrichment program is its effect in stimulating not only gifted learners but also the other students in the class and the teacher. When gifted learners are afforded opportunities to work with other students in the class, they provide new insights into assigned problems, provide leadership, and direct the group toward new avenues of learning.

Another advantage of this type of approach is its sensitivity to providing individualization for gifted learners within the most natural context—the classroom. Enrichment not only provides activities for the gifted to develop their areas of interest but also allows for maximum flexibility in the assignment of such activities based on the student's abilities, motivation, and depth of concentration.

Disadvantages

While there do exist some concerns about the concept of enrichment, none of these concerns appears seriously detrimental to the gifted learner. The questions surrounding enrichment center more on whether such an approach can prove beneficial.

For example, one of the major concerns about enrichment is the fact that the concept of enrichment often implies at best the provision of more activities, rather than qualitatively different ones, for the gifted learner. Even though providing gifted learners with more experiences is not in essence what is meant by a true enrichment program, this approach would seem more acceptable than having the student idle in the classroom.

A difficulty that arises in providing any type of supplemental activities to learners as well as encouraging them to pursue topics of interest is the risk that there will be no logical organization to what is learned. For example, skills may at times be taught without considering whether any knowledge or abilities are needed prior to that stage of learning.

A third concern involves the wide range of differences found in the regular classroom; thus, it is unrealistic to assume that a teacher, without guidance or assistance, could accurately identify and plan the type of individualized enrichment program needed by gifted learners. A factor that should be mentioned here is the necessity for the teacher to provide the necessary guidance and stimulation that will continue to heighten the students' motivation and stimulate their curiosity to the point where they can independently assume the responsibility for pursuing these activities—a very difficult task for classroom teachers to undertake along with the regular demands of their jobs. Consequently, without adequate consistency, control, and cooperation among the separate components of the enrichment program, gifted learners may find themselves doing more of the same kind of work as everyone else around them, often simply at a faster rate.

Types of Enrichment Formats

Although enrichment programs may take on many descriptions, there are several types that can be mentioned here.

Extracurricular Interest Groups. This approach provides the gifted learner the opportunity to work with individuals who share common interests so that these interests may be collectively pursued. Clubs or organizations that focus on special topics can be effective stimulators of intellectual growth.

Independent Studies. An independent study approach enables a gifted learner to make an in-depth investigation into an area of interest under the guidance of an instructor.

Contracting. Similar in framework to an independent studies organization, contracting is a method whereby the gifted individual and an instructor work out a written agreement. This written agreement outlines not only the topic or area of study, but the criteria of successful accomplishment within each stage of topic development.

Learning Packets and Learning Centers. More of a teaching strategy than a variety of enrichment, the employment of learning packets and centers, especially when developed at several ability levels and around student interests, can be effective sources of enrichment within the classroom.

Floating Teachers. A rather unique approach to enrichment, the floating teacher system allows the gifted learner to function within the context of the regular classroom. Yet the students' curriculum and the work of the regular classroom teacher are supervised and supported by a special gifted teacher who circulates through the school system providing expertise and assistance wherever needed.

Implications of an Enrichment Format

With the growing concern over the mainstreaming of exceptional students, enrichment is one category of program organization that cannot be overlooked as a potential force in comprehensive education of the gifted. If we view gifted programming on some form of continuum, the enrichment approach would appear at the relative center. However, for the enrichment format to be effective and to become more than a chance to do nothing or more of it under the auspices of the gifted movement, several facets of the program must be carefully developed.

In the consideration of enrichment for gifted programming, it becomes important that the needs of gifted learners are adequately identified. Once an accurate evaluation of the gifted learner's instructional level is complete, it is essential that the enrichment activities are accurately designed at that level. Knowing the ability levels of students is not sufficient to ensure the formulation of a successful program for them. Knowing the students also involves having some understanding of their interests, attitudes, and activities. Their potential will be better achieved by tapping the natural sources of interest and enthusiasm that are present.

If having an adequate understanding of a gifted student is one prerequisite to the enrichment program's success, having an understanding of the school curriculum is another. An understanding of the total educational curriculum is important in order to ensure that the activities provided for gifted learners are not presented in ways already experienced in past settings. A thorough knowledge of the total educational program will better ensure diversity of experience in attainment of student objectives within the sequence of the already existing curriculum.

Exclusive Groupings

Exclusive grouping can be considered an organizational and instructional procedure whereby gifted students are homogeneously grouped in special classes or special schools in order to utilize fully their unique abilities. Any variation of exclusive groupings that a school system may wish to put in operation requires some method of identification of gifted students by means of specific criteria. The assumption of this type of program format appears to be that gifted students benefit from interaction with others of similar cognitive ability and that such separate or exclusive instruction can better meet the special needs of the gifted.

While exclusive grouping is a reorganization of gifted learners and thus a deviation from regular procedures, this relocation may or may not involve a major adjustment in the present curriculum. In other words, the scope or sequence of the operating curriculum need not be altered by the inclusion of an exclusive grouping format. However, program initiators may determine that more than the setting within which the instructional content is presented needs to be restructured for the gifted learner. In this instance, instructional as well as procedural changes can be made in the existing curriculum.

It would seem that even though the underlying assumption of an exclusive groupings approach would be the belief that a gifted learner profits from interaction with other gifted learners, there has been a misinterpretation of this format. This misinterpretation centers around a common misunderstanding that the exclusive groupings approach advocates the total exclusion of gifted learners from the mainstream of students. While this view may be a commonly held belief, the actual organization underlying exclusive groupings can be structured in numerous ways to permit varying degrees of exclusivity.

If exclusive grouping is to be successfully implemented in some way, however, it will be extremely important that it be undertaken with a keen awareness of its advantages and disadvantages.

Advantages

One of the obvious advantages of exclusive grouping is the opportunity it provides for the gifted to work cooperatively with other gifted learners, to share the knowledge they gain, to stimulate each other cognitively, and to provide different insights in particular areas of interest. Because of the high level of abilities within these classes, the curriculum can be restructured to that level, providing gifted learners with new and more challenging situations than might be possible within a more heterogeneous setting. Consequently, learning can be stimulated not only by interaction with other gifted learners but also by interaction with a more specialized curriculum.

This interaction, as the focus of the exclusive grouping format, is further heightened by the potential influence of teacher selectivity. Generally, if the present organization of the school's curriculum is markedly altered to accommodate the homogeneous grouping of gifted learners, it would seem logical for program developers to exercise selectivity in appointing personnel to staff such grouping. A teacher with interest, expertise, and experience in working with the gifted would be a reasonable choice to guide the instruction in an exclusive grouping program.

Disadvantages

One of the major disadvantages of exclusive grouping is the constant complaint that the gifted learner is given little opportunity to interact wtih learners of varying levels of cognitive development. This fear would seem to have more justification as the amount of exclusivity increases. Certainly, those who advocate a mainstreaming approach would argue that a program that separates exceptional learners from supposedly "normal" students for a large portion of school experiences would deprive both groups of sufficient interaction with one another—an interaction that is valuable to both.

Another factor to be considered here is the social effect that special placement has on the gifted learner. As was briefly considered under the category of acceleration, there is a persistent, if unfounded, attitude that exclusive grouping leads to the social stigmatization of gifted learners. This social stigma can be analyzed in two ways. First, the gifted learner may be ostracized by average learners because of the special treatment or added attention received. This is the image of gifted learners being looked on as "different" by those who are not given the opportunity to know or relate to them individually. However, such social isolation could be two-directional, that is, gifted learners may somehow perceive themselves as "different" and seek to restrict their own scope of interaction. Of course, these are only theoretical possibilities that are susceptible to individual differences and in need of further empirical testing.

The second social consideration is that taking gifted learners out of the regular mainstream leads to society's perception of these students as an elitist group. Another difficulty that deserves adequate consideration within the category of exclusive grouping is the effect of inadequate or inaccurate diagnosis on the placement of gifted learners. If admission to a gifted program is dependent on identification procedures and if these procedures are insufficient, two obvious problems can arise. First, certain individuals who are not actually of gifted potential may be placed in a highly structured situation with which they will have difficulty coping. Second, a student of gifted potential may be needlessly overlooked. These two shortcomings are inherent in any system of programming that provides services to students only on the basis of placement decisions. In acceleration and exclusive groupings, these misplacements are more problematic because of the removal of students from regular classroom context.

Types of Exclusive Grouping

Several examples of exclusive grouping which have found popularity as gifted program formats include the following:

Summer or Weekend Schools. Offered outside the regular educational curriculum, these special programs provide gifted learners with an opportunity to work on specific talents and interests with students of similar abilities and interests. Such an approach can be placed into operation when exclusive grouping does not fit into the structure of the regular curriculum but is felt by program developers to be important enough to pursue by alternative means.

Part-time Special Classes or Groups. In this program, the student is removed for a portion of the school day or school week to take part in activities designed to supplement the regular curriculum. In some systems, resource rooms have been organized to service the gifted learner in much the same way as they service other special learners. In addition, gifted learners may periodically meet to take advantage of experiences that involve group dialogue and discussion and seminars focusing on certain subject areas.

Full-time Special Classes. When gifted learners are participants in full-time classes, they spend the entire school day in homogeneously grouped classes.

Mentorship. In this type of program, the gifted learner is given the opportunity to pursue an area of interest under the guidance of an individual with expertise in that particular field. Under this system the gifted learner is allowed to seek knowledge within the context of the real world.

Implications of Exclusive Grouping

It is essential when considering a program of exclusive grouping to view the homogeneous grouping of gifted learners as the first step in effective programming and not as an end in itself; merely placing gifted students together will not result in heightened educational experiences for these individuals. Undoubtedly, interaction is the focus of exclusive grouping, but interaction between the gifted must be accompanied by their interaction with an appropriate curriculum and an effective instructor.

In addition, it should be noted that even within an exclusive grouping of the gifted there will remain a range of abilities, interests, and needs that must be dealt with. Often within these exclusive groupings there will be a need to place students into small groups or clusters or to provide the individual student with instructional guidance.

Finally, because of the nature of exclusive grouping, this format can be more numerically restrictive than an enrichment approach. When the basis for the program is placement in a special class or school rather than in the setting of the regular classroom, only a specified number of individuals can generally be accommodated.

Program Formats Compared

Now that program formats have been individually described and analyzed, the question may remain as to which type of program structure would be the most appropriate for a particular school or school system. First, as has been pointed out previously within this chapter, appropriateness is a unique quality. Appropriateness can only be determined on an individual basis with a clear understanding of the theoretical objectives and practical aspects of the academic environment into which the program will be structured. However, with the idea firmly established that no one means of achieving effective educational programming for the gifted far surpasses any other, several comparisons can be made.

The first comparison that can be described is based on the center of adjustment created by each format. "Center of adjustment" is a term used to designate the segment of the school population or curriculum on which the burden of adaptation to the gifted program tends to fall. If a continuum is constructed to display this concept, the word "curriculum" would be placed at one end and the word "learner" at the other (see Figure 5-8). A format of acceleration, in which the gifted learner is placed into an already existing curriculum, would be the type of gifted program structuring that places the burden of adjustment clearly in the lap of the gifted learner.

More to the opposite end of this continuum the exclusive grouping format would be situated. This positioning of exclusive grouping is based on the fact that the curriculum within the special class or school is brought up to the higher cognitive level of the gifted learners. At least in theory, it is the curriculum that is modified to meet the needs of the homogeneously grouped, gifted students.

Enrichment is located more to the center of this continuum because while it does require curricular changes, these changes are tempered by the heterogeneous situation of the regular classroom. It would seem that the degree of curricular adjustment is somewhat diminished by the time and expertise demanded of the classroom teacher, as well.

Another comparison that can be made among the three types of gifted program structures regards the amount of reorganization required for each. As this comparison is made, it must be pointed out that these are simplified situations, employed to make such a comparison more readily visible. With this clarification, it would appear that the installation of an accelerated program format would require the least amount of reorganization to the present curriculum than either of the other formats. After careful screening of the student is made and the appropriate evaluation achieved, little more remains but to match the individual to the suitable level and area of the curriculum in operation (see Figure 5-9). Enrichment, on the

Figure 5-8 Gifted Program Formats: Center of Adjustment

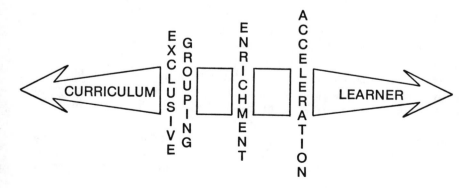

Figure 5-9 Gifted Program Formats: Degree of Reorganization

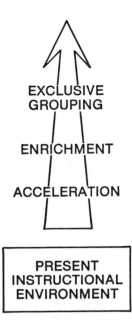

other hand, requires somewhat more adjustment to the present curriculum. While the regular structure of the classroom is maintained, the curriculum is modified, to some degree, within the classroom to satisfy the needs of the gifted learners present.

In general, it would seem that the implementation of an exclusive grouping approach would result in the greatest amount of alterations to the existing curriculum. In this instance, not only is the curriculum modified, but the gifted student population is relocated as well. Often this student relocation is accompanied by a readjustment among the ranks of the personnel, as the most suitably trained and experienced instructor is placed with the gifted.

Another important comparison that needs to be addressed pertains to the adaptability or flexibility of each program format. Stated differently, this is an analysis of the format's ability to function as the basis for an entire gifted program. In this regard, it would appear as if either an enrichment or exclusive grouping approach could readily function as the principal organization of a gifted program. Both of these formats exhibit the adaptability needed to serve the majority of gifted learners if adequately implemented. The acceleration format, while not as practi-

cal as a baseline organization for the gifted program, provides a valuable alternative procedure especially for the highly gifted learner or the learner with a
specialized ability or talent.

Although these various program formats have been presented singly within
this chapter, it must be understood that a school or school system may choose to
implement one or more variations of these formats (see Figure 5-10). It is not
uncommon for school systems to specify several types of arrangements for the
gifted within one format type, such as part-time and some full-time classes, or to
designate the inclusion of several alternatives across format lines, as in an independent study approach and advanced placement. The choice of format must suit
the many criteria discussed within this chapter and will take on a unique appearance as it is ultimately put into effect within a particular instructional unit. No two
institutions have the exact same needs, populations, personnel, or environment as
the next. Therefore, while the program formats have been presented in general
terms, they will take on the qualities and characteristics of the program in which
they are implemented.

Figure 5-10 Program Arrangements by Format and Location

	In School	In Community	Across Schools
Acceleration	Continuous pro- gress Grade Telescoping Grade Skipping Increased Aca- demic Load		Advanced Placement
Exclusive Grouping	Part-time special classes or groups Full-time special classes	Mentorship	Weekend in Summer Schools
Enrichment	Contracting learning pack- ets and centers Independent studies Extracurricular activities		Floating Teachers

SUMMARY

While the destination of more effective education for the gifted can be reached by the implementation of acceleration, enrichment, or exclusive groupings format, the choice of route that the gifted program will take must be carefully determined. The decision as to which format, variation, or combination of formats should be put into operation must be based on a clear understanding of the advantages and disadvantages associated with each type of administrative design and the implications the format would have on the remaining program development.

Also, the consideration of an appropriate program design warrants the analysis of the principal factors affecting the organization of gifted programs. These include the following: the philosophical viewpoint of the educational system; the financial considerations; the physical setting of the school and community; the staffing requirements; and, most importantly, the needs of the individual student. The decision on program format arises from the interaction of theoretical considerations and practical guidelines and is, in essence, a compromise between what is desired and what is attainable.

The selection of an appropriate program format should be based, as well, on a comparison of the formats available. If the principal consideration of program developers is the amount of adjustment required by the gifted learner, more emphasis might be placed on an exclusive grouping or enrichment approach than on an acceleration format. However, if the amount of reorganization required is the main concern for program planners, they may look more favorably on an acceleration approach.

The choice of an appropriate program organization is somewhat like a balancing act, in which we attempt to equalize the ideal against the practical. No single program will suit all the needs of the program planners. What must be done is to find the most acceptable and workable approach and transform it to the type of program organization that can best be applied within a given context.

REFERENCES

Bish, C., & Fliegler, L. Summary of research on the academically talented student. *Review of Educational Research*, 1959, *39*, 408-450.

Durr, W. *The gifted student*. New York: Oxford University Press, 1964.

Gallagher, J. *Teaching the gifted child* (2nd ed.). Boston: Allyn & Bacon, 1975.

Lehman, H. *Age and achievement: American Philosophical Society Memoirs (Vol. 33)*. Princeton, N.J.: Princeton University Press, 1953.

Pressey, S. Concerning the nature and nurture of genius. *Science*, 1955, *31*, 123-129.

Pressey, S. Educational acceleration: Occasional procedure or major issue. *Personnel and Guidance Journal*, September, 1962.

Renzulli, J. S. *The enrichment triad model: A guide for developing defensible programs for the gifted and talented*. Mansfield, Connecticut: Creative Learning Press, 1977.

Rice, J., & Banks, G. Opinions of gifted students regarding secondary school programs. In. S. Kirk and F. Lord (Eds.), *Exceptional children: Educational resources and perspectives*. Boston: Houghton Mifflin, 1974.

Stanley, J. Identifying and nurturing the intellectually gifted. *Phi Delta Kappan*, 1976, *58*, 85-89.

Chapter 6

Outlining Roles and Responsibilities

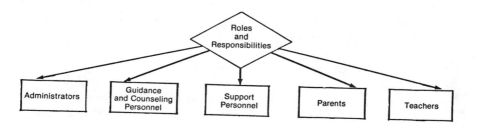

There are many individuals from various segments of the school and community setting who have much to contribute to the gifted program. These people can serve as valuable resources in the education of gifted learners and include administrators, counselors and guidance staff, school support personnel, parents, and, of course, teachers. Within this chapter the roles and responsiblities of these potential contributors will be detailed and discussed for the purpose of determining ways they can enhance the education of the gifted and promote the growth of the gifted program. Administrators, guidance counselors, support personnel, teachers, and parents can work within their special domains, as well as cooperatively, to furnish the firm foundations upon which gifted instruction can continue to develop. These individuals can, ultimately, provide the gifted program with a deeper commitment and sense of direction as it moves along the road to success.

THE ADMINISTRATOR

Those individuals entrusted with the responsibility of designing and implementing gifted educational programs should be fully aware of the important role the administrator plays in ensuring the success of any program. All too often, however, administrators are perceived by their staffs as individuals who are not part of the group. Rather, administrators are viewed as outsiders whose goals and objec-

163

tives differ from the educational mainstream. This feeling can be accentuated by the "them against us" attitude that might exist in certain educational institutions.

Yet, the success of the gifted program will depend largely on how well all involved in the planning and implementing of that program can act as a well-coordinated and cohesive group. From the very beginning, administrators should not only be considered group members who will work cooperatively for the benefit of the gifted program but also as members whose wealth of experiences should be invaluable assets in program development. This cooperative group effort is plausible only if (1) the administrators are viewed in a positive manner; (2) their roles are clearly defined and understood by themselves and their staffs; and, (3) they are given the opportunity to become actively involved in the development of the gifted program.

To develop a relatively complete picture of the administrator in respect to the education of the gifted, the needed characteristics of administrators will be discussed, along with their responsibilities and competencies.

Positive Characteristics of Administrators

There are numerous qualities a good administrator should possess. It is unreasonable to assume, however, that administrators would possess all these positive qualities. Yet, there are three specific characteristics that appear to have particular relevance to the gifted program. These characteristics are awareness, flexibility, and a positive attitude.

Awareness

Before administrators at any level can become committed to differentiated educational programming for the gifted, they must first be cognizant of gifted learners' capabilities and needs that require specialized instruction. Such administrative awareness can be either achieved by direct experience in gifted education or acquired, in part, through knowledge assimilated from the existing literature, or both. Taking a more active role in program development from its initial stages would provide the administrator with a great opportunity to increase experiential awareness. Furthermore, program planners can supply administrators with essential information that will assist them in establishing a broader understanding of the gifted, as well as specific information concerned with the gifted program under development. Without question, administrators will eventually be called on to make decisions that will have a direct bearing on the gifted program. Effective decisions demand that administrators possess knowledge about gifted learners, in general, and information about the workings of the gifted program under their supervision. This general knowledge and specific information can come only from a concerted effort on the part of administrators to achieve a greater understanding.

Flexibility

The establishment of any educational program requires change or modification in the existing situation, and the gifted programs based on the exceptional needs of exceptional students are no different. The degree of alteration imposed by the planned gifted program will vary from educational institution to educational institution, and the level of change will be dependent on many factors, such as quality and openness of the existing program. The level of change is also highly related to the restructuring permitted by the administration. Administrators who are well aware of the needs of the gifted, are involved from the outset in the design of the program, and are flexible enough to sanction necessary changes in the regular school program provide the kind of leadership needed in gifted education. It should be cautioned at this point that change for change sake should not be considered desirable in gifted programming. Knowing what *should* be done, however, must be accompanied by the willingness to initiate the type of instructional environment that will have positive educational results. This quality of flexibility requires a willingness on the part of the administrator to accept the fact that all gifted programs will not fit neatly into the school's present structure. Thus, what is required is a degree of open-mindedness in working toward a program design that will match the diversity of gifted learners.

Positive Attitude

Probably no other quality possessed by the administrator is as important as a positive attitude toward gifted programming. The administrator who feels confident about the development of a gifted program will convey this feeling to other school staff, parents, and the community, providing them with the encouragement and motivation needed for continued growth.

In all instructional settings, the administrators' educational priorities, whether stated or unstated, soon become evident to those around them. The value administrators place on gifted programming often becomes the standard to be followed by many around them.

Also, there will be times throughout development and continuation when the gifted program may produce frustrations for administrators and staff alike. Without a positive attitude it would be far more difficult for administrators to face patiently and tolerantly the minor irritations and setbacks. Educational growth cannot occur overnight, nor can gifted programming flourish in a negative atmosphere. Therefore, the gifted program must carry the support of administrators who convey their belief in its development and continuation.

Administrative Competencies and Program Responsibilities

Throughout the previous section, the discussion of the administrator focused on the personal qualities that should be possessed by those individuals in an administrative capacity—supervisors, program coordinators, principals, and school superintendents. Presently, attention will be focused on the specific program responsibilities and the competencies the administrators should possess. Although there will be, undoubtedly, some relationship between the characteristics described within this and the previous section, the distinction lies in the difference between one's personal qualities and the professional performance that may be affected by those qualities. Clearly, it would be extremely difficult for administrators to motivate others involved in the gifted program if they themselves lack a positive attitude toward the gifted program.

Even though differences will exist in how gifted programs are organized and what specific roles the administrator may have, there are basically five specific functions of administrators related to gifted programming (see Figure 6-1). These functions are:

1. the administrator as motivator
2. the administrator as information seeker
3. the administrator as disseminator of information
4. the administrator as a partner in program planning
5. the administrator as evaluator.

The Administrator as Motivator

One of the most important functions of the administrator is to be the impetus behind the initiation of the gifted program and the prime motivator during the course of the program's development. The administrator as a motivator influences individuals who may be directly or indirectly involved in gifted education, the school staff, parents, community, gifted learners, and other educators at the national, state, or district level.

School Staff. The administrator motivates the school staff in several ways. First, prior to and during the gifted program's development the administrator provides the staff with the support and encouragement necessary to proceed to develop such a program. In this setting the administrator encourages school staff to generate ideas about the formulation of the gifted program and accepts and is open to these ideas.

During the actual implementation of the program, the administrator regularly meets with the program developers to provide them with constructive comments about the program, which may include words of encouragement or reemphasis of the administrator's commitment in providing special programming for the gifted.

Parents and Community. Parents and community members represent a population that has the potential to be among the most ardent supporters of the gifted program. Yet, it often falls to the administrator to provide the first spark that

Figure 6-1 The Responsibilities and Related Competencies of Administrators in the Gifted Program

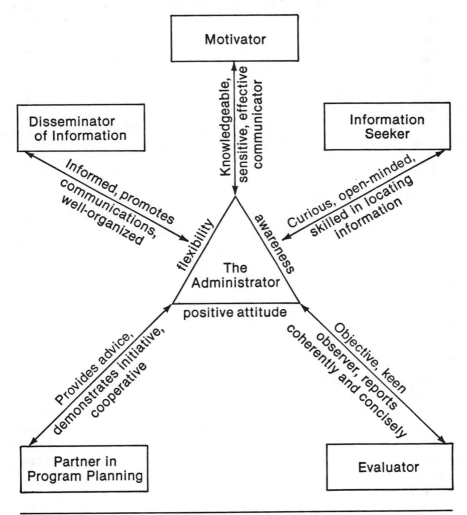

ignites this support. As a motivator of parents and community, administrators should tap the natural concerns of parents about the educational experiences of their children and should build on the interest of the community in the workings of the local school system for which they furnish financial support. Administrators should find the opportunity to let these parents and community persons know that their concerns and interests are important and that there is a role for them in the development and continued success of the gifted program. As a motivator in this setting, the administrator imparts to parents and community the idea that they serve as a vital link in the education of the gifted and encourages their active involvement in program development.

Gifted Learners. Administrators can motivate gifted learners by their caring, interest, and receptiveness. Administrators must make gifted learners realize that they care about them and are sensitive to their needs as a special population. Acknowledging the existence of the gifted in a positive manner is the first step in the motivational process.

Second, administrators should display a continued interest in the educational endeavors of the gifted. They should be alert to what gifted learners are doing and what type of projects they are undertaking in and out of the classroom to demonstrate their abilities, interests, and talents. Whenever warranted, these gifted learners must be offered the positive reinforcement that is deserved or the constructive criticism that is required.

Finally, administrators must show the gifted that they are sensitive to these learners' concerns and ideas about their own educational experiences. A "receptive ear" by administrators conveys the notion to the gifted that they do have some input into their own instructional destiny. This, in turn, may elicit more pride and enthusiasm from these learners in their educational programs.

National, State, or District Administrators. Often, many effective gifted programs go unnoticed or fall by the wayside because administrators fail to fulfill their responsibility as motivator. What they forget is that their role as program "cheerleader" operates in two directions. Not only do those under the administrator's authority or service need to be told how vital and effective the gifted program is, but also those to whom the administrator must report deserve to hear encouraging words.

Because of the frequent opportunities administrators have to meet and talk with other school personnel and administrators at the national, state, and district levels, they should learn to use these encounters as opportunities to promote the gifted program. Administrators should also encourage their staff to promote the gifted program at national, state, and local meetings and gatherings.

Related Competencies. In order for administrators to carry out their responsibilities as motivators, it is necessary for them to possess certain competencies. First, administrators must be knowledgeable about the objectives and development of the gifted program. For administrators to adequately portray the gifted program they must know that program well. Second, and perhaps most importantly, administrators must be sensitive to the feelings and ideas of others. For those in authority to effectively encourage others to give their time and energies to the cause of gifted education, they must first show others that what they say or what they think has importance. Third, not only must administrators know what is occurring in the gifted program, and be sensitive to the beliefs and concerns of others, but they also must be able to convey that knowledge and sensitivity. Therefore, administrators must be effective communicators if they are to function satisfactorily in the capacity of motivator.

The Administrator as Information Seeker

In the role of information seeker, the administrator has two major responsibilities. First, the administrator attempts to collect information that is needed to justify the development and operation of the gifted program. This type of knowledge can be defined as project-specific data. Second, it is also important for administrators to gather information about gifted education, in general, that may prove helpful in program planning. The information sought in this instance is knowledge of a theoretical framework.

Project-specific information may encompass such data as how many children will be served by the gifted program and what expenditures are to be anticipated in program development. In regard to the issue of costs vs. benefits, the administrator must be attuned to the financial requirements of supplying the gifted program with persons and materials. The administrator must also try to utilize all available resources in putting together the most efficient and effective educational program for gifted learners. This cannot be accomplished without an adequate knowledge base.

In the second role as information seeker, administrators need to establish a theoretical framework around which educational programming for the gifted can be constructed. Within this capacity, administrators should become acquainted with the gifted literature even when the principal responsibility for program development rests with a program coordinator or designated staff member. To some extent, program planners and others familiar with gifted education can provide administrators with assistance in gaining answers to their questions, at the same time increasing their understanding of these exceptional learners.

Related Competencies. Several competencies are required by administrators for fulfillment of their responsibilities as information seekers. Coupled with a natural curiosity, eagerness to learn, and a mind open to new ideas and innovations, administrators must have the foresight to pose relevant questions. Once pertinent questions have been postulated, whether those questions are project-specific or theoretical in nature, administrators must know where and how to locate the information that could supply adequate answers. By keeping abreast of current trends in education the administrator should have access to a wealth of important information that will be beneficial to the gifted program. The skill of locating information is one competency, therefore, that should be possessed by all administrators.

The Administrator as Information Disseminator

As information disseminator, administrators are assigned the responsibility of providing information about the gifted to their staff, parents, community, and other educators. While there may appear to be some overlap between the administrative roles of motivator and information disseminator, there is a difference. Within the responsibility of information disseminator, administrators must deal with theoretical as well as project-specific data. As with the task of motivator, this responsibility is "bi-directional." Administrators bring information to the schools that is amassed from the national, state, and local levels. In addition, knowledge gained from school level developments is brought to the attention of educators at the upper stages of instructional planning.

School Personnel. The administrator, in an attempt to keep school personnel aware of current developments in gifted education, should initiate some type of periodic communication with and for these individuals. At the school level, these periodic interactions may take the form of in-service sessions or discussions at faculty meetings. While in-service training may be provided at the district level, it is also important to bring individuals involved in gifted programming at the school level together for an exchange of observations and ideas. Problems and successes shared in this way provide administrators with a line of communication between district and school that furnishes information valuable to administrators and faculty alike. Interested personnel should be encouraged to attend and become involved in conferences and professional organizations concerned with the education of the gifted. Such conferences and organizations are frequently useful sources of information and innovations relevant to the gifted movement.

The role played by consultants to the gifted program should not be overlooked either. The administrator should recognize the amount of knowledge that can be gained through the services of consultants whose expertise lies in the field of gifted education. Consequently, opportunities should be provided for these consultants to participate in the gifted program by means of in-service activities designed to utilize their expertise to the fullest.

School Boards. Important to the success of the gifted program is the continued support of the Board of Education. The administrator as disseminator of information can provide valuable information to school boards that will enable them to make valid decisions about the gifted program. Data concerned with the number of gifted being served and the approximate costs of and benefits incurred from the gifted program should be presented.

Parents. The administrator has a responsibility to see that the parents of the gifted are directly involved in planning the gifted program. Administrators as disseminators should schedule periodic meetings with parents to solicit their ideas and to offer them information regarding the education their children are receiving. Furthermore, some type of communication network should be established so that parents receive regular feedback about the gifted program and their children's role in that program. Parents should be furnished with knowledge about gifted learners in general as well as information specific to the school's gifted curriculum. In addition, parents should be involved in workshops in which they can learn about their gifted children and ways to assist them in meeting their potential. Parents should be encouraged to visit schools and observe first hand the workings of the gifted program. In some instructional settings, parents may even be sought as volunteers for the gifted program, donating their time to work in or outside the classroom. At times, schools may hold special assemblies and programs centering around the gifted to which parents can be invited.

Community. As previously mentioned, the community must be seen as a vital link to the success of the gifted program. Consequently, administrators must make a conscious effort to keep the community aware of the school's attempts to provide suitable education for the gifted. Local newspapers, radio stations, service and professional clubs and organizations, and community leaders can be utilized as mediums through which information about the gifted program can be communicated.

National and State Educators. Innovations do not always develop first at the national or state levels of education and then filter down to local levels. Many worthwhile undertakings emerge from the grassroots level of instruction and eventually find their way into state and national curriculum designs. Therefore, the administrator's responsibility to keep school personnel abreast of happenings in gifted education at the state and national levels is balanced by an equally important responsibility to alert individuals in upper level administrative positions to changes and innovations taking place in the gifted program.

Related Competencies. To be effective in disseminating information, the administrator must possess several important competencies. While administrators should certainly be well informed in the area of gifted education, they should also be efficient and well organized in their dissemination attempts. Important information vital to the success of the gifted program must be organized into some understandable and useful components that do not overwhelm or confuse those they are suppose to enlighten. This information must not only be outlined in a concise and coherent manner, but it must also then be distributed to the appropriate individuals. Administrators should maintain good interpersonal relationships with people connected in some way with the gifted program and should promote frequent and positive contacts with these individuals.

The Administrator as a Partner in Program Planning

As a partner in program planning, the administrator assumes a number of responsibilities that relate directly to the development, implementation, and maintenance of the gifted program. Initially, administrators may provide program initiators with suggestions, guidelines, or procedures to follow in getting the gifted program off the ground. Once the program has become operational, administrators can perform numerous functions, such as assisting in the selection of gifted learners, seeking resources needed for the program (e.g., finances, facilities, materials), and participating in the appointment of the program staff.

It should be remembered that the degree of involvement for administrators will vary greatly from individual to individual. This involvement can move from a more intense stage of initiator to that of advisor, and finally to that of approver, the least involved administrative role.

Whatever form their input takes, administrators will have some part in various phases of program development, including the determination of the format, strategies, and materials to be applied. As a partner in program planning, the administrator applies all the competencies displayed within the other areas of responsibility discussed and combines them with a stated interest in being a full or partial participant in program development. For example, the administrator must offer advice or make decisions based on knowledge and experiences accumulated and must actively seek the information or knowledge needed to answer questions that arise in program development. In addition, throughout the planning and development process the administrator must supply the positive reinforcement and enthusiastic support that is involved in the role of motivator. As a part of their job as program planning partner, administrators must be willing to take on assignments, as well as to assign others to various tasks. While administrators will be called on to voice an opinion in matters, they in turn should listen objectively to the opinions of others. Finally, throughout program planning, implementation, and maintenance, administrators need to be alert to those situations when the gifted program would be best served by the delegation of authority or responsibility to others. No matter how personally involved and professionally concerned in gifted education administrators may be, it is important to establish a support system among staff, parents, and community. This can be accomplished, to some degree, by allowing these individuals to assume important roles in the planning process.

The Administrator as Evaluator

The process of evaluation is a critical one that signals the strengths and weaknesses of educational programs such as those planned for gifted learners. Although this process of evaluation will be presented in detail in Chapter 9, a brief discussion of the administrative responsibilities and competencies related to evaluation will be offered here. Evaluation is ongoing and requires an influx of information and objectivity on the part of those involved. Because it is so essential to program success and continuance, administrators should come to view their role in the evaluative process as positive and potent. Therefore, administrators need to establish their positions as evaluators around the purpose of making the gifted program more effective and efficient. This requires that administrators, in cooperation with others, carefully determine the approaches to evaluation that will be taken throughout the existence of the gifted program. If administrators do not already have a knowledge of strategies and options available in the objective scrutiny of the program, they must seek out this information. It is crucial that the framework of program development follows closely the procedures that will be employed to evaluate it. Program initiators, in cooperation with administrators, must decide on the types of methods to be used in evaluating the instruction of the gifted and must also determine what instruments and methods will be utilized to collect data needed in adequate decision making.

Also as part of the evaluation process, administrators will be expected to complete various reports, surveys, and summaries. Although such paperwork is usually time consuming, it is still a necessary and useful element in evaluation. Administrators should be able to complete these forms and reports coherently and concisely, portraying the program in the most accurate light possible.

Not only must administrators be objective in the evaluation process, but they also must possess several other competencies. As previously noted, those in administrative positions must be able to record and report their findings concisely and coherently. By doing so, data that are important in determining the efficiency and effectiveness of the gifted program can be understood and appreciated by those who will eventually judge the program's merits. Finally, in order to amass needed information, administrators must be keen observers of the educational programming established for gifted learners to be capable of assessing accurately the instructional environment of which they are a part.

A checklist of the duties of administrators as evaluators and in their other roles discussed previously is provided in Exhibit 6-1.

GUIDANCE AND COUNSELING PERSONNEL

The task of providing for the needs of gifted learners is monumental. No one segment of the educational community can assume sole responsibility for the nurturance of the gifted. For their educations to be comprehensive and meaningful, gifted learners need contact with and support from a variety of individuals within the school and community. These exceptionally bright learners, plagued at times by concomitant problems associated with their giftedness, require the warmth, support, and understanding of competent, caring persons—a job description suited to the school's guidance and counseling personnel.

Exhibit 6-1 Checklist of Administrative Responsibilities and
Competencies

	Yes	No
The Administrator as Motivator		
Encourages school staff to plan, organize, and develop the gifted program.	___	___
Enthusiastically promotes the gifted program within the community.	___	___
Actively seeks community support for the gifted program.	___	___
Gives school staff opportunities to implement their own ideas as to what should be included in programs for the gifted.	___	___
Promotes the school's gifted program at the national, state, and local levels.	___	___
Allows teachers to be flexible in planning and implementing the gifted program.	___	___
Encourages gifted learners in their various endeavors.	___	___
The Administrator as Information Seeker		
Takes the initiative to learn more about the needs and characteristics of gifted learners.	___	___
Tries to determine community attitudes toward gifted education.	___	___
Asks appropriate questions of program planners concerning the program.	___	___
Attempts to determine the attitudes of teachers, parents, and personnel toward the gifted.	___	___
Attempts to identify different federal, state, and local resources that may provide support for the gifted program.	___	___
Seeks to understand more about types of identification procedures available.	___	___
Plans strategies for analyzing student and staff needs.	___	___

Exhibit 6-1 continued

	Yes	No
Determines the roles various local community agencies can play in the gifted program.	___	___
Is concerned with ways the gifted program can meet the needs of children from diverse backgrounds.	___	___
Attempts to find out what services are presently available to the gifted at the school, district, state, and national levels.	___	___

The Administrator as Disseminator of Information

Designs in-service training workshops for staff and parents.	___	___
Plans public awareness activities that assist the community in understanding more about the gifted program.	___	___
Keeps school faculty aware of any contemplated changes in the gifted curriculum.	___	___
Meets with parents of the gifted both individually and in a group setting to discuss individual children or the gifted program in general.	___	___
Makes information about the school's gifted program available to other educators at the national, state, and local levels.	___	___
Provides school staff with information about federal and state developments in gifted education.	___	___
Makes consultants who might assist in program improvement available to school staff and parents.	___	___
Assists in promoting teachers' and parents' active involvement in professional organizations that are concerned with the gifted.	___	___
Keeps Boards of Education aware of the developments concerning the gifted program.	___	___

Exhibit 6-1 continued

	Yes	No
The Administrator as a Partner in Program Planning		
Establishes identification criteria in cooperation with program staff.	——	——
Assists teachers in acquiring materials and resources needed to implement the gifted program.	——	——
Assists in establishing guidelines by which teachers of the gifted may be selected.	——	——
Provides program planners with information concerning the appropriate administrative procedures to follow in developing the gifted program.	——	——
Assists in the selection of the appropriate gifted program format suitable to the school population.	——	——
The Administrator as Evaluator		
Outlines an evaluation plan implementing both formative and summative forms of evaluation in conjunction with program planners.	——	——
Determines methods for evaluating classroom effectiveness.	——	——
Reviews the methods for obtaining evaluation information on students (e.g., tests, parent and teacher questionnaires).	——	——
Determines if the gifted program is providing learning experiences to meet the educational, social, physical, mental, and emotional needs of all gifted learners.	——	——
Records evaluative data concisely and coherently.	——	——
Employs good observational techniques in the acquiring of evaluation information.	——	——

Characteristics of Guidance and Counseling Personnel

Regardless of the population served, individuals who provide guidance and counseling services generally must possess a number of traits that allow them to function effectively. Counselors should project sincerity and concern for the students and must develop a rapport and sense of trust with their clients. Basic to the competencies required by the school counselor are communication skills. Verbal and nonverbal interactions are the core of the counseling role, and listening as well as speaking abilities are necessary tools for the guidance personnel. Another important asset for the school counselor would be a wide range of experiences with individuals from diverse backgrounds. These experiences could lead the guidance and counseling personnel to a greater awareness and sensitivity.

Because of the uniqueness of gifted learners, counselors who serve this special population should possess several additional qualities. First, if counselors are to furnish the guidance appropriate to the gifted, they, at the very least, must have some knowledge and understanding of the needs, strengths, and goals of this exceptional group. As guidance and counseling personnel should develop an adequate picture of gifted learners, they must also know well the workings of the gifted program. This knowledge is essential if the guidance personnel are to play any role in the gifted program or in the *Specific Learner's Instructional Plan (SLIP)*.

Furthermore, it is crucial that every member of the guidance staff have confidence in the abilities of the gifted and encourage them to participate in challenging experiences. To perform this function satisfactorily, counselors need to know what educational and intellectual opportunities are available to these learners. Information as to these opportunities should extend outward from instructional institutions to the private and business sectors, in a search for all avenues that may serve the diverse and advanced interests and abilities of the gifted.

Roles and Responsibilities of Guidance and Counseling Personnel

To attain maximum success in the gifted program, counselors must fulfill obligations to various individuals directly and indirectly involved in the education of the gifted. The responsibilities to be discussed will include those related to gifted learners, teachers of the gifted, administrators, parents, and community members.

Responsibilities to the Gifted Learner

Identification. Perhaps the most important work performed by counselors and guidance personnel revolves around their contacts and interactions with gifted learners, for whom they serve a number of important functions. To be effective in this role, the counselor must recognize that the learner identified as gifted by virtue of membership in this unique population will possess special needs and abilities that must be recognized and addressed. As decribed in the literature, the gifted may be plagued by various difficulties associated with their exceptional abilities and with situations that may arise from those abilities. These difficulties can occur in any number of areas—social, emotional, physical, educational, cultural—and may require the assistance of the school counselor or guidance personnel. By prior identification of potential problem areas or anticipation of individual needs, these counseling personnel can provide guidance before problems are allowed to develop.

This concept of identification of gifted needs is not restricted solely to the issues and concerns relevant to the population as a whole. Instead, this awareness of strengths and needs has a second more personal dimension: the attention to the individual. Gifted learners, by virtue of their shared experiences, may have some of the same concerns and questions that can be collectively addressed; however, it cannot be forgotten that regardless of common needs each gifted learner is an individual, with unique interests, abilities, goals, fears, and dreams that must be recognized and dealt with by the counselor. Counselors must sharpen their skills in developing a profile of the gifted that encompasses their understanding of that individual first as a unique person and second as a gifted learner.

Interaction. If identification of potential needs among gifted learners is one area of concern to counselors and guidance personnel, then this must be followed closely by the provision of interaction. This interaction may take several forms. Possibly the most frequently considered mode of interaction is the one-to-one approach involving the counselor and the gifted client (see Figure 6-2). Within these sessions, situations of a highly personal nature can be shared. These personal situations may include discussions of social or emotional difficulties or questions about educational programming and intellectual endeavors. Owing to the personal information that may be communicated within these private discussions, the counselor and the gifted learner must come to an understanding about confidentiality. In certain instances, the learner might wish to have the knowledge shared with the counselor kept confidential. This question of students' right to confidentiality remains controversial, and guidance personnel should be prepared to tackle this issue before the problem arises.

However, one-to-one interactions need not be restricted to the counselor and student only. In some higher educational levels, programs have been instituted that provide for peer counseling. In this way, one gifted student may share feelings, concerns, and experiences with another gifted learner. These peer discussions can furnish opportunities for the gifted to establish lines of communications and a sense of cohesion within their ranks. The role of the counselor within these peer

Figure 6-2 A Model for One-to-One Counseling and Guidance Interaction

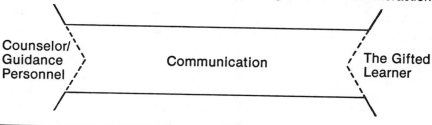

Counselor/
Guidance
Personnel

Communication

The Gifted
Learner

interactions can be defined more as a facilitator or observer than as an actual verbal participant.

Other modes of interaction are available to counselors in their dialogue with the gifted. One type of alternative approach is the triad model (see Figure 6-3). This model involves not only the counselor and a gifted learner but a third party as well. The third party included in the triad form of communication could be a parent, another student, a member of the school staff, or others who have a vested interest in the topic under consideration.

Still, at other times, counselors may prefer to initiate communication between small or large groups of individuals, including gifted learners and perhaps additional parties such as parents, educators, or community persons. As a consequence of this form of interaction, topics discussed must be of general rather than personal concern. Again, the counselors must view their roles as facilitators of the communication or learning process that should unfold.

Figure 6-3 A Triad Model of Counseling Interaction

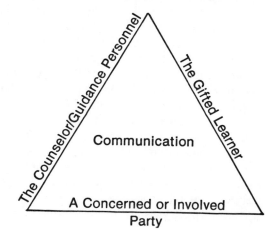

The Counselor/Guidance Personnel

The Gifted Learner

Communication

A Concerned or Involved
Party

Wherever the counselor or guidance personnel and gifted learners decide to meet and engage in communication should be perceived as suitable. An office or designated room is not the only location where counseling can occur; any classroom, corner, hall, or lot that satisfies those who wish to interact will do fine. Also, while counselors will need to establish some regular hours, there should be time set aside for other activities, such as classroom involvement, in-service presentations, and parent discussions. Finally, the gifted learners should be given the means to refer themselves to the counselor whenever they feel it necessary. This can be accomplished through the development of a simple form on which learners (elementary, middle, or secondary) indicate their desire to see the counselor. Not all referrals must come from teachers or parents, especially in the case of the gifted, who are frequently acutely aware of their own needs and problems.

Information and Encouragement. Because of the depth and scope of gifted potential, a vast array of opportunities is open to these exceptional learners. Gifted individuals may remain unaware of many of these options or perhaps unconvinced that their own abilities can lead to certain ends. To assist the gifted in fulfilling their potential, counselors must furnish them with both information and encouragement. Counselors should have access to a wealth of information about suitable careers, educational and intellectual activities, and community projects. By becoming cognizant of the many choices open to them, the gifted are more apt to make adequate decisions about their immediate and distant futures.

Information is a two-pronged tool, however. While counselors should be busily involved in providing their gifted clients with information about career and educational choices, they must also consciously make these learners aware of who they, the counselors, are and what they do. This may be especially true at the elementary or middle school levels where students have not formed concepts of the counselor's role in their educational experience. Orientation of younger learners to counseling can be achieved by puppet shows, slide presentations, role playing, question and answer sessions, and coloring books that teach visually, for example. Muro and Dinkmeyer (1977) outline the points that should be covered in a discussion with students about counseling in Exhibit 6-2.

Along with this information, counselors should offer the gifted learner the appropriate encouragement they require and deserve. The word "appropriate" is carefully added for several reasons. First, for counselors to perform their duties of channeling gifted learners, they must have a clear understanding of that student's interests, abilities, needs, and concerns. Knowing the gifted well is a prime prerequisite in furnishing guidance. Second, guidance personnel must view their role as pointing the way for the gifted learner, not pushing or pressuring the individual in any way. Choices or decisions must be those of the gifted learner and not those of the counselor. Certainly, because of their experience and perceptions, counselors may be aware of the talents and abilities of the gifted learner and the

Exhibit 6-2 Counseling: Orientation Discussion

I. Introduce yourself. Tell who you are and what your job is.

II. Outline the broad guidance function. Tell about guidance services in the areas of counseling.

III. Define counseling in a way that the students will understand what you mean:
   A. Stress that counseling is available for all students.
   B. Discuss "typical" concerns that are brought to the counselor (peer problems, making friends).
   C. Emphasize the helping aspect of the office; introduce confidentiality to the students.
   D. Encourage self-referral; show students how to make an appointment.
   E. Elaborate on the nature of the process; tell students what they can expect from interaction with the counselor—what behaviors are expected of the student, of the counselor.

IV. Make and use a tape recording of a demonstration counseling session (ask a colleague or friend to role-play a student on the tape). Stop the tape at appropriate points and discuss what is going on.

V. Pass out three- by five-inch cards and ask students to write out any questions they may have about counseling. To avoid embarrassment ask them not to sign their names. Collect the cards and respond to the questions.

VI. Terminate the meeting by asking the class, "What have you learned about counseling today?" (This will enable you to get some "feel" for how well you are conveying the message.)

Source: From Muro, James J., and Don C. Dinkmeyer, *Counseling in the Elementary and Middle Schools,* © 1977 Wm. C. Brown Company Publishers, Dubuque, Iowa. Reprinted by permission.

relationship of those talents and abilities to certain career or educational goals, but they can only express their opinions in these matters. Ultimately, it will be up to the learners to follow certain social, emotional, or intellectual paths. By their praise, warmth, and understanding, counselors can encourage these gifted individuals to make choices that will lead them closer to the fulfillment of their potential. The greatest service that can be provided by the counselor is to listen and eagerly respond to the feelings and ideas of the gifted.

Responsibilities to the Teacher and Administrator

Commitment. For comprehensive programming of the gifted to flourish, it must exist within an atmosphere of holistic education. One aspect of the gifted learner's personality, whether intellectual, social, emotional, cultural, or physical, cannot be isolated and treated separately. All these components come together and overlap to create the gifted individual. Consequently, all these aspects of the person must be a part of the educational experience.

For this reason, counselors should see themselves as playing a valuable role on a team—a team that includes teachers, administrators, and support staff. Counselors and guidance personnel, as a result of their experiences and training, tend to possess competencies and expertise in certain areas. It is this expertise that counselors must willingly share with others involved in the comprehensive education of the gifted.

Counselors must not assume that other educators outside their specialized field are aware of the services they have to offer the gifted program. It is up to these individuals to inform teachers and administrators of the interests and abilities they can commit to the gifted movement. Guidance counselors must voice their willingness to donate time and energy to the success of the gifted program.

Consultation. As noted, counseling and guidance personnel have knowledge and skills that they should share with other staff members. Within this capacity, information tends to flow outward from the counselors to be received and interpreted by those with whom they attempt to communicate. There are so many ways counselors can be of service to the gifted program in this function as consultant. To begin with, there are useful materials and kits familiar to those in the guidance field that can be employed by teachers of the gifted within the classroom setting. These materials include, for example, *Developing Understanding of Self and Others (DUSO) D-1 and D-2* (Dinkmeyer, 1970; 1973), *Values Clarification* (Raths, Harmin, & Simon, 1966), and others.

The most important abilities possessed by counselors and guidance personnel are their communication skills. Effective counselors must learn well the art of listening and responding to others, an art that also should be in the teacher's and the administrator's repertoire. Those in the guidance and counseling areas could assist the gifted program and the entire educational community by sharing this knowledge through instructing staff members in the techniques of active listening. Certainly, those who work with the gifted in the confines of the classroom cannot be expected to be effective counselors, but they can become more efficient in the communication skills that are at the heart of all educational endeavors.

As previously noted, counselors should not labor under the assumption that other school staff are aware of the services they perform. It would be logical for counselors to clarify and outline their philosophy, approaches, and objectives to the educators with whom they work. They should demonstrate the common goals and interests they share with teachers and administrators and do so early in the school year. They should emphasize the fact that their focus is not limited in scope to therapeutic or behavioral counseling alone. For many counselors, especially at the elementary and middle school levels, there is an enthusiastic, professional investment in the developmental aspects of all learners. Therefore, as it relates to the gifted program, the guidance or counseling personnel should become an integral part of the educational experience of all gifted learners—not merely those exhibiting social or emotional difficulties.

Cooperation. If counseling should be perceived as more than a service for problem or troubled students, then counseling should be seen as taking place in places other than the guidance office. Through cooperative efforts, guidance and counseling personnel and faculty and administrative staff can move counseling functions out of the office and directly into the classrooms and lounges.

Two obvious ways teachers, administrators, and counselors can work together are by organizing and conducting units of study and in-service sessions. Such topics as career awareness, values clarification, and student interactions are natural realms of investigation that can fit well into the normal classroom curriculum. The amount of input on the part of the counselor and the exact nature of the guidance personnel's role can vary, depending on the specific situation and the views of all participants. In-service sessions can differ in the same context. These in-service meetings can be developed around the general issue of the counselor's role in the education of the gifted or can be organized on more specific topics such as active listening or values clarification in the classroom.

As the demand for the planned, individual programs for the gifted gains momentum, one of the increasing modes of cooperation between counselors and other educators will be their shared input into *SLIP* or similar individualized program formats. On such outlines of personalized curriculum, counselors are given the opportunity to inject their views and priorities, and they should employ this opportunity to its fullest potential.

Responsibilities to Parents

Without question, the home environment of gifted learners plays a crucial role in their overall development. As noted by Muro and Dinkmeyer (1977), the values, attitudes, and life style of learners can be influenced by (1) their relationship with parents, (2) the training procedures used by parents, and (3) the individual's position in the family constellation.

To ignore such a powerful component in the gifted learner's life may affect the chances of the program to achieve its desired goals and objectives. Those involved in counseling and guidance should look at parent counseling and consulting tasks as among the most significant they can undertake. These responsibilities are identified as involvment, communication, and contact (see Figure 6-4).

Figure 6-4 The Responsibilities of Counselors to the Gifted Learner, Teachers and Administrators, and Parents

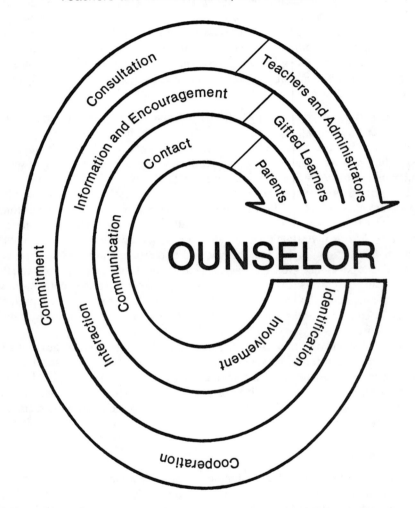

Involvement. In general, it can be stated that parents of the gifted view the school as primarily responsible for the intellectual development of their children and less accountable for development in other areas of personality. However, the education of the gifted should be holistic in nature. Although the cognitive development of these exceptional learners remains focal, it cannot be dealt with in isolation.

All these components are intertwined and must be considered in totality. The first chore of counseling personnel is to enlighten parents of the gifted of this fact and to demonstrate to them their importance in the education of their gifted child. Such a task is perhaps complicated by a tendency of parents to look on the counselor in narrow terms as a specialist not integrally related to the schooling process. Further encumbering the job of the guidance staff is the negative belief held by many parents that the counselor only works with "bad" or "problem" students. Before any positive inroads in parental involvement can be made, pains must be taken to eliminate these barriers. Parents must be made to see the importance of counseling in the healthy development of all gifted learners and then must be shown that their contributions are important and encouraged.

Communication and Contact. In their communications with parents, counselors must clearly demonstrate the scope of their skills and responsibilities in the education of the gifted. Along with these skills and responsibilities, guidance counselors should be able to demonstrate their understanding of the gifted population and the concerns, questions, and problems that are associated with this special group. In addition to this knowledge of a general nature relative to counseling and the gifted, guidance staff must also be conversant about the individual learner and the counselor's role in relation to that gifted learner's skills, needs, abilities, and questions. It is also up to the counselors to provide the positive atmosphere and suitable platform for such communication.

This communication is by no means a one-way process in which the counselor furnishes all information while parents dutifully listen. It is, instead, a process of sharing, reflecting, and responding through which parents and counselors alike offer and receive information. The contacts between parent and counselor should become an ongoing and natural part of gifted education and must never be conceived as a one-time encounter.

The format of these contacts can vary in similar fashion to the types of interaction possible between counselors and gifted learners. For example, the counselor may select an individual mode of contact in communication with parents of the gifted comparable to that pictured in Figure 6-3. Certainly, this form of interaction injects a personal quality to the communication process and may well be the most effective means of sharing information, but it is not without its disadvantages. These one-to-one encounters between parent and counselor are extremely time consuming and difficult to organize for all parents of learners identified as gifted. One means of alleviating this problem is to work these meetings into the conferences arranged between the gifted teacher and parents or between parent and gifted learner (see Figure 6-4). An alternative to the individual interaction and the triad form of communication is the contact arranged between the counselor and a small group of parents. The advantage of these small group interactions is that some personal involvement can be achieved by all participants.

Whatever method of contact is chosen, parents of the gifted should meet with the counselors. Through these positive associations, parents should be helped to see the role of counselors in the comprehensive education of their children and should be shown how important their input into the instructional process really is.

SUPPORT PERSONNEL

There are other individuals at work in the schools who have much to offer the gifted learner. Among these support personnel are the reading specialist, learning disabilities teacher, health staff, social worker, school psychologist, and others. While their training, perception, expertise, and concerns will vary, these support personnel will be looked on as possessing some common characteristics, competencies, and responsibilities useful to program development and successful continuance.

Essential Characteristics and Competencies of Support Staff

Specifying from among the many characteristics and competencies possessed by support personnel the few that are deemed essential to the gifted program is a difficult if not impossible task. Yet, several of these characteristics and competencies are central enough to the education of the gifted to warrant consideration. Primary among these essentials is the fact that these individuals must be knowledgeable and capable within their own areas of expertise. It is this core of specialized information that makes these persons valuable to program initiators. Along with the body of knowledge particular to each area of specialization, these support personnel must be trained to effectively implement what they know in the educational setting.

If expertise and training are two of the essential qualities required by support personnel, a third must be an awareness of the gifted movement, in general, and the school or school system's gifted program, in particular. It is through an understanding and interaction of these three spheres of knowledge, (1) expertise and training in a specialized area, (2) awareness of the gifted movement, and (3) familiarity with the gifted program, that support personnel can begin to discern the exact nature and degree of their involvement. To illustrate further, support personnel may find that the philosophy and objectives of the gifted program duplicate, to some extent, their own professional goals and beliefs. By working cooperatively, these specialists and the developers of the gifted program can assist one another to achieve their desired ends.

Although these three spheres of knowledge help shape the nature and intensity of support personnel involvement in the education of the gifted, there remain additional outside forces that can exert influence on this situation. Among those characteristics that can alter the basic design of support staff involvement should include interest, availability, commitment, rapport, and relevance.

The aspect of interest is probably self-explanatory for it seems apparent that no amount of knowledge can be of use if the individual chooses to remain a disinterested onlooker. Hand in hand with this idea of interest is the potential influence of commitment. There may be those among the support staff who may have an interest in the gifted but do not transform these internal motivations into external actions. A third factor that can mold the nature and degree of their involvement in gifted instruction is the amount of time support personnel have available for such participation. Most of us in education are acutely aware of the responsibilities and duties frequently placed on already overburdened support staff members. These staff members may have the interest and commitment called for but may lack the time and opportunity to take on more active roles. However, the more relevant the goals and objectives of the gifted program appear to their own professional duties, the more apt these individuals in support roles are to find the time necessary to participate. Equally as important as the external factors already listed is the rapport and cooperative atmosphere at work in the instructional environment. Individuals laboring within the various facets of the school system must see themselves as members of the broader educational community. Such membership should enable these individuals to willingly share ideas, seek advice, and offer opinions. Without this rapport among the support personnel and instructional and administrative staff no program can realize its full potential.

Roles and Responsibilities of Support Personnel

The cooperative atmosphere between regular and support personnel just described as so necessary in the ultimate success of the gifted program does not come about accidentally. This working relationship is the result of a deliberate and concerted effort. It is far too easy for gifted program initiators to overlook the valuable role that could be played by personnel in support positions. Support personnel should be seen as important contributors in a comprehensive educational program developed for the gifted learner. The expertise in training of these individuals coupled with their unique perspective of the instructional process can enrich the gifted program and make it more likely that the diverse needs and strengths of the gifted can be interpreted and satisfied. The task of seeking out these support staff members, acquainting them to the gifted curriculum, and demonstrating the desire for broad-based participation falls to program organizers. Once communication has been initiated, it is up to the support personnel to make their interests, abilities, and opinions known. Crucial in this process of establishing lines of communication between program developers and support personnel is the need to clearly define the roles to be played by these auxiliary specialized staff.

At the very least, support personnel should be directly involved in the development of the *SLIP* in those instances when it is deemed appropriate. Input in the *SLIP* for support staffers may encompass such responsibilities as testing and/or diagnosis, identification of objectives, provision of materials and techniques, and follow-up of objectives.

Testing and/or Diagnosis

Owing to their specialized training and unique educational perspective, support personnel may become aware of an individual gifted learner who warrants additional diagnostic attention. This diagnosis may include the administration of a particular test or battery of tests with which the support personnel are familiar. Administering and interpreting these tests will be responsibilities that fall to the support staff under such conditions.

Identification of Objectives

Whenever their expertise is solicited in the writing of a learner's *SLIP*, the opinions of the support staff find their way into a formal, objective statement. The objective statement should reflect what the support personnel perceive as a desired instructional aim for that particular learner based on specific strengths and needs. The actual construction of the objective should be completed with some consideration of how the objective could be carried out and by what means it would be evaluated.

Provision of Materials and Techniques

Support staffers may also have information on various materials and instructional techniques that may be employed by gifted learners and their teachers in fulfillment of the stated objectives. As described in the section on counselors, knowledge of this type may be shared with teachers and administrators on an individual or group basis inside or outside the classroom setting.

Follow-up of Objectives

Diagnosing a particular strength or need, writing a suitable learner-specific objective, and providing suitable materials and techniques for objective completion are all important responsibilities of support personnel. However, one additional responsibility must be described—evaluation of objectives. Without the necessary follow-up on the part of the support staff, an objective remains only a meaningless group of words. Those who take part in the writing of the *SLIP* objectives should also participate in the evaluation of those objectives.

PARENTS OF GIFTED LEARNERS

Equally important as school staff and support personnel, another population that has a deep-felt impact on the gifted program and on the achievements of the specific gifted learners with whom they come in contact are parents. Throughout this book references have been made to the influence of parents on their children and the necessity of establishing channels of communication between the home and school. It is crucial for educators to realize that the gifted's education does not begin or end when these individuals enter or leave the school building. Education is a continuous process that involves all the experiences and environments with which the learner has contact. Consequently, the school and the home must work together to produce the best educational climate for the exceptionally capable. The positive attitudes and experiences present in one environment must receive reinforcement in the other. Likewise, we cannot expect the gifted to reach their potential without the support of key individuals from the environment outside the school. While this discussion speaks specifically to parents it must be remembered that the information presented and the comments made pertain equally well to those "significant others," who play an important part in the life of the gifted learner, for example, grandparents, or older brothers and sisters. Various topics will be discussed that have direct bearing on the relationship between parent and child and parent and school, including such issues as coping with the responsibilities of being the parent of the gifted, establishing goals for the child, and working with the school.

Coping and Communicating

Being a parent is not always an easy task, and being the parent of a gifted learner can make that task even more complex. Our job as educators concerned with the gifted is to help these parents see that while their parenting role may well be more complex as a result of their children's exceptional abilities it can be, nonetheless, a rewarding and stimulating experience. It is helpful to remind parents, and occasionally ourselves, that their sons and daughters with whom they have been interacting and communicating for any number of years do not change overnight as the result of any label, even when that label is "gifted." Certainly the parents of gifted learners have a great wealth of knowledge to share about their offspring. They are frequently well aware of their children's particular strengths and weaknesses, as well as the various ups and downs of their personalities and behaviors. This knowledge can be invaluable in preparing an instructional plan for gifted learners that adequately fits their specific talents and needs.

It is not uncommon for parents of the gifted to be the first to identify the uniqueness of their children long before they enter the classroom. Also, it is not uncommon for parents of the gifted to feel apprehensive or concerned when others recognize their children as exceptional. Many questions are raised: What does it mean to be ''gifted''? How will this identification as ''gifted'' change my child's education? Will other children treat my child differently? Am I to treat my child differently now? With all these issues and more rising to the surface the first job for educators is to help these persons cope with their roles as parents of gifted learners.

There are many pieces of information that programmers can furnish the mothers and fathers of the gifted. It is perhaps advisable to offer this information freely, without waiting for parents to express a particular need or initiate the first contact. Frequently, parents may not know that they are allowed to have doubts or concerns or that these questions can be shared with others. Consequently, it falls to those entrusted with organizing and maintaining the gifted program to make the first contacts and open the channel of communication.

There are several ways that this communication can be fostered on the topic of coping with the gifted child. One principal resource is the school counselor. The issue of coping with a child's giftedness may be just the question for group discussion that leads parents to express ideas and share common concerns, situations, or problems. The list of suggestions presented in Exhibit 6-3 may serve as a springboard for group dialogue and interaction. It is important to caution parents that there are many ideas offered, some of which may or may not relate to their own special circumstances.

Coping with the gifted child is only one of the many issues that need to be brought out into the open and shared, and direct dialogue between the interested parties (teachers, parents, counselors, gifted learners) is by far the best method to foster communication. The ideal situation is not always achievable, however. Many parents work outside the home or have other children to care for. Too often parents are either too busy, too apprehensive, or too disinterested to come and participate in small, large, or individual conferences with school personnel. This should not be the end of the attempts to reach all parents of the gifted, and certainly other alternatives must be considered. The first and last contact with the parents should not be their signature on the *SLIP,* or the goal of establishing a working relationship between home and school cannot be met.

If face to face communication with parents does not appear feasible within the immediate future, or as a supplement to more direct communication, teachers or school personnel may find the phone or letters to be useful alternatives. Phone calls should be set up with parents so that they are informed about and in agreement with the topic and time for discussion. Letters can be written with either the individual or a group in mind. Individual letters can focus, of course, on the specific learner, emphasizing the contributions being made and activities or interests being pursued within school. When written communications are aimed at groups of parents, their style and purpose will vary. School newsletters about the gifted should be more upbeat and visually lively and their information far more general in focus. Class

Exhibit 6-3 Eleven Commandments for Living and Coping Well with Gifted Children

Know it is alright to have questions, doubts, and problems about your children's unique abilities. Being the parent of gifted children is not easy.

Seek advice, help, and information of others who may be of assistance. You do not have to go it alone.

Acknowledge your children's interests and abilities, even when they are extremely different from your own.

Encourage your children to pursue and develop their ideas and abilities. Remember, you do not have to sing yourself to admire a beautiful song.

Try to provide your children with the experiences they need to develop their abilities fully but never feel guilty if you cannot give them everything they may want or need.

Participate in things with your children. Showing off your interest is more important than showing off, so do not think you must equal or excel your children's talents or abilities.

Listen to and talk with your children. Let them share their views and ideas freely even when the final word is yours.

Bring your children in on the decisions that will affect their lives directly or indirectly. Just letting them know their ideas are important counts.

Be prepared to answer many questions. Gifted children are notorious for asking "why." Also, teach your children to find answers to some of their own questions.

Praise your children when they deserve it, and correct them when necessary. However, do not overdo either the praise or the criticism.

Accept your children for what they are and not for what you feel they should be.

activities, projects, and goals can be presented, and gifted students may even be encouraged to contribute in some way to this communication.

Whatever format the communication between school and home takes, it is vital to keep the information flowing. It is helpful to combine various forms of parent-teacher interactions. Personal phone calls can be highlighted by class newsletters or followed by a personal visit. Two important points about communication must be emphasized, however.

First, the burden of initating communication rests with the educators of the gifted. As educators have frequently realized, you cannot expect all parents to seek out the school. The school personnel must, therefore, seek out parents of the gifted and reach them in some manner. Ideally, this channel of communication will be routinely used by both parties. Regular dialogue between home and school is a worthwhile goal for any gifted program.

Second, the initial communication between parent and school should be positive in nature. The first impression made by the gifted program is crucial. Therefore, every effort should be made to get off on the right foot. Do not wait for difficulties to develop before a call is made or a letter is written. Find a very positive reason to call, write, or visit. Parents deserve to see their gifted children and the gifted program in the best light, at least initially. Problems are too easily found and shared. Program developers must be good enough at public relations to seek out favorable and positive incidents and share those incidents with parents. Informing the community as to the achievements of the gifted program can be effectively accomplished through the utilization of local media. A community that has a positive opinion of the gifted program will have little difficulty enthusiastically supporting such a program.

Establishing Goals for the Gifted Child

One principal goal of the communication between parent and school should be the realization that the gifted learner's success should be everyone's concern. Some parents and teachers may have erroneously assumed that education is only the business of educators and that home and school are separate and unrelated aspects of a learner's experiences. In reality, a learner's experiences are all combined and intertwined. The eventual success of a gifted program in structuring an educational environment best suited to a particular learner requires a cooperative effort among all those individuals who have positive contributions to make. Parents are a key component in this cooperative effort. As has been pointed out on several occasions, parents have a special knowledge of their children and can offer much information and provide positive input into the development of their gifted children's school programs.

Putting their signature to the *SLIP* is not enough. Parents should be given every opportunity to express their views on what they consider to be important goals for their children. These may be either short-term instructional objectives or long-range educational or career goals. As is the case with other contributors to the *SLIP*, parents' views, attitudes, and beliefs must be carefully balanced against the objectives shared by others and stated within the program philosophy.

For parents perhaps the most difficult part of their participation in their children's educational program planning is establishing realistic and attainable goals. Most parents want the best for their children, and it is often hard for them to temper their enthusiasm and objectively evaluate their offsprings' strengths and needs. Educators can provide some guidance in this matter. It should also be remembered that a parent's suggestions are not blindly accepted but are considered within the context of the entire school gifted program.

Again, as has been mentioned repeatedly, no one, whether teacher, parent, or administrator, can be expected to make reasonable and appropriate decisions for the gifted learner without knowledge of program goals and how those goals relate to the specific population being dealt with and ultimately to the individual gifted learner. Dissemination of this type of information to those who must make decisions relevant to the learner's educational future is crucial. Parent workshops, conferences, and assemblies are several methods of getting out this information that can be employed within the program framework. General, large group interactions that present more global information can be effectively followed with individual sessions between parents and teachers.

Within the area of goal setting, parents should also be made aware of the educational and career opportunities and alternatives available to their children. A few examples of these options would be scholarships, early admissions programs, and after-school, weekend, and summer projects built around special talents and abilities. Program developers need to provide parents with such information. Parents may also require information about "giftedness," in general, and knowledge of the gifted program, in particular, if they are to make appropriate suggestions about their children's present and future educational goals. Again, educators must look on the input by parents as a very positive element in the overall success of the gifted program. Parents can offer much needed information and input that can enlarge the knowledge of gifted learners and make gifted education more meaningful.

Parent Participation

As it relates to parents, the principal aim of program initiators perhaps should be to produce active participation and eliminate passivity. Such passivity by parents in the gifted program will bring little satisfaction and a decreased likelihood of success. If parents wish to contribute most effectively in their children's education, they must actively interact with those who administer and staff the gifted program. Also, much can be gained by organized and informal conversations among those directly outside the educational realm who have a vested interest in the curriculum and objectives of the gifted program. By discussing their personal joys and tribulations encountered in the rearing of gifted children, as well as issues relevant to the gifted program, parents can develop a useful support network for one another. If parent support groups do not exist in the school program, developers may wish to suggest or initiate such a group. This support group may provide support not only for the parents themselves but also for the gifted program. Those parents who have committed themselves to active involvement in the gifted program and who see the need to contribute to the eductional growth of their gifted children become valuable resources volunteering their time and services.

Dedicated parents can serve in a number of capacities within the framework of the gifted programs. For one example, parents can assist in the classrooms. Many programs have found parents to be excellent aides within the school setting, taking on tasks as diverse as making materials, tutoring, organizing outings, and sharing special hobbies, abilities, and talents. Parents with unique talents and abilities may also serve effectively as mentors for gifted learners who express an interest in similar areas. Parents can also work with teachers and gifted learners by helping develop special classroom projects or activities, such as plays, exhibits, and conferences.

However, the parent does not have to be "in the classroom" to be an asset to the gifted program as a volunteer or helper. There are many other jobs that can be taken on by parent volunteers, including telephoning, typing, and chauffeuring, that are important to the smooth functioning of the gifted program.

No matter what form of participation parents choose they should be seen as a natural part of the gifted program. The doors of the gifted classroom should always be open to parents and their presence welcomed. It might be useful for schools to invite parents to sit in on the gifted program whenever it can be arranged. This open-door policy should make parents feel more at home in the school setting and more a part of their children's education. Schools and the gifted program can benefit as well from such a cooperative relationship. In the final analysis it is probably the gifted learners who gain the most when parents participate and interact with the school for the purpose of maximizing the success of the gifted program. A list of suggestions for parental participation is provided below:

1. Meet with teachers, guidance counselors, and other gifted staff members at least once during the school term.
2. Observe in your child's classroom.
3. Attend any special meetings or workshops that can provide you important information about your child or about your child's educational program.
4. Offer any assistance that suits your interests and inclinations.
5. Make suggestions or offer your opinions about the program or your child's education.
6. See yourself as a partner with the school in providing your gifted child the best education possible.

TEACHERS OF THE GIFTED

Any textbook that attempts to identify the factors that influence the way students learn must certainly include a discussion of the teacher. As attention has been focused in education on identifying the most productive ways to meet children's needs there has been interest centered on the identification of those personal characteristics of teachers that may be associated with effective instruction.

Behaviors such as understanding, sympathy, cheerfulness, acceptance, flexibility, fairness, and cooperativeness are just a sampling of the overwhelming number of general behaviors that have been identified, studied, and linked to the effectiveness of teachers. The difficulty, however, with linking such behaviors to effective instruction is the unlikelihood that there exists teachers who possess all of the identified behaviors mentioned in the literature. Additionally, becoming an effective teacher of the gifted may require more than the mere possession of such behaviors. The way one uses such behaviors in relationship to the goals and populations to which they are applied and the positive changes in learners' behaviors that may result ultimately determine teacher effectiveness.

In addition to the attempts at identifying the personal characteristics of effective teachers, there has also been a great deal of attention focused on identifying the qualities, skills, and attitudes that characterize competent instruction. One such attempt has been within the field of gifted education in which there continues to arise a genuine concern for the accurate identification of those qualities and competencies of teachers that will enable gifted learners to approach their potential. Owing to the uniqueness of the gifted population as a whole, there is a strong need to locate those individuals who can complement this uniqueness within the framework of the gifted program. This section of the chapter will focus on a discussion of teachers of the gifted learner, bringing to light some important factors to consider in developing a classroom atmosphere that is most conducive to the growth of gifted learners. A self-evaluation procedure will be discussed so that prospective teachers of the gifted can evaluate their positions, and an analysis of gifted characteristics in relation to the instructional behaviors which may foster them is presented.

The Gifted Teacher—A Facilitator of Learning

While there will continue to be interest in determining the various personal characteristics of competent instructors the one fact that remains is that teachers, in their endeavors to help individuals grow, are constantly involved in bringing about positive change in learners. Withall (1970) explains this point further:

> Learning is a highly complex process that is evident primarily in changed behaviors, perceptions and hypotheses by the one who has learned. The changed behaviors encompass all the behaviors of the individual, both covert and overt, including, for example, reversing phenomena, developing new perceptions, mastering and employing skill, developing new attitudes, and setting up hypotheses and ways of testing them. (p. 41)

Maker (1978) considers this idea of the teacher as a facilitator of change. In her comprehensive treatment of training procedure for teachers of the gifted and talented, she points out that as an agent of change the teacher of the gifted will work at bringing students to the acquisition of skills and attitudes, not only to help them deal effectively with the present but also to assist them in acquiring those abilities essential for understanding, adapting, and functioning effectively in the future. Because of the very nature of the classroom setting, teachers have a range of behavioral options from which to select in dealing with gifted learners. It may be pointed out here that learning can be facilitated or debilitated depending on the option chosen.

Surely, facilitating learning and thereby changing learners' behaviors positively is not an easy task, especially in view of daily pressures on teachers and students. The level of verbal interaction between teacher and student is often an excellent barometer of the learning climate that exists. Consequently, a gap in the line of communication between teacher and learner may signal the presence of some barrier to facilitation that could lead to frustration or the eventual breakdown of learning. The monitoring of dialogue between teacher and gifted learner, therefore, is a valuable undertaking that can be pursued informally or through such formal measures as the Flanders' *Interaction Analysis Scale* (1949) or the Withall's *Social-Emotional Climate Index* (1969) (see Exhibit 6-4). Other such instruments useful to monitor verbal interaction are reviewed by Rosenshine and Furst (1973).

A positive step that will assist teachers of the gifted in overcoming communication barriers while assuming a role of change agent is to adopt, as Withall (1973) indicates, trust, respect, and caring for the learner:

- *Trust* for the learner means that teachers internalize and convey to their students the belief that there is a natural desire for learning.

- *Respect* for the learner assumes a mutually rewarding experience will result, whereby both teacher and learner help each other.

- *Caring* for the learner conveys the notion that learners are viewed as important individuals by the teacher and will be given the guidance and assistance they need to succeed.

There must be an underlying assumption in this situation that may remain unverbalized and unwritten. That assumption communicates the belief that regardless of any difficulties that may arise, the personal growth of the students will be the result of a cooperative effort between teacher and learner built on a foundation of mutual respect and concern.

Exhibit 6-4 Withall Social-Emotional Climate Index

Criteria of Teacher-Statement Categories

1. LEARNER SUPPORTIVE statements or questions

   These are teacher-statements or questions that express agreement with the ideas, actions or opinions of the learner, or that commend or reassure the learner. Agreement is frequently expressed by a monosyllabic response such as "Yes," "Right," "Uh huh," and the like. Commendation or reassurance may be stated in terms of:

   a. class-accepted criteria or goals

   or

   b. the private goals and subjective criteria of the teacher.

   The *dominant intent* of these statements or questions is to *praise, encourage* or *bolster the learner.*

2. ACCEPTANT OR CLARIFYING statements or questions

   These are teacher-statements or questions which either:

   a. accept, that is, evidence considerable understanding by the teacher of, or

   b. clarify, that is, restate clearly and succinctly in the teacher's words

   the ideational or the feeling content of the learner's statement. The *dominant intent* of these teacher-responses is *to help the learner* to gain insight into his/her problem, that is, define his/her "real" problem and its solution in more operational terms.

3. PROBLEM-STRUCTURING statements or questions

   Problem-structuring responses by the teacher offer facts or ideas or opinions to the learner about

   a. phenomena
   b. procedures

   in a nonthreatening and objective manner. These responses contain NO element of advising or recommending the adoption of certain ideas or procedures. Problem-structuring responses are frequently posed as questions which seek further information from the learner about the problem confronting him/her; or they may be statements which offer information to the learner about his/her problem. The learner is free to accept or to reject in part or in entirety the facts or opinions that are presented to him/her. Problem-structuring responses may be questions which the teacher asks (1) to further increase his/her own understanding of what the learner has

Exhibit 6-4 continued

said or (2) to increase the precision of the learner's statement of the problem. Problem-structuring responses are problem-centered rather than either teacher or learner-centered; nevertheless, they do tend to sustain the learner by facilitating his/her problem-solving activities.

4. NEUTRAL statements evidencing no supportive intent

These statements are neither teacher-sustaining nor learner-sustaining nor problem-centered. They constitute a small percentage of the total teacher-responses. These responses include statements in which the teacher: (1) questions himself/herself aloud; (2) repeats verbatim a statement that the learner just made; (3) uses a polite formality, et cetera. Statements having to do with administrative procedure—the room in which the class will meet, the hour at which a conference will occur (especially after consensus has been been achieved)—fall into this category.

5. DIRECTIVE statements or questions

These are teacher-statements or questions which advise the learner regarding a course of action or his/her future behavior and which narrowly limit his/her choice or offer no choice. These statements recommend to the learner the facts or procedures that the teacher proffers him/her. These statements or questions convey the impression to the learner that the teacher expects and hopes that he/she will follow his/her prompting and that he/she will approve if he does. The *intent* of these responses is to have the learner take up the teacher's point of view and pursue a course of action that he/she advocates.

6. REPROVING, DISAPPROVING, OR DISPARAGING statements or questions

By means of these statements a teacher may express complete or partial disapproval of the ideas, behavior, and to him/her, personality weaknesses of the learner. The teacher's internalized societal values largely enter into these responses. By means of these statements some teachers believe they are fulfilling their responsibility of inculcating in young people society's standards of acceptable and desirable behavior and achievement. The *intent* of these statements is:

  a. to represent to the learner societal values as the teacher sees them;
  b. to admonish the learner for unacceptable behavior and to deter him/her from repeating it in the future;
  c. to impress on the learner the fact that he/she has not met the criteria for successful achievement which the teacher accepts.

Exhibit 6-4 continued

7. TEACHER-SUPPORTIVE statements or questions

These are statements or questions in which the teacher refers to himself /herself and expresses a defensive attitude, or refers to his/her present or past interests, activities or possessions with the purpose of reassuring himself/herself and of confirming his/her position or his/her ideas in the eyes of those around him/her. The *dominant intent* of these teacher-responses is to *assert,* to *defend* or to *justify* the teacher. Statements in which the teacher perseverates on an idea, a belief or a suggestion would fall in this category. By "perseveration" is meant a persisting in, a reiteration of, and a rigid advocacy of an idea or opinion by the teacher despite additional data being presented to him/her which calls for a reexamination of the original idea or opinion.

A Frame of Reference and Procedure to Facilitate
Categorization of Teacher-Statements

Each teacher-statement contains *one* of two dominant kinds of intent. These are:

either (a) intent to sustain the teacher and his/her behavior (teacher-centered statements)

or (b) intent to sustain the learner and his/her behavior (learner-centered statements and issue-centered statements are included under this intent).

By analysis of both the CONTEXT and the CONTENT of a teacher-statement it may be possible to determine whether the dominant intent of a statement is to sustain the teacher or the learner.

Once the dominant intent of a teacher-statement has been ascertained, one can proceed to determine the technique by which the support is conveyed.

1. If the statement is intended primarily to *sustain the teacher,* one or possibly a combination of the two following techniques may be used:

    (a) reproof of the learner (category 6),
    (b) directing or advising the learner (category 5).

Frequently, the intent of the statement is to sustain the teacher yet neither of the above techniques is used. In that event the statement is simply a self-supportive remark which defends the teacher or evidences perseveration in support of the teacher's position or ideas (category 7).

Exhibit 6-4 continued

2. If the intent of a statement is to *sustain the learner,* then one or possibly a combination of the two following techniques may be used:
   (a) clarification and acceptance of the learner's feelings or ideas (category 2),
   (b) problem-structuring statements (category 3).

Frequently the intent of a statement is to sustain the learner yet neither of the above techniques is used. In that event the statement is simply one that reassures, commends, agrees with or otherwise sustained the learner (category 1).

Infrequently a teacher-statement may have no dominant intent to sustain either the teacher or the learner. If the statement represents neither of the techniques in the two intent areas nor gives evidence of being one of the more general kinds of supporting statements, then the statement can be considered to have no intent to support and should be placed in category 4.

Recourse to the learner-statement or behavior before and after a teacher response, particularly when one encounters a statement in which the intent is difficult to ascertain, is sometimes helpful in categorizing the teacher's statements.

Source: Reprinted from the Withall Social-Emotional Climate Index by permission of John Withall, Ph.D, 1969.

As mentioned above, it becomes the teachers' responsibility to facilitate learning in the classroom. Research into classroom practices and their effect on learning has uncovered three teaching styles, identified here as group-directed, teacher-directed, and self-directed. In group-directed practices, the teacher and gifted learners cooperatively take part in decision making, while a teacher-directed approach places the burden for decision making squarely on the shoulders of the teacher. Within a self-directed framework, the teacher assumes a more passive role, allowing decisions to emerge from the situation that freely operates. The use of any one or combination of these teaching styles is largely dependent on several factors:

- the subject matter or curriculum to be learned
- the influence of teacher personality on the classroom setting
- the program goals and philosophy to be addressed
- the uniqueness of the gifted learners.

The interactions and reactions of teachers with these key factors help to shape their ability to bring about growth of the gifted learners with whom they deal (see Figure 6-5).

Figure 6-5 Interactions and Reactions That Influence the Style and Approach of Teachers of the Gifted

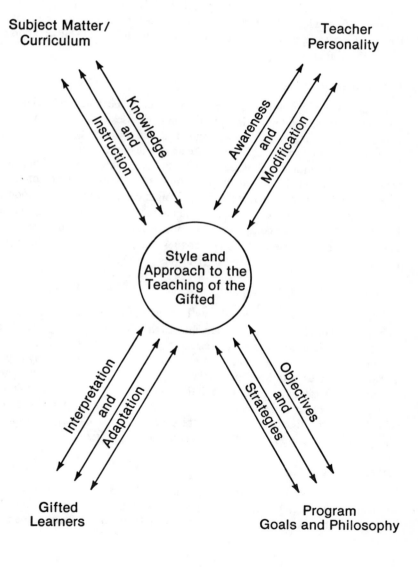

Subject Matter/Curriculum

Within each subject matter area or discipline there is a core of knowledge that must be possessed by someone who is to teach that curriculum. Knowledge of the laws, skills, rules, or concepts relevant to a particular field of study and the details that accompany them is indeed necessary for the teacher of the gifted. However, the acquisition of this core knowledge is, by itself, not sufficient to facilitate learning. What is also required of teachers is the ability to make this knowledge accessible to gifted learners. It is frequently the case that an individual may possess a wealth of knowledge but lacks the talent to teach others or has the knack within the classroom to relate well with others only to fall short of the information critical to a subject area.

Teacher Personality

Perhaps the most important factor influencing the teachers' selection of a particular instructional mode is their own uniquenesses. It is quite obvious that no two individuals are exactly alike, and it is equally true that no two teachers approach their jobs in the same way. The uniqueness of the teacher's personality is mirrored in the uniqueness of teaching style. As a consequence of this situation, those who instruct the gifted must become attuned to or aware of their own personality traits and the effect these traits might have within the classroom. Once awareness has been achieved, teachers can make necessary modifications in their instructional styles that complement the positive aspects of their behaviors while compensating for those that are perhaps less favorable. More of these personal characteristics will be discussed later in this chapter.

Program Goals and Philosophy

While instructors of the gifted may be teaching for a specific body of knowledge, they should, ultimately, be teaching to the philosophy and goals that are the heart of the gifted program. For this reason, the selection of a teaching approach should carefully consider the objectives outlined for the gifted. It may appear that certain objectives could be best achieved by the implementation of a particular instructional strategy. Furthermore, it may become apparent that a certain strategy could best operate within one or another learning environment. Consequently, selection or modification of one's teaching approach can clearly be influenced by the goals or philosophy established for the gifted program.

Gifted Learners

It is quite understandable that the unique behavioral characteristics of gifted students should be a powerful influence on the instructional style adopted by the teacher. Each gifted student comes to the classroom situation with a special set of abilities, interests, and needs fashioned within a personalized learning modality. For teaching to have positive, desired effects it must adapt to the uniqueness of the gifted individual. Yet, this adaptation can only occur when the behaviors and performances of the gifted have been adequately interpreted. First, teachers must have an understanding of the gifted individual before they can ever be expected to adapt their teaching styles to suit the needs of that individual.

It must be emphasized at this point that while there are several approaches to the instruction of the gifted available, because of the multiplicity of factors existing in schools, there is no one style that can clearly be shown to be superior for all learners and for all settings. However, regardless of our approach or particular mode of instruction it is essential that as teachers we strive toward acquiring behaviors that are, as Withall (1979) describes, more accepting, problem structuring, and challenging in nature. It is the acquisition and utilization of these behaviors in the classroom that facilitate learning and assist learners in uncovering and realizing their potential. Consequently, teachers can only become cognizant of the factors that influence teaching style and select or modify their behaviors through systematic observation of their instruction. What would also be useful, however, is for teachers to assess their current attitudes or preferences as they tend to reflect one mode of instruction over another. A short self-evaluation questionnaire offered in Exhibit 6-5 may aid teachers in determining their present choice of instructional style.

Personal Characteristics of Teachers of the Gifted

A survey of the literature in gifted education presents references to many specific personal characteristics that appear highly desirable for teachers of the gifted. Behaviors such as intelligence, flexibility, enthusiasm, and understanding are a few examples of the characteristics that have been generated. These characteristics, it might be added, are frequently associated with effective teachers in general and are not strictly the domain of educators of the gifted. The principal purpose of formulating such lists is to enhance the selection of those teachers better suited to the task of educating the gifted along the dimension of personality. However, there are several disadvantages to the implementation of such characteristics checklists that should be addressed.

Inappropriate Uses of Personality Checklists

Several obvious shortcomings of rather lengthy lists of positive personality characteristics are the ridiculous notion that any teacher could measure up completely to the qualities identified and the possibility that these characteristics during the evaluation process may be inappropriately used for assessing teacher effectiveness. Consequently, no teacher should be included or excluded from

Exhibit 6-5 Teaching Style: A Self-Evaluation Questionnaire

		Yes	No
1.	I am the type of teacher who is orderly and systematic in my classroom approach.	___	___
2.	As a teacher I generally determine the direction for the class and establish the class goals.	___	___
3.	As a teacher I tend to allow students to work on activities and assignments that they think are best for them.	___	___
4.	As a teacher I give the learners a lot of responsibility and guide them through group discussion in selecting the classroom goals.	___	___
5.	I am the type of teacher who appreciates independence but prefers "disciplined conformity."	___	___
6.	As a teacher I believe that students should determine their own direction and freely express themselves.	___	___
7.	I am the type of teacher who plans lessons carefully and requires specific objectives to be achieved.	___	___
8.	I am the type of teacher who enjoys involving students in planning classroom activities.	___	___
9.	I am the type of teacher who is comfortable giving students the responsibility for establishing, monitoring, and reinforcing classroom guidelines.	___	___
10.	I am the type of teacher who once students are set to work on activities tends to remain in the background.	___	___
11.	I am the type of teacher who guides the students in making choices as to their learning.	___	___
12.	I am the type of teacher who helps students become aware of the materials and resources available in the classroom and then expects the students to follow through on the tasks independently.	___	___
13.	I am the type of teacher who sees evaluation of students' work secondary to the student's individual expression and creativity.	___	___
14.	I am the type of teacher who believes that students should plan their own learning.	___	___
15.	I am the type of teacher who likes to teach by asking students questions and stimulating discussion in problem solving.	___	___

group-directed statements: 4, 8, 9, 11, and 15
teacher-directed statements: 1, 2, 5, 7, and 10
self-directed statements: 3, 6, 12, 13, and 14

working with gifted learners solely on the basis of such imperfect and highly subjective lists of characteristics. These characteristics should basically be viewed as guidelines by which teachers can enter into a self-evaluation process either alone or with their administrators for the purposes of learning more about themselves and identifying specific goals for future improvement. In Exhibit 6-6, research on teacher characteristics has been summarized into a series of statements that teachers can utilize to introspectively evaluate their own particular personality strengths and weaknesses as they relate to gifted learners. In the administrator-teacher dialogue that may ensue, the teacher and administrator may establish a rapport that can lead naturally to future and frequent interactions and can cooperatively strive to improve the learning environment for the gifted.

The Context-Dependent Nature of Personality

A second disadvantage of personality checklists is that they tend to portray their characteristics as one-dimensional, overlooking the fact that teachers must operate within the ever-changing context of the classroom, school, and society. Consequently, as the environment around them is modified and altered, teachers of the gifted must allow their behaviors to adjust accordingly if they are to meet the needs of their gifted learners. Considering the fluid nature of the surrounding context, those traits that were emphasized in one situation might be deemphasized in another. Those characteristics that were deemed important for gifted learners may be viewed as less important, and perhaps even new characteristics will be added while others are eliminated. Generally, it is important to remember that no trait shown by research to be possessed by effective teachers of the gifted is set in stone. As changes occur in education and society and as teachers encounter new populations of gifted learners, the characteristics they employ and the characteristics valued in gifted education may be modified or changed.

While some potential disadvantages of employing lists of personality traits have been analyzed, their major purpose or advantage should not be overlooked. The research generated around this topic of the characteristics of effective gifted teachers provides educators with guidelines for greater understanding of their own personalities in relation to the task of instructing the gifted. It is not merely knowing ourselves better as teachers, although this is indeed valuable, it is applying that knowledge with the purpose of helping our gifted learners make the most of their own personalities and the abilities, interests, and attitudes that are part of them.

Competencies Important to Teachers of the Gifted

In the previous section of this chapter a procedure was presented that will assist teachers in classifying and analyzing their own personality characteristics. Just as certain teacher traits are more suited to the needs of gifted learners so, too, should

Exhibit 6-6 Teacher Characteristics: A Selection Checklist
for Self-Evaluation

	Yes	No
1. I have an interest in working with gifted learners because of a personal belief that because of their uniqueness they need and deserve differentiated educational instruction (e.g., Alexander & Muia, 1980; Bishop, 1968).	___	___
2. I am the type of person who is usually not threatened or intimidated by learners who possess exceptional potential (e.g., Newland, 1976; Sisk, 1976).	___	___
3. I have developed a philosophy of education that can accommodate the need to identify and provide differentiated instruction for gifted learners who come from culturally diverse groups (e.g., Sisk, 1976).	___	___
4. I am a teacher who encourages student responsibility and can allow students to make decisions regarding their learning (e.g., Feldhusen & Kolloff, 1978; Nelson & Cleland, 1967; Shelby, 1978).	___	___
5. I am a teacher who has grown because of the interaction with learners and, as a result, I have developed a more complete understanding of myself (e.g., Withall, 1969).	___	___
6. I consider myself an intelligent individual who learns quickly and enjoys pursuing intellectual, literary, and cultural interests (e.g., Bishop, 1968; Nelson & Cleland, 1967; Baldwin, Gear, & Lucito, 1978).	___	___
7. I am a patient person who empathizes with gifted learners and has a grasp of the difficulties gifted learners might encounter in their endeavors to reach their potential (e.g., Bishop, 1968; Nelson & Cleland, 1967; Baldwin, Gear, & Lucito, 1978).	___	___
8. I am an imaginative person who enjoys stimulating learning through a variety of teaching approaches (e.g., Bishop, 1967).	___	___
9. I enjoy teaching and I am dedicated to the demands of teaching which require extra time and effort (e.g., Nelson & Cleland, 1967).	___	___
10. I am a flexible teacher who is not restrained by grades or time demands (e.g., Bernal, 1976; Brodbelt, 1979; Cangemi, 1979; French, 1957).	___	___
11. I am a well-organized and businesslike individual who can deviate from this structure in order to		

Exhibit 6-6 continued

	Yes	No
pursue learners' interests (e.g., Bishop, 1967; Bishop, 1968; Gibson, 1976).	___	___
12. I am a teacher who can interact with learners in an open manner but earn the respect and maintain the discipline necessary to ensure a quality classroom atmosphere (e.g., Sisk, 1976).	___	___
13. I am a confident person who has a clear understanding of my role as a teacher (e.g., Torrance & Kaufmann, 1977).	___	___
14. I am the type of person who tends to pursue a leadership role in activities rather than wait for someone else to initiate the activity (e.g., Gibson, 1976).	___	___
15. I am an individual who likes to take part in activities which seek alternate solutions to problems (e.g., Whitmore, 1980).	___	___
16. I tend to be an emotionally strong person who feels good about myself (e.g., Brieter, 1979; Ryan & Cooper, 1972).	___	___
17. I am a person who has a particular talent in one or more of the arts and enjoy expressing myself in these modes (e.g., Vernon, Adamson, & Vernon, 1977).	___	___
18. I am a creative individual and often strive to demonstrate creativeness in various ways (e.g., Whitmore, 1980).	___	___
19. I am a teacher who views each of my students as a unique human being (e. g., Cangemi, 1979).	___	___
20. I am a tolerant person who is not upset by the divergent types of behavior and thinking often displayed by gifted students (e.g., Brodbelt, 1979; Thomas, 1976; Vernon, Adamson, & Vernon, 1977).	___	___
21. I am an educator who values the learning process as much or more than the end result of that learning (e.g., Nelson & Cleland, 1967; Cobb, Cobb, & Dow, 1978; Shelby, 1978).	___	___
22. I consider myself as student-centered and utilize this attitude through encouraging learner participation in daily activities and through respecting and valuing the opinions of these learners (e.g., Bernal, 1976; Bishop, 1968).	___	___
23. I enjoy teaching, am enthusiastic about facilitating the learning of gifted pupils, and utilize stimulating, creative activities to make such learning exciting (e.g., Bishop, 1968; French, 1957).	___	___

teachers of the gifted possess a repertoire of competencies. In Exhibit 6-7 a list of competencies identified in the literature as being important for teachers of the gifted have been also converted to a series of statements that can be applied in a self-evaluation process.

Because of the changing nature of the context in which the gifted learner and teacher must function, it is to be understood that these competencies will vary. Also, on first evaluation, teachers of the gifted may not feel capable or proficient within each of the areas outlined. Yet, this checklist may assist teachers of the gifted in identifying the competencies they do possess and those that need further attention.

Exhibit 6-7 Important Competencies for Teachers of
the Gifted: A Self-Evaluation Instrument

	Yes	No
1. I am familiar with the instruments used in the identification and selection of gifted learners (e.g., Nelson & Cleland, 1967; Sullivan, 1973).	___	___
2. I understand the limitations in using standardized test scores to select gifted learners from culturally diverse groups and can apply alternative means of identification (e.g., Baldwin, Gear & Lucito, 1978; Bishop, 1967; Frasier, 1979).	___	___
3. I have an understanding of theories of learning and human development and the implications of the theories to gifted learners (e.g., Nelson & Cleland, 1967; Thomas, 1976; Torrance & Kaufmann, 1977).	___	___
4. I am aware of current trends in gifted education, (e.g., Nelson & Cleland, 1967).	___	___
5. I am competent in my subject matter area and am well informed about new developments in my field (e.g., Baldwin, Gear, & Lucito, 1978; Bishop, 1967; Newland, 1976).	___	___
6. I feel that I have developed my teaching skills as a result of my interactions with learners (e.g., Baldwin, Gear, & Lucito, 1978; Gibson, 1976).	___	___
7. I have an understanding of the characteristics of gifted children and of their social, emotional, and educational needs (e.g., Baldwin, Gear, & Lucito, 1978; Nelson & Cleland, 1967).	___	___
8. I have developed, as a result of my teaching experiences, the capability to plan and implement various strategies and activities for gifted learners, whether they		

Exhibit 6-7 continued

	Yes	No
are from dominant or subdominant cultural groups (e.g., Baldwin, Gear, & Lucito, 1978; Frasier, 1979).	___	___
9. I have an understanding of some of the needs of the special gifted (i.e., learning disabled; handicapped; physically impaired) (e.g., Bernal, 1976; Maker, 1977).	___	___
10. I feel competent in activities that stimulate higher level thinking skills (e.g., Feldhusen & Kolloff, 1978; Torrance & Kaufmann, 1977).	___	___
11. As a result of my contact with learners, I have developed effective methods of providing feedback and reinforcement to learners and fostering their self-concept (e.g., Henjum, 1977; Maker, 1977; Ryan & Cooper, 1972; Shelby, 1978).	___	___
12. I feel competent in identifying children as being gifted without letting my decision be influenced only by any single criteria or characteristic (e.g., Baldwin, Gear, & Lucito, 1978; Sullivan, 1973).	___	___
13. I feel competent in varying instruction according to the learner's needs and evaluating the appropriateness and success of the lesson (e.g., Bishop, 1968; Gibson, 1976).	___	___
14. I am proficient in communication skills and feel comfortable in the way I convey information to my students (e.g., Bishop, 1968; Whitmore, 1980).	___	___
15. I feel competent in my ability to build rapport with learners, teachers, administrators, parents, and community members (e.g., Breiter, 1979).	___	___
16. I feel capable of utilizing a classroom approach in which my role will be one of a facilitator of learning (e.g., Nelson & Cleland, 1967; Shelby, 1978).	___	___
17. I am able to select, construct, or modify instructional materials to meet the needs of my gifted learners (e.g., Ryan & Cooper, 1972).	___	___
18. I feel competent in planning and utilizing activities that will enhance students' self-concepts, such as small group discussions, student presentations of particularly meaningful work, and values clarification exercises (e.g., Henjum, 1977; Maker, 1977, 1978).	___	___
19. While I feel competent in providing activities that allow my students to enjoy success, I put an emphasis on feeling good about one's work rather than on achieving perfection (e.g., Maker, 1977).	___	___

Relationship of Teacher Characteristics and Competencies to Particular Gifted Performance Criteria

Within this chapter the various characteristics and competencies important to teachers of the gifted have been separated and scrutinized. What is even more essential in this look at teachers of the gifted is to understand how these particular characteristics and competencies relate to the development of desired performance criteria. In Table 6-1 several positive performance criteria have been presented along with the teacher characteristics and competencies that may interact to produce that performance within gifted learners. This chart offers only a preliminary overview of an extremely complex set of interactions that might warrant further investigation.

Table 6-1 An Overview of Teacher Characteristics and Competencies in Relationship to Particular Performance Criteria of Gifted Learners

	Teacher Characteristics	Teacher Competencies
Critical thinking and problem-solving skills	Seeks justification or support for ideas and beliefs Rational in nature Reflective and open-minded in thinking Constantly questioning or probing Curious, eager to discover	Skilled in logical reasoning Able to identify a problem Able to formulate appropriate and meaningful questions Able to focus or identify suitable direction Organizes ideas into systematic framework Accumulates evidence—relevant vs. irrelevant; fact vs. opinion Arrives at a logical conclusion
Divergent thinking	Accepting of new ideas and differences in themselves and others Insightful; views things in creative and enlightening ways Willing to give ideas time to grow and develop Not rule bound Has varied interests Inquisitive	Capable at creating a suitable atmosphere for student response Skilled at developing open-ended questions Competent in providing opportunities that foster divergent production Skilled at monitoring and guiding the behaviors of others Capable of evaluating end products

Table 6-1 continued

	Teacher Characteristics	Teacher Competencies
		Possesses a repertoire of alternatives that can be demonstrated or shared
Persistence and commitment to task	Self-disciplined; self-controlled Reliable; dependable Systematic and dedicated Seeks structure and closure	Knows the worth of a particular task or project Capable of establishing realistic goals Able to recognize the subtasks within a task Skilled in organizing and prioritizing the various subtasks Capable of sensing when each subtask has been effectively completed Able to compare desired goals with visible outcomes
Basic skill development process oriented curriculum	Attuned to the holistic nature of knowledge Recognizes a core of knowledge within a field of inquiry Views learning within a hierarchical framework Diagnostic in nature	Knows subject matter Capable of conveying information to others Able to relate knowledge to the needs of particular learners Knows various methods of formal and informal assessment Able to construct and select appropriate instructional materials and strategies Capable of determining when learner has achieved competency in a skill area Able to stimulate interest in learning
Leadership qualities	Likes to initiate actions and ideas Looks for opportunities to demonstrate capabilities Views self in a positive manner Assertive and confident Facilitates interaction and relates well with others Not afraid of responsibility Seeks challenges Adaptable in approach Accepts constructive criticism	Capable of assessing accurately the behaviors and reactions of others Competent in the application of persuasion skills Skilled in motivating others Able to synthesize the ideas of a group Able to assign responsibilities to others commensurate with their interests and abilities Capable of clarifying the goals and purposes of a group

Table 6-1 continued

	Teacher Competencies	Teacher Characteristics
Self-directed learning	Likes to work through problems independently with little guidance Internally motivational Probes and questions Orderly in thinking Looks at problems in many directions	Capable of establishing realistic goals Able to identify a meaningful task Able to locate sources of information Knows various resources Capable of organizing information Able to pursue solutions in a systematic method Skilled in evaluating outcomes
Self awareness/ acceptance	Cognizant of personal strengths Acknowledges and adjusts for personal limitations Introspective in nature Open and genuine about feelings Accepting of differences in others	Knows how to assess the reactions and actions of others to own behaviors Ability to locate situations complementary to our personalities Capable of controlling elements of our character that are not conducive to learning Cognizant of activities that promote self-awareness and self-acceptance Able to provide positive feedback and reinforcement to others
Adaptive behaviors	Sense of humor Resourceful and adventurous Learns from experience Flexible and open to change Quick to assess the situation and act accordingly	Understands various sociocultural value systems Capable of relating present to past experiences Able to assess situations adequately to identify appropriate behaviors Skilled at selecting language and actions suitable to a given context
Communication: verbal and nonverbal	Can get ideas across Comfortable in sharing thoughts, ideas, or beliefs/self-confident Shapes the message to suit the audience	Possesses an adequate vocabulary and language skills Organizes and conveys thoughts in a coherent fashion Capable of using expressions and gestures that enhance ideas

Table 6-1 continued

	Teacher Competencies	*Teacher Characteristics*
	Some flair for the dramatic Eager to relate experiences	Able to provide clarification by furnishing examples and illustrations Skilled in various techniques that foster interaction
Interpretation of ideas: verbal and nonverbal	Sensitive to thoughts and ideas Aware of facial expressions and body language Listens and looks for discrepancies in behavior and ideas Mentally questions Listens intently to what is being said Relates what is said to what is felt, known, or experienced	Capable of following other's line of reasoning Skilled in organizing the ideas of others Able to identify main ideas and supporting details Capable at structuring information within the proper sequence Able to critically evaluate the ideas of others
Interest and expression in the arts	Appreciates unique or divergent expression in self or others Enjoys artistic modes of expression Sensitive, open minded, and nonconfronting Pursues a variety of hobbies and interests	Knows excellent models or examples of specific forms of art Able to analyze artistic products fairly and accurately Capable of designing settings in which others can display their talents and abilities Skilled at relating artistic expression to specific subject matter areas
Physical capabilities and adaptability	Strives for "wellness" Participates in various physical activities Aware of physical strengths and limitations and adjusts accordingly Views the individual in a holistic manner Is energetic and displays vitality	Engages in a variety of physical psychomotor activities Possesses information related to nutrition and health Skilled in diagnosing the physical abilities and disabilities of others Capable of providing a learning environment that considers the physical development of the learners

SUMMARY

Any individual who is concerned about and interested in the maximum growth of gifted learners can assume a vital role and undertake important responsibilities within the gifted program. It has been the goal of this chapter to consider in detail the potential roles and responsibilities that can be and perhaps should be taken on by certain groups working within and outside the school setting. Among the specific populations scrutinized within this discussion were the administrators, guidance staff, support personnel, parents, and teachers. In general, administrators were viewed as the directors of the activities that were in operation; guidance counselors as the facilitators of dialogue among the various program participants; support personnel as the providers of specific expertise; parents as links between home and school environment; and teachers as the transmitters of information.

The key to the ultimate success of the gifted program would appear to rest in the cooperative efforts and enthusiastic support of these individuals described. While rather specific roles and responsibilities have been summarized for these persons important to the gifted program, it should not be assumed that these duties and characteristics are either exhaustive or inflexible. As programs change and because learners vary, these roles and responsibilities will need to be expanded and modified. It has been the objective of this section to provide a suitable and applicable set of guidelines from which additional ideas can be generated. Above all, it must be remembered that no program can exist long and function well without the cooperative input of many individuals such as those presented here.

REFERENCES

Alexander, P., & Muia, J. A. Gifted reading programs: Uncovering the hidden potential. *Reading Horizons*, 1980, *20*, 302-310.

Baldwin, A., Gear, G., & Lucito, L. (Eds.). *Educational planning for the gifted*. Reston, Va.: The Council for Exceptional Children, 1978.

Bernal, E. M. Gifted programs for the culturally different. *NASSP Bulletin*, 1976, *60*, 67-76.

Bishop, W. E. Characteristics of teachers judged successful by intellectually gifted, high-achieving high school students. *Dissertation Abstracts International*, 1967, *28A*, 487-88.

Bishop, W. E. Successful teachers of the gifted. *Exceptional Children*, 1968, *34*, 317-325.

Breiter, J. Survey: *Teachers of gifted elementary students*. Iowa: Iowa State University of Science and Technology, 1979. (ERIC Document Reproduction Service No. ED 170 987)

Brodbelt, S. Key program considerations for selecting and guiding gifted students. *The High School Journal*, 1979, *62*, 272-77.

Cangemi, J. P. How culturally different, gifted, and creative students perceive their teachers. *Clearinghouse*, 1979, *52*, 419-20.

Cobb, S. G., Cobb, P. H., & Dow, C. M. E. *Conn-Cept. III. Once upon a building: Creating a differentiated learning environment for the gifted and talented*. Hartford: Connecticut State Department of Education, Bureau of Pupil Personnel and Special Education Services, 1978. (ERIC Document Reproduction Service No. ED 154 598)

Dinkmeyer, D. C. *Developing understanding of self and others: D-1.* Circle Pines, Minnesota: American Guidance Service, 1970.

Dinkmeyer, D. C. *Developing understanding of self and others: D-2.* Circle Pines, Minnesota: American Guidance Service, 1973.

Feldhusen, J. F., & Kolloff, M. B. A three stage model for gifted education. *G/C/T,* 1978, *1,* 3-5; 53-57.

Flanders, N. A. *Personal-social anxiety as a factor in learning.* Unpublished doctoral dissertation, The University of Chicago, 1949.

Frasier, M. M. Rethinking the issues regarding the culturally disadvantaged gifted. *Exceptional Children,* 1979, *45,* 538-542.

French, J. L. (Ed.) *Educating the gifted.* New York: Henry Holt & Company, 1957.

Gibson, J. T. *Psychology for the classroom.* Englewood Cliffs, N.J.: Prentice-Hall, 1976.

Henjum, A. E. A response to the needs of rural gifted and talented youth. University of Minnesota at Morris, 1977. (ERIC Document Reproduction Service No. ED 144 303)

Maker, C. J. *Providing programs for the gifted handicapped.* Reston, Va.: The Council for Exceptional Children, 1977.

Maker, C. J. *Training teachers for the gifted and talented: A comparison of models.* Reston, Va.: The Council for Exceptional Children, 1978.

Muro, J. J., & Dinkmeyer, D. C. *Counseling in the elementary and middle schools: A pragmatic approach.* Dubuque, Iowa: William C. Brown Co., 1977.

Nelson, J. B., & Cleland, D. L. The role of the teacher of the gifted. *Education,* 1967, *88,* 47-51.

Newland, T. E. *The gifted in educational perspective.* Englewood Cliffs, N.J.: Prentice-Hall, 1976.

Raths, L. E., Harmin, M., & Simon, S. *Values and teaching.* Columbus, Ohio: Charles E. Merrill, 1966.

Rosenshine, B., & Furst, N. The use of direct observation to study teaching. In R.M.W. Travers (Ed.), *Second handbook of research on teaching.* Chicago: Rand McNally College Publishing Co., 1973.

Ryan, K., & Cooper, J. M. *Those who can, teach.* Boston: Houghton Mifflin Company, 1972.

Shelby, M. E. Who should teach the gifted? Paper presented at the World Congress on Future Special Education, June 1978. (ERIC Document Reproduction Service No. ED 157 336)

Sisk, D. Teaching gifted children. 1976. (ERIC Document Reproduction Service No. ED 150 810)

Sullivan, A. R. The identification of gifted and academically talented black students: A hidden exceptionality. *Journal of Special Ed.,* 1973, *7,* 373-379.

Thomas, D. Gifted and talented children: The neglected minority. *The National Association of Secondary School Principals Bulletin,* 1976, *60,* 21-24.

Torrance, E. P., & Kaufmann, F. Teacher education for career education of the gifted and talented. *Gifted Child Quarterly,* 1977, *21,* 176.

Vernon, P. E., Adamson, G., & Vernon, D. F. *The psychology and education of gifted children.* Boulder, Colo.: Westview Press, 1977.

Whitmore, J. R. *Giftedness, conflict and underachievement.* Boston: Allyn & Bacon, 1980.

Withall, J. Evaluation of classroom climate. *Childhood Education,* 1969, *45,* 403-408.

Withall, J. A modest proposal for teacher education and teaching. *West African Journal of Education,* 1970, *14,* 40-44.

Withall, J. *Learning: Social psychological conditions that may enhance it.* Mimeographed paper, 1973.

Withall, J. Taking the threat out of classroom observation and feedback. *Journal of Teacher Education,* 1979, *30,* 55-58.

Chapter 7

The Gifted Curriculum: A Holistic Approach

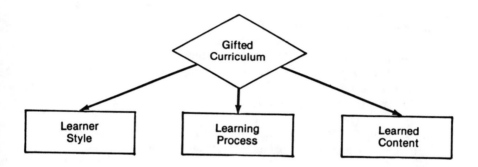

When discussing the development of educational programs for the gifted, one must look long and hard at the issue of curriculum. Certainly, curriculum is the heart of the gifted program, and much of what else transpires is merely the selection, modification, and evaluation of that curriculum. Yet, providing a curriculum innovative and appropriate enough for exceptionally able learners is an overwhelming task. There are many questions that must be asked and answered: What is curriculum? How is curriculum for the gifted determined? How do project developers know they have implemented a curriculum that is suitable to the unique needs of gifted learners? It will be the purpose of this chapter, therefore, to give an in-depth consideration to the determination, development, and evaluation of curriculum for the gifted learner. An innovative and holistic curriculum for the gifted will be introduced with discussion of its three basic components: learning styles, learning processes, and learned content. Within the area of learning styles, the "who" of curriculum will be described, emphasizing the various ways the gifted may approach the learning situation. In the section on learning processes, the "what" of the gifted curriculum will be presented, focusing on the underlying goals of instruction. Finally, with the topic of learned content, the holistic curriculum will be portrayed in operation in various content areas: language arts, math, science, social science, art, and music.

THE HOLISTIC CURRICULUM: ITS PURPOSE AND ITS PARTS

One of the first facts that should become apparent to educators as they process the information in this chapter is that the curriculum is presented here in a unique fashion. When reading books or articles about gifted programming, it is most common to find the curriculum sectioned into traditional content areas such as language arts or math, with suggested activities, materials, and strategies offered for each. However, this will not be the case in this chapter, since a critical requirement in developing a unique, innovative educational program for the gifted is that the curriculum designed for that project be just as unique and innovative. Thus, curriculum developers would do well to remember that any program of planned instructional experiences that ignores the special characteristics and learning modalities of the gifted or that does not seek to unify the educational experiences through common goals will fail to achieve maximum success. In accordance, this chapter presents a holistic curriculum for the gifted that relates the three essential elements of a curriculum: the learner, the goals of learning, and the content to be learned. Furthermore, this innovative approach to curriculum development for the gifted has been constructed to attain four basic characteristics:

1. *Interaction.* Curriculum is much more than a summary sheet of various activities conducted in separate content areas. Curriculum involves the interaction of a particular individual with a unique learning style with all areas of instructional content (see Figure 7-1). It is this special learner who forms the core of the curricular model and around whom the educational program must revolve. In addition, there are common learning processes that link the gifted learner to these areas of content and without which the curriculum could not operate smoothly. Therefore, for a curriculum for the gifted to be truly appropriate it must be interactive, combining all three key elements into a functioning system.

2. *Integration.* While the gifted curriculum must be vertically organized, it must be horizontally cohesive as well. If educators persist in treating curriculum in isolated chunks of content, they will never succeed in identifying the common threads of learning that run through all bodies of knowledge. It is important for the gifted to see the relationship between the traditional content areas and to transfer readily what is learned in one field of study to the next. Unless the curriculum of the gifted program is integrative, it will not facilitate this transfer of learning across content lines.

3. *Timeliness.* When a curriculum is produced around specific activities and skill lists, it frequently becomes outdated and, thus, less useful. This is especially true if the curriculum is product rather than process oriented. In explanation, a process-oriented curriculum is one that has a broad, rather than narrow or restricted, purpose and is concerned with developing a wide

Figure 7-1 The Holistic Curriculum

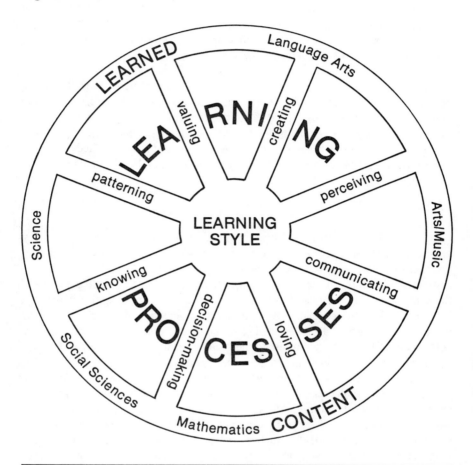

range of intellectual skills, rather than catering to far more specific but less meaningful objectives. Because the curriculum is centered around these basic, more general processes, it remains more flexible and adaptable to the ever-changing needs of school and society. For the curriculum to survive in its fluid surroundings, it must be based on those rudimentary processes that remain timely.

4. *Self-perpetuation.* Every educator must realize that it is impossible to provide the gifted with every piece of knowledge they will require in every content area. Even if we could assume that we have furnished gifted learners with everything they need to succeed in today's world, that may not be

enough to ensure their success tomorrow. Consequently, those who develop the gifted program must aim for a curriculum that not only teaches content but also teaches the gifted how to learn. By being independent thinkers, the gifted are able to locate and utilize whatever knowledge is needed, thus becoming self-perpetuating learners.

No traditional curriculum can satisfy all of these requirements as well as can a holistic curriculum that combines the learner, content, and learning processes into one manageable framework. It is this holistic curriculum that sets out to unite the educational experiences of the gifted in both a horizontally and vertically consistent system and does so by centering on both the uniqueness of the gifted and on the basic processes that ensure their greater success in school and in society.

LEARNING STYLE

The central characters in the educational drama identified as the gifted program are the learners themselves. All gifted students, whether they are male or female, younger or older, approach the learning process in a way that reflects their own distinctiveness. It is this manner of interaction and reaction between the gifted and the educational environment that is referred to here as learning style. In its most basic form, learning style encompasses three dimensions of the student's total personality: cognitive, affective, and physiological (Keefe, 1979). The cognitive component of learning style refers to the typical method by which gifted learners process information, which incorporates their modes of perceiving, remembering, ordering, and recalling knowledge. Affective style, on the other hand, is described by Keefe (1979) as the learner's typical motivating processes, which relate to the characteristics of attention, emotion, and valuing and which include the gifted's way of arousing, directing, and sustaining behaviors. While perhaps the most superficial and most evident influences on the educational process, the psychomotor factors in learning style incorporate the biologically based response patterns and the expected reactions of the gifted to certain physical environments.

In the past, the concept of learning style has been largely ignored in the literature on curriculum and in the development, selection, and implementation of instructional materials. The fact that certain classroom environments, modes of teaching, and educational materials might influence different types of learners in different ways apparently was not implemented, perhaps owing to the immensity of the task of adjusting the curriculum to suit the diverse learning styles of the gifted students in any one classroom. Perhaps also this was not given serious consideration because of the difficulty of implementing it into the curriculum. Therefore, with the possible exception of some superficial consideration of auditory or visual modalities of students, little was said about learning style and even less was done.

Why has this idea of learning style, which has been overlooked in educational planning for years, been purposely situated at the very core of the holistic curriculum being proposed here? Although the concept of learning style has only recently begun to command some attention, educators *have* succumbed to the basic notion that certain groups of learners learn in different ways; why else would we teach children differently from adults, younger children differently from older children, and less able youngsters differently from their more able counterparts? Educators have sensed this need to adjust instruction to certain learning styles and have done so in a very rudimentary and unorganized fashion. In the holistic curriculum, the idea of learning style is purposely, centrally, and systematically pursued at two levels: group and individual.

Group Planning

If educators did not believe that gifted learners, as a group, represent a unique population, there would be no reason to construct an educational program designed specifically for these learners. Therefore, the planning and implementation of a gifted program presupposes that the gifted population possesses certain characteristics and behaviors that set them apart from the educational mainstream and that must be treated differently in the classroom setting. The behavioral checklists employed in the identification of the gifted and the common descriptors used in defining giftedness are frequently the same words that signify the general learning style of that population. The difference here is that these terms become forces in curriculum planning and not merely adjectives that are used to identify the gifted and then promptly discarded.

In accordance, the common learning traits exhibited by this distinct population of learners must be considered in the organization of the program curriculum. Among the traits Dunn and Price (1980) identify for gifted students in grades four to eight are that, compared with nongifted peers, they are more persistent, require less structure, and favor a more formal design in their instructional environment. Griggs and Price (1979) found seventh and ninth grade gifted learners to be less teacher motivated, more persistent, and more likely to appreciate some sound in their learning environments. These gifted students also demonstrated a preference for learning alone rather than in groups.

Gifted learners, as a whole, also appear to be more field independent than field dependent. The learner who is basically field independent is more analytical and is generally a high achiever who is well in control of the instructional environment. The field-dependent individual, on the other hand, is more distracted by the surroundings and may have more difficulty in identifying relevant information.

Also, the gifted population tends to be more conceptual than perceptual. This means that they are better able to complete novel and complex tasks and generally possess a greater facility for conceptual behaviors and perhaps less for those of a perceptual-motor nature, especially as they become mature learners.

Even within the gifted population there may be some distinguishing differences between groups of gifted learners. Saurerman and Michael (1980), for example, found that high achieving gifteds in grades four, five, and six tend to be more creative in divergent production tasks, more field independent, and more interested in academic achievement than those identified as low achievers.

Certainly, utilization of learning styles is an attempt to better match the instructional climate and approach to the gifted population as a whole. It is far more than a consideration of intelligence and involves an analysis of the entire gifted personality. While no clear conceptual match exists between gifted behaviors and curriculum at the present, it is essential for those entrusted with the development of the program's curriculum to ponder carefully the potential reactions that might be expected from the gifted within certain instructional contexts. It is through the consideration of learning styles of gifted populations that a greater likelihood of curriculum match is possible.

Individualization

It is a stated purpose of this text to emphasize the importance of providing gifted learners with personalized instruction, that is, instruction that is built on a learner's specific strengths, needs, and interests. In developing the *Specific Learner's Instructional Plan (SLIP)* (see Chapter 4) for each individual, there should be concern for the way the student appears to learn best as well as for what knowledge or skills we want the child to acquire. Consequently, the *SLIP* should reflect the teacher's awareness of various learning styles through the identification of instructional strategies that would best complement the individual's unique approach to learning. It should be understood that no teacher can be expected to plot every gifted learner along a continuum for each of the many learning style characteristics. What teachers of the gifted can be expected to do is to develop their understanding of these various learning traits and recognize the reflection of these traits in gifted students by demonstrated interaction and reaction with their curriculum. Finally, educators can learn to provide educational experiences that might be better suited to the learning modalities of the gifted in the cognitive, affective, and psychomotor domains. Several of the key cognitive and affective learning traits with some description of accompanying behaviors that might be demonstrated within the classroom are shown in Figure 7-2.

The following case studies demonstrate how a teacher's understanding of various learning styles may be incorporated in the instructional planning for the gifted students within the classroom.

Figure 7-2 Dichotomous Display of Cognitive and Affective Styles of Learning

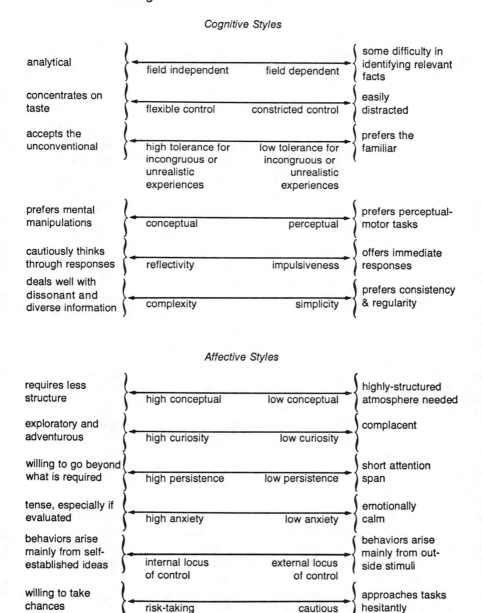

Cognitive Styles

analytical	field independent field dependent	some difficulty in identifying relevant facts
concentrates on taste	flexible control constricted control	easily distracted
accepts the unconventional	high tolerance for incongruous or unrealistic experiences low tolerance for incongruous or unrealistic experiences	prefers the familiar
prefers mental manipulations	conceptual perceptual	prefers perceptual-motor tasks
cautiously thinks through responses	reflectivity impulsiveness	offers immediate responses
deals well with dissonant and diverse information	complexity simplicity	prefers consistency & regularity

Affective Styles

requires less structure	high conceptual low conceptual	highly-structured atmosphere needed
exploratory and adventurous	high curiosity low curiosity	complacent
willing to go beyond what is required	high persistence low persistence	short attention span
tense, especially if evaluated	high anxiety low anxiety	emotionally calm
behaviors arise mainly from self-established ideas	internal locus of control external locus of control	behaviors arise mainly from out-side stimuli
willing to take chances	risk-taking cautious	approaches tasks hesitantly

Case Studies

Miss Skrobak is a fourth-grade teacher who is well organized and very structured in her approach to instruction. She prefers to use a lecture-discussion format followed by teacher-directed, large group activities. In Miss Skrobak's classroom, two students, Kristen and John, have been identified as gifted. Even though both students demonstrated high intellectual abilities, Miss Skrobak noted some distinct differences in the behaviors of these two students.

Case 1

Kristen is a very perceptive and insightful girl who prefers the classroom activities that require her to deal more in depth with a particular topic or problem. She enjoys searching out information and finding alternate solutions to problems presented. While she excels in these activities, Kristen has been frequently reprimanded for inattentive behavior during whole group discussions and lectures. Kristen's persistence and attention to task is noticeably related to the atmosphere in which that activity occurs.

Since Miss Skrobak realized Kristen's preference for more independent, problem-solving activities, she planned to provide Kristen with opportunities to work on such projects in social studies and reading. With Miss Skrobak's assistance, Kristen outlined several topics in current events that she would like to pursue. It was decided by both that Kristen could share her information with the class and possibly help other interested classmates investigate this problem. In reading, Kristen was given the opportunity to select books of special interest to her. Through a contract method, Miss Skrobak and Kristen agreed on the topic areas for reading and the follow-up activities that Kristen would pursue. Periodically, during the course of the contract, Miss Skrobak had individual conferences with Kristen to determine how she was progressing.

Case 2

Unlike Kristen, John is observed to be a gifted child who works better in situations where all tasks are clearly outlined and criteria for evaluation are specifically stated. John appears to prefer regularity in his environment and becomes highly anxious when presented with new tasks, especially those slightly unfamiliar activities for which he will receive a grade. John also seems to work better in small groups and frequently assumes a leadership role in this situation.

To meet John's educational needs more effectively, Miss Skrobak modified her teaching procedure slightly to accommodate John and several others like him in her classroom; for their needs, Miss Skrobak incorporated more small group discussions and activities in her instructional program. In addition, she was careful to outline to the students what was expected of them when they engaged in some less familiar instructional activities. Miss Skrobak also made it a point to talk over classwork with John and provide him with the opportunity to help in establishing the criteria for evaluation for his special, less routine assignments.

In attempting to meet the needs of these gifted students in her class, Miss Skrobak realized that she would need to make some adjustments in her classroom structure. It was unrealistic to assume that any major alteration in her approach was either possible or preferable. However, she did realize that several key changes or additions could effectively accommodate these students' styles of learning. Acting on this realization, Miss Skrobak effectively employed her awareness of gifted learning styles to improve the curriculum for these individuals.

LEARNING PROCESSES

The second dimension of the holistic curriculum is the various learning processes that form the spokes of the curricular structure. Radiating from the core of this model, which is the learner style, are those common and cohesive threads of learning that vertically link the gifted to the content and that horizontally unite knowledge across all content areas. It is because of their most basic and yet flexible nature that these processes create a gifted curriculum that is both timely and manageable. Perhaps the hardest task is to dissect what we do in education down to its barest bones and then put appropriate labels on the parts that remain. One of the best attempts at this difficult task was undertaken by Berman (1968). In her text, *New Priorities in the Curriculum,* Berman succeeded in producing a listing of these essential learning processes, which will be incorporated into this discussion of the holistic curriculum for the gifted. These learning processes include the following components: perceiving, communicating, loving, decision making, knowing, patterning, valuing, and creating. Each of these processes will be described briefly and then related more specifically to gifted programming.

Perceiving

The process defined as perceiving refers to the way in which individuals view, interpret, and organize the world around them. It is through the process of perceiving that the gifted learner builds a theory of the world, using ideas, concepts, and beliefs rooted in experience. In education, it is important that we help others see the value in looking openly at what takes place around them. They must be receptive to new sights and ideas and must be willing to observe things in many different ways and from many different perspectives. They must also learn to categorize and organize their perceptions so that they can make maximum use of the knowledge they have obtained and interpreted. Furthermore, learners must be able to see how ideas and events, people, and principles all interrelate, and they must allow their view of the world to be panoramic, encompassing as much of their surroundings as they can, yet not overlooking the details that create the entire picture.

What meaning does all this have for the gifted curriculum? First, educators must assist the gifted in understanding how they view the world and how these perceptions might influence the choices they make or the actions they take. The curriculum itself should be constructed on what program initiators perceive to be the needs of the gifted population with whom they will deal. Not only should the curriculum concern itself with the knowledge base of the gifted, but it must also incorporate the social, cultural, physical, and emotional aspects of their personalities. For the holistic curriculum to operate, it must begin with an understanding of the whole learner and then, based on this knowledge, must move outwardly.

Another characteristic of the holistic curriculum is that it should understand and appreciate the diversity among gifted learners rather than attempt to mold them into one preconceived acceptable form; eventually, it would be hoped that the gifted would also become more aware and accepting of diversity within others and the world around them. In adjusting to the diversified personalities of the gifted, the holistic curriculum must also seek to make learning experiences more relevant. The gifted may acquire greater understanding if they are helped to see how the information presented to them relates to their existing theory of the world and, therefore, has personal meaning to them.

Communicating

All individuals have the need to communicate. That is to say that all people must send and receive information in one form or another. Communication, as a learning process, goes far beyond the conventional notion of speaking, writing, or listening to messages transmitted within a language framework. It also entails one's ability to interpret nonverbal information or symbols, such as those present in math, science, art, or music that are nonlinguistic in nature. Indeed, communication goes far beyond mastery of a language.

At the center of all communications, however, is the individual, and it is up to that individual to receive, interpret, and transmit ideas. Without effective skills in communication, gifted learners will be unable to reduce the uncertainty that exists around them and will not have a clear sense of the world in which they live.

Accordingly, communication is an essential process in education and a focal point in a holistic curriculum. To function as effective communicators, gifted learners must possess many skills. They must be good listeners, attentive to the message being delivered. They must learn to question themselves and others about the information they encounter. Also, it is important that gifted students skillfully compare the ideas communicated with the knowledge that they already possess, carefully weighing one against the other. In this same vein, educators must help gifted learners identify inconsistent information and distinguish fact from opinion, or fact from fiction. The holistic curriculum should also aim to instruct gifted learners in recognizing main and supporting ideas, in organizing the information that is received, and in recalling or transmitting information in varied and appropriate formats.

Everywhere we turn in our world we are being bombarded with messages. These messages come in all forms, transmitted in many symbols and within varying contexts. If our gifted learners are not able to interpret what is communicated, in relation to when, where, and how it is communicated, they will not be able to receive information vital to their maximum growth. Thus, a primary task of the holistic curriculum is to focus on this process of communication throughout all areas of content, as delineated and discussed later in this chapter.

Loving

The appearance of a word like "loving" among a listing of basic learning processes is perhaps startling to some. However, educators quickly realize that imparting knowledge to an individual is not an impersonal task but a highly interpersonal one. Schools are the social settings in which information is shared between teacher and student, as well as between student and student, and thus learning requires the gifted to function in a social context with others. Within the context of the classroom, emotional interactions are frequently intertwined with concepts, facts, and thoughts that are to be learned; it is thus impossible to separate intellectual activities from the social and emotional ties that bind them together.

Loving or caring or responding is not a new process to the gifted learners entering the classroom, because interpersonal relationships are an integral part of their preschool environment. The difference is that the context for human interaction changes along with the members and diversity of persons to whom the gifted learner must respond. The process of loving is continued, expanded, and varied as the gifted move from home to school and, later, from school into society at large.

The holistic curriculum must prepare the gifted to respond personally to the diverse individuals they will encounter throughout their lives. It can do this, in part, by providing them with frequent opportunities to interact with persons of differing ages and abilities and of varied beliefs, interests, and behaviors. Certainly, within the educational setting, the gifted should be given the chance to deal with those who may be dissimilar. The holistic curriculum should function as the positive atmosphere in which the gifted learn to coexist with others.

Understanding ourselves as feeling and thinking human beings is a phenomenon that occurs as we monitor and modify the effect our behaviors have on others. Understanding ourselves is truly a reflective process, and it is, therefore, essential that the holistic curriculum for the gifted serve as a forum from which these learners can test out their hypotheses about themselves. The holistic curriculum should thus furnish the gifted with the tools and skills to realistically assess both their own humanistic qualities and the effect that their behaviors have on others.

Finally, in the holistic curriculum, it is crucial that teachers see themselves as role models in loving and caring. Teachers should thus impart to all gifted learners that their feelings, ideas, and beliefs are important. Teachers should be honest in their own feelings and share these emotions with gifted learners whenever appropriate. Teachers of the gifted must act as they want their students to become.

Decision Making

Soon after individuals are born they begin to make choices. While many of the decisions made are relatively insignificant, there are those that have or could have far-reaching influences on an individual's existence. Yet, too little educational time is appropriated to teaching learners how to effectively make decisions, and freedom of choice is still a relatively uncommon occurrence even in gifted programs. It is essential that a holistic curriculum for the gifted tackle this issue of decision making and bring it to the forefront of educational experiences, where it rightly belongs. If our gifted learners are to make quality decisions throughout their educational careers and afterward, then they must be given the opportunity to make meaningful choices. Experience, even in decision making, is frequently the best teacher. Gifted learners, therefore, could have input into, among other elements, their assignments, activities, and evaluation. Certainly, such exceptionally able learners can make some positive contributions to their own instructional plans as well as to the instructional program in general.

There is much that the gifted should learn about decision making. The gifted must begin to see that decisions vary in complexity and that there are often priorities that must be considered. They must also be made to understand that in selecting from existing alternatives, the external conditions and consequences of each choice must be balanced against the internal desires and motivations.

Also, within the holistic curriculum, care should be taken to demonstrate that information is an essential component of the decision-making process. Gifted learners need to recognize what information would be appropriate in a given situation, where such knowledge could be found, and how much information to seek. They should also be shown that even when supporting data are available, no decision is without risks. Those instructing the gifted should provide the kind of learning environment that can tolerate risk taking and thus demonstrates to the gifted that it is sometimes suitable or even advisable to take chances. These individuals must learn to expect some frustration and disappointment when they accept responsibility for their own choices and behaviors, although they should strive to grow from whatever mistakes or circumstances result.

Knowing

Often in education those who plan instructional experiences become overly concerned with the specific facts, figures, formulas, skills, and symbols that are part of particular content areas. As a result, some of the fundamental processes that lead individuals into becoming independent and capable learners are bypassed. As was stated at the outset of this chapter, and earlier in Chapter 4, no teacher can be expected to impart all the information that will be important to gifted learners throughout their lifetimes. Knowledge is an ever-expanding, ever-changing body of information that can only be touched on in the educational experiences incorporated in gifted programs. Therefore, while the gifted must come to realize that knowledge can be segmented into particular fields of study, it may be of equal or greater importance to help them recognize the relationships of these knowledge areas. The holistic curriculum must thus assist gifted learners in assimilating and accommodating new information. This may be achieved by focusing on the underlying concepts, ideas, and generalizations appearing throughout the curriculum. What we must do in our holistic curriculum is help our gifted realize what they already know and provide them with the skills to locate and utilize whatever further information they find to be necessary or worthwhile. The most important skill we can furnish our gifted students with is the ability to learn for themselves—the skill of knowing how to learn.

Patterning

There is a natural tendency for thinking beings to seek out and attempt to impose some order on their existence. This need for order is evident, too, in our efforts to organize the bits and pieces of information we receive. For those individuals, such as the gifted, who must deal with extremely complex and challenging questions and problems, this need to schematize knowledge is probably much greater. To some degree, this ability to look over amounts of information and sense some pattern or system among its symbols and ideas is a developmental process (Flavell,

1977). However, to some extent this is also a practiced or learned effect, and, as a learned skill, patterning is an essential process to be included in a holistic curriculum. In addition, while patterning is an important ability in itself, it also aids the gifted in getting the most out of the content knowledge to which educators will expose them.

Basically, patterning conveys to the gifted that information does not exist as isolated chunks of knowledge within the brain. Instead, the knowledge already possessed is probably classified and categorized into information networks referred to by Piaget as "schemas." In our mental computers, this information is ordered, in some fashion, according to its importance, with supporting details being slotted under main concepts or schemata (Rumelhart, 1980). Also, the mind seems able to link thoughts, moving quickly from one schema to another. In the holistic curriculum, educators must aid the gifted in recognizing how organization of information is vital to its reception, utilization, and transmission.

Gifted learners should be taught that an effective and efficient mental organization is one in which useful categories are established, outdated ones are discarded or modified, and the most appropriate information is stored within the appropriate category. This may sound like a confusing, and maybe an impossible, task, but it is a critical one, especially for gifted learners. Educators should begin by explaining the mental framework to the gifted even in simple terms of a computer that receives, stores, and then emits information in an efficient way. Also, in the holistic curriculum, the gifted can be provided with opportunities to take unstructured pieces of information within a content area and place it into some manageable framework. Outlining, for example, and similar organizational tasks are written parallels to what we attempt to do mentally with information.

Unless we demonstrate to gifted learners the necessity of efficiently ordering the information they wish to retain, they will become far less able thinkers. After all, knowledge can be learned but then stored away in some fashion that the individual cannot retrieve it upon demand; we can easily draw a comparison here to the secretary who has put away an important folder of information only to forget how it was filed. Certainly, helping gifted learners become even more proficient receivers, organizers, and retrievers of knowledge should be one of the principal goals of the holistic curriculum. Because the minds of our gifted learners hold the potential for greatness, it would be tragic to let that knowledge be unlearned as a result of disorganization or remain in some unordered maze from which it may never emerge.

Valuing

People do not act or react in random fashion. Generally they operate according to certain internalized principles that have arisen from their encounters with the world around them. We call these guiding precepts "values," and it is these values that place some constraints on the way people behave toward others. Valuing is the process that leads an individual to the recognition and formulation of the internalized set of principles that direct one's own actions. Formation of values is a slow, continuous process that is greatly influenced by external factors, such as parental relationships, cultural heritage, and religious training, and is equally molded by internal forces, such as emotional stability, openness and flexibility to change, perceptional intensity, and personal aims or motivations. Valuing is less likely to occur in isolation because it is through interactions with others in society that we define and refine the feelings and beliefs we have about ourselves as social creatures. Because no two people share the same experiences in life, it is understandable that the values they hold and the depth of their commitments will vary accordingly; what is valued in one group or population might be of little significance to the next.

Since all gifted learners must act in the educational setting according to a developing value system and must interact with others who operate within a framework of differing precepts, the process of valuing should become one of the central themes in the holistic curriculum. As teachers of the gifted, it is important that we help these learners identify the principles that influence their behaviors—the biases and beliefs that shade their view of the world. Once the gifted have some awareness of their own values, they can compare them with the beliefs and biases of those they encounter. From this point, the gifted can attempt to assign priorities to clarify, and justify the particular values they hold. Putting values into words is a difficult assignment, requiring the gifted to use concrete terms to describe abstract feelings or thoughts.

Through education, the gifted may also understand how and why their values change. They can identify the internal and external forces that have the greatest impact on the principles they defend. In the holistic curriculum, discussions and activities should promote the gifted's understanding of the way values react with the surrounding context and how those who profess certain values attempt to rationalize or justify the relationship between their own values and what appears to be reality. Balancing the scales between the values of the gifted individual and the common good for the gifted population must also take place in the gifted programming, and gifted learners must be shown how such judgments are made.

Again, teachers must serve as behavior models in this process of valuing. They must demonstrate their willingness to accept and explore their own values and those of others. They must create a classroom environment that permits the existence of diverse, yet justifiable values, and they must provide their students with the opportunities to communicate and test their own beliefs and biases against the backdrop of acceptance and openness. Before gifted learners move upward in their journey to achieve full potential they must first know what values direct their course and where these values are likely to lead them.

Creating

In all of us there has been that momentary desire or goal to do something no one else has done before, to succeed where others have failed, or to place our marks upon the world in which we live. Perhaps this need to stand out from the group and to prove our own uniqueness is the best description of the process called creating. At the heart of creation is the knowledge that all individuals perceive the world in a unique fashion and that whatever contributions are made arise from their perceptions.

The process of creating, however, involves more than these perceptions and more than the desire to produce some unique and original expression. Creating or creativity also requires an ample dose of special skills or talents, along with the necessary cognitive skills that can bring the product to its fruition. The ability to create also involves an emotional investment on the part of the individual. Every product we assemble is in some way an expression of ourselves; thus, the rejection of our work carries with it the potential for self-rejection. However, the truly creative person must be willing to take the necessary risks. Not only do the gifted run the risk of having their personal expressions rejected, but they must also face the possibility that they will be unable to achieve their desired outcomes. Many people would like to create a painting as renowned as da Vinci's *Mona Lisa*, but very few have the skills, abilities, or perceptions to complete such a task.

In a holistic curriculum, however, there are ample opportunities to foster creativity through the content areas. First, since creating relates directly to perception, it is important for the gifted program to furnish its learners with richness of experience. Exposing students to a wide range of experiences can help them to expand and elaborate their view of the world. Second, the gifted classrooms should be places that are accepting and encouraging of creative expression. Such a classroom would be flexible and open to diversity and would provide learners with the private time they need to create.

Another critical factor to consider in the holistic curriculum is the issue of evaluation, especially as it relates to personal expression. As was noted, a creative act is to some degree an individual's reflection of self. While criteria are important in assessing a creative product, it is vital that these criteria merely serve as guides by which the gifted can examine, value, and improve their mode of creative expression. In judging the products, teachers must be extremely careful not to place judgment on learners in such a way as to stifle future creative attempts. It is most important for the learners themselves to become aware of the strengths of their own products and ways in which later products can be improved or strengthened. Therefore, educators must help the gifted ask themselves appropriate questions about their creations and provide suggestions for modifications when suitable. The goal of the holistic curriculum, then, is to encourage the development of the creative self that resides within each gifted learner and to furnish the type of atmosphere in which creativity can flourish.

LEARNED CONTENT

Traditionally, school curriculums have taken the published form of printed volumes of specific skills and accompanying activities that should be taught in a sharply defined area of content at some particular stage in the learners' educational career. It is the purpose of this chapter to modify this format to a certain extent in a manner that is most beneficial to gifted learners and those responsible for their education. What has been proposed in this discussion of a holistic curriculum is that content areas are of little importance in isolation. They are important as they relate to the gifted's learning style and the learning processes that should be central concerns in all segments of knowledge. To continue in this vein, it is vital for those who have been directed to implement the gifted curriculum to have some clear sense of how this holistic curriculum will appear in actual practice. They do not disregard the theoretical significance of this curricular approach but are equally interested in its relationship to practice. To address this relevant dilemma, the key content areas (social sciences, mathematics, science, language arts, art and music) are presented along with suitable learning activities for the gifted that relate to the various processes central to this holistic curriculum. It should also be noted that each activity is described in such a way as to be easily implemented in any classroom setting and is accompanied by suggested variations. Additionally, these activities have the added benefits of low or no expense and, because learners are given primary responsibility, reduced work load for the already overworked educator.

Language Arts

The curricular area defined as language arts encompasses several more specialized components, including speaking, listening, writing, reading, and spelling. Language arts, as a field of study, is generally concerned with the learners' proficiency in using and comprehending information transmitted through language symbols. In accordance, the following activities can be implemented within the language arts area:

Perceiving: Detailed Descriptions

Because of the importance of careful observation and accurate description in our day-to-day lives, this activity centers on enhancing these skill areas. Working individually or in groups, gifted students are asked to generate descriptive words or phrases—as many as possible—for a particular object, person, situation, or event. Once a list has been formulated, it can serve as the basis for a written or orally shared product. They should also be directed to study the object carefully and closely, looking for ideas or characteristics others may have overlooked. For example, gifted students may be asked to describe snow and may structure their response into a free-flowing verse, as follows:

SNOW
White, melts,
Like angels' tears,
Clean, blinding,
Soundless.

Variation. With younger gifteds, this activity might focus on a concrete object that they can manipulate or on a person or event they can actually experience with their senses. With older gifted learners, this descriptive task can move into more abstract, conceptual areas such as love, prejudice, thoughts, or friendships.

Communicating: Body Language

Nonverbal communication is interesting to gifted learners of all ages; charades is still a familiar game even to adults. In language arts, an appropriate activity to enhance nonverbal communication is to prepare lists of objects, events, or even persons that students can act out without speaking. Explain to them that they must *become*, rather than demonstrate, whatever object they draw at random and that they can use any movement, gesture, or expression to convey their idea. Some useful objects for this activity might be a banana, a tire jack, a coffeepot, a television, or a merry-go-round. With younger gifteds, teachers might find it helpful to model first their own interpretation of the object, event, or person.

Variation. With older gifted students, the activity might be modified to incorporate more elaborate actions rather than single objects. Examples include walking through a blizzard, competing in a pie-eating contest, or going to your first dance. These nonverbal activities can also be done in pairs, allowing the student to plan out and present the action with someone else.

Loving: Characterization

Gifted learners will interact throughout life with many different types of people and thus would do well to be familiar with and tolerant of different individuals. To assist in fulfilling this objective, teachers might prepare a visual display of expressive and diverse faces. The display should include portraits of young, middle-aged, and older individuals, along with representatives of various cultural or ethnic groups. Using this display, the teacher should engage gifted learners in a discussion by asking a variety of questions: What do you think these people are like? How does this person feel? Where do these people live, and what do they do for a living? Which of these people would you like to invite to your house?

Students should be asked to supply justifications for the answers and the various responses given could be compared or contrasted.

Variation. One way to vary this particular activity is to use tapes of various persons of different ages, cultures, or dialectic groups reading the same short passage. The same kinds of questions can then be posed.

Decision Making: Word Accuracy

In the content area of spelling, most gifted learners are required to master lists of selected words. Generally, all students are given the same sheet and are graded under the same criteria. One alternative to this procedure, and one that would foster decision making in the gifted, is to furnish the students with the term's master list of spelling words. In cooperation with the teacher the students could determine how many words they each would be responsible for each week. Also, they would agree on a particular criteria for judging their level of performance. The responsibility for selecting each week's words would be the students' and every student would be expected to chart any progress during the term. In this way, modifications could be made as necessary in the number of words learned or in the criteria used for evaluation of performance.

Variation. Rather than using a prepared master list of spelling words, the teacher might ask gifted students to decide what words they would like to learn to spell and then create a master list using these words.

Knowing: Fact or Opinion?

With the amount of information that bombards gifted learners daily, it is essential that they learn how to separate factual statements from those that are opinions. One way to teach this concept in language arts is to read students a series of statements related to some current topic (e.g., the energy crisis). As the statements are read, have the students decide whether they are fact or opinion. Then, as a follow-up, ask them to find written support for each of those statements they identified as factual and to share their supporting evidence with the class. Gifted students could also be allowed to find proof that the statements made were not based in fact and thus disprove the evidence found by others.

Variation. With younger gifteds, teachers might prefer to present a pair of statements about events significant to the children or about meaningful objects in the environment and ask students to decide which is fact and which is opinion and why. For example, the following sentences could be employed:

      A. Sunday is the best day of the week.

1.

      B. Sunday follows Saturday.

  A. Everyone should wear shoes.

2.

  B. Shoes help protect our feet.

Patterning: Critical Reading

Very important in reading is the ability to identify topic sentences and locate supporting details in a reading selection. In this activity, gifted learners are given a series of sentences selected from their reading material and are asked to rank order these according to their importance or chronologically.

Variation. Younger gifted learners might be asked to listen to a short reading selection and then individually create an appropriate title. Each student could then be given the opportunity to share the titles that were developed and compare and contrast them to those generated by the other learners.

Valuing: What a Character!

An important aspect in teaching literature to gifted learners is providing them with activities that develop the ability to identify mood, plot, and character development. This activity focuses on sharpening gifted students' skills in interpreting why characters acted as they did in a story. For this activity, teachers can have the students study a particular character and show how the actions or personality of that character changed over the course of the story and what affect these changes had on the outcome. Appropriate characters, for example, include Scrooge in *A Christmas Carol*, or Captain Ahab in *Moby Dick*.

Variation. Younger gifted learners could be involved in the same activity with minor changes in the leading material. Stories such as "Jack and the Beanstalk," or books such as *Pinocchio* and *The Grinch Who Stole Christmas* might be used with these children.

Creating: Let Me Write You a Story!

Important in every curriculum program is the need to develop activities that are relevant to the learner's interests and experiences. Therefore, in this activity, gifted learners are given the opportunity to demonstrate their creative writing abilities through a story or play. The teacher should assist gifted learners in focusing on areas in which they have some knowledge and interest. The individual stories can either be added to a collection of stories developed by the entire class or placed into the student's individual collection of stories to be later shared with other class members.

Variation. Younger gifted learners might concentrate on writing personal experience type stories. Topics might include the funniest thing that ever happened to me or the most embarrassing event in my life. The students might then develop puppet characters and perform skits of their experiences for the rest of the class.

Social Sciences

Perceiving: Social and Self-Awareness

Throughout the course of their lives, gifted students will come into contact with many types of people. The purpose of this activity, therefore, is to assist them in identifying their present feelings about others. In this activity, the teacher can develop a survey that identifies gifted students' perceptions about a particular cultural, ethnic, or special population of individuals, with the purpose of the survey being to determine students' real feelings about such individuals. After administering the survey, the teacher presents the students with a lesson that focuses on this particular group, including information about their life styles, their cultural values, their beliefs, and what kinds of work they do. After the lesson, the teacher readministers the survey and then allows the gifted students to compare their perceptions and engage in group discussion.

Variation. A variation of this activity for younger gifted children might involve the use of occupations related to their community. Before and after assessment of the students' perceptions about various occupations can be carried out in the same manner.

Communicating: Here's What I Think

There are many individuals whose actions have had a significant impact on shaping history and thus are of interest to gifted students. To initiate this activity, the teacher asks each gifted learner to select a historical figure whose actions, in the learner's estimation, have influenced particular events in history. The student prepares a brief oration and presents this to the class, attempting to persuade the audience that the actions of the selected historical figure truly had a tremendous effect in history. The class can then vote for the most influential historical figure.

Variation. To vary this activity, gifted students might be asked to assume the identity of the historical figure whom they would most like to be and give reasons for their choice.

Loving: Personal Solutions

As humans, we are constantly becoming involved in situations that are uncomfortable for us. Thus, an important part of life is learning how to cope with such situations in our own lives as well as empathizing with others who find themselves in similar predicaments. In this activity, gifted learners are first presented with profiles of individuals who are facing different situations and then asked how they personally would react to the same situation. Profiles might include, for example:

- the new child on the block
- the boy who didn't get toys for Christmas
- the individual who is disabled or handicapped in some way
- the adult who cannot find a job and support a family.

Variation. Teachers might have the students become the individual faced with an uncomfortable situation and role play how, in their opinions, the person should react to the situation. In a similar vein, one student can role play the selected individual, while other class members react to this student as they would to the actual troubled person. Afterwards, the "actors" can discuss with the rest of the class their feelings about the way they were treated.

Decision Making: You Decide!

Because of the importance of making wise judgments in day-to-day life, the purpose of this activity is to assist students in making logical decisions after carefully considering the facts. Gifted learners are assigned roles as jurors in a mock trial. After the teacher explains all the pertinent facts in the case, the students must deliberate and reach a verdict as to the innocence or guilt of the defendant. The jurors must then give the pertinent facts that helped them each make a decision.

Variation. To vary this activity the teacher might present the gifted learners with facts regarding a decision that was made and affected the lives of many people (e.g., the bombing of Hiroshima). After knowing all the facts, the students are asked to consider the situation carefully and conclude whether or not they would have made the same decision, giving reasons for their conclusions. Additionally, the students can form small groups, communicate their ideas to one another, and try to reach a single group decision.

Knowing: Cause and Effect

In this activity, the teacher's purpose is to give learners skill in identifying cause and effect relationships. The teacher presents gifted learners with the factors that influenced a significant historical event, such as the outbreak of the Revolutionary War. Once the facts have been presented, the teacher asks the students what would have occurred if some of the actual events had not turned out the way they did (e.g., what if the colonists had been represented in Parliament?).

Variation. Cause and effect can also be taught by having students think of worthwhile community fund-raising projects and then indicate what effect their fund-raising efforts might have in the future (e.g., funds for the Cancer Society might support research to find a cure for cancer).

Patterning: Time Is of the Essence

Developing a time line of important historical events is one method of teaching patterning using the social sciences. In this activity, the teacher asks the students to place a sequence of historical events, or the names of individuals who have influenced history, on a time line. Students can select different periods in history or different countries. As a group activity, students can explain their time lines and give other classmates an opportunity to review them.

Variation. As a variation, young gifted children might be asked to make a time line of the significant events in their own lives. As additional motivation, the students might construct a movie box screen, so that time lines can then be placed on a wooden roller that is used to roll the events onto the screen as the student narrates.

Valuing: Media Manipulation

Gifted learners are constantly being exposed to various media events that attempt to influence their values and beliefs. Consequently, this activity is designed to assist gifted learners in closely analyzing a type of media that has impact on all people—television. In this activity, gifted learners review various television commercials with the teacher. Afterward, the teacher asks them to work in small groups and describe the characteristics of the television commercial that tended to sway them to choose between the alternatives. The groups then present their results to the rest of the class.

Variation. As a variation for this activity, teachers might provide gifted learners with various magazines in which they can locate advertisements that promote similar products. The teacher can then ask the students to carefully examine these advertisements and to decide which one best convinced them to buy the product.

Creating: Designing a City

With our society rapidly changing, it is important that we teach gifted children to look forward to the future. Therefore, in this activity the gifted learners are given an opportunity to develop a model city of the future. The teacher asks the students to focus on such questions as: What would this city look like? What kind of problems would it face? In what ways would it be different from their own cities?

For this project, the class could be working in small groups with each developing their own city or assigned to develop various aspects on one model city.

Variation. The teacher might have younger gifted learners describe their conceptions of the ideal neighborhood. The students might be guided in focusing on questions such as: What kind of people would you find in your neighborhood? What types of jobs would people have? What kinds of fun things would there be to do?

Mathematical Skills

Perceiving: The Long and Short of It!

Weights and measurement are crucial mathematical areas and, thus, ones in which gifted students need to develop skills. At present, the conversion to the metric system requires additional mathematics skills. The purpose of this activity is to help students be more aware of things in their environment and at the same time learn measurement skills. In the classroom the teacher organizes a scavenger hunt. The purpose of the hunt is to find objects in the room that are the longest; shortest, lightest, heaviest, widest, narrowest. The students are to identify the object and present the weight or measurement required.

Variation. Younger gifted students might be asked to give all the dimensions of a single object (e.g., desk).

Communicating: Symbol Dictionary

Since mathematics is another type of language, it is important for gifted learners to master the symbols that are necessary for this language system. In this activity, the teacher explains that the students will take part in developing a mathematics dictionary. Located in this dictionary will be various mathematics symbols and the words that they represent (e.g., $=$, equals; $>$, greater than; and $\leq$, less than or equal to).

Variation. Shapes can be used as a variation for younger gifted learners. The teacher can assist the learners in developing their own picture book. Only pictures of the shapes are included, and the students review their entries by identifying the shapes. The relationship of various shapes can also be explored. For example, the picture book can show how triangles repeated can form other shapes such as a rectangle or a square.

Loving: Looking Ahead

With many problems facing the world, gifted learners should be given the opportunities to use their creative abilities to generate some answers to the perplexing questions that face society in the future. Consequently, in this activity, gifted learners are asked to analyze a potential problem facing society and, as a group, to brainstorm ways of solving this problem. For example, the teacher might present the fact that with the continuous and rapid expansion of the population, in the 21st century there may not be enough food available. In addition to developing their own ideas, gifted learners can also be asked to research what ideas are presently being worked on to prevent these problems from occurring.

Variation. Younger gifted learners might be asked to take an imaginary allowance that is given to them and outline how they would spend/save their money, explaining why they would budget their allowance this way.

Decision Making: Making and Testing Hypotheses

Problem-solving situations in daily life often require us to consider data, make reasonable hypotheses, and test the validity of our assertions. Thus, gifted learners are asked in this activity to take part in hypothesis testing. The teacher presents the students with a situation (e.g., two different shaped cylinders holding the same amount of water). The teacher then presents the problem statement. Do the two cylinders hold the same amount of water? The gifted learners are then required to state the hypothesis and test it.

Variation. To vary this activity the teacher might assist the learners by generating the hypothesis and having the students test it.

Knowing: Figure This One Out!

In order to build logical reasoning skills, the teacher might utilize riddles with gifted learners. For this activity, the teacher presents the students with various problems in logic in the form of riddles (e.g., **Q.** How far into a forest can a dog run? **A.** Half way—because the other half, it is coming out.)

Variation. Gifted learners might be asked to formulate their own riddles and ask them of other class members.

Patterning: Numberless Number Problems

In this activity, the teacher presents gifted learners with math problems in a nondigit form. The students, utilizing patterning-related skills, must then figure out the numbers represented by the graphic symbols. For example:

Problem:	DBE	Answer:	513
	+ ABC		+ 412
	FCD		925

Variation. Teachers can develop a message for the class written in numerical code and supply the corresponding letters. This activity can be a regular activity with the children, for example, being presented with a morning message delivered by a mystery person.

Valuing: You Deserve It!

Everywhere we turn today we are asked to make judgments about other people and things. In this activity gifted students work on developing a value for work and for other peoples' merits. With the aid of the teacher, the students work out a token payment system for activities they complete during the school day.

The students are also given a certain number of tokens that they may give to other class members who do something that is worth rewarding. The earned tokens can then later be redeemed for quiet personal time.

Variation. As a variation, the teacher might break the class into three small groups. Each group becomes a company and all manufacture the same product. Each company is allotted a certain amount of money, and the students must decide how to spend it. The teacher might outline categories in which money should be spent (advertising, cost of materials, labor). The students are then required to develop and carry out an advertising campaign.

Creating: Playing by the Rules

An activity that can stimulate creativity and simultaneously build problem-solving skills involves the use of games. Teachers can bring in a math game and engage the students in playing the game without specifying the rules. The students then must generate their own rules and play accordingly.

Variation. As a small group activity, gifted learners can be guided in developing their own games. The groups can then share the design of their game and engage members of other groups into playing.

Science

Perceiving: How Does It Work?

In science, being able to examine things closely, noting their characteristics and methods of functioning, is an important skill. In this activity, gifted learners are presented with an object whose functioning depends on a number of interrelated parts, such as a bicycle. The students are asked to carefully examine the bicycle or other object and describe these interrelated parts and how they function together. This activity can be done in small groups or as an independent project.

Variation. This same activity can be used with younger gifted children by utilizing less complex objects or by having the students work in groups in which each member assumes the representative movements of a single component of a complex machine, such as a sewing machine.

Communicating: Listening to Nature

There are many new scientific discoveries being made daily, and these can provide the basis for interesting classroom activities. One such discovery, which serves as a useful example, is the whale songs. In this activity, the students might be asked first to listen to the National Geographics' record of the whale songs and then to re-create in words the message they believe is being transmitted by the whales.

Variation. A variation of this activity might involve listening to various bird calls and then attempting to imitate them or translate them.

Loving: A Matter of Life or Death

Recently, there has been great attention paid to the subject of death with dignity. This activity permits older gifteds to explore their feelings about gravely ill individuals' rights to maintain or end their lives. The students are given cases of individuals who are facing various medical problems and whose prognosis is bleak. The students are asked to freely express their feelings as to whether medical treatment should be continued for these individuals or whether the person should be allowed to die. The students are asked to give their reasons for their decisions and are encouraged to discuss their conclusions with other class members. It must be cautioned that such a controversial topic must be handled with sensitivity by the instructor and group.

Variation. For younger gifted learners, this activity might involve the subject of putting stray animals to sleep because of a potential problem with overpopulation. Gifted students might be asked to deal with this topic in a discussion format after first being given an opportunity to thoroughly gather information on the subject.

Decision Making: Science Surprise!

In science, gifted learners will need to utilize decision-making skills as they follow through with various experiments. In this activity, gifted learners are presented with the materials needed to complete a particular experiment without telling the students what experiment they are to complete. The students' task is to manipulate the materials they were provided and to develop a valid experiment, both stating and proving a hypothesis.

Variation. In this activity, teachers present gifted students with a box containing various items. On the front of the box is a printed statement of the box's contents in the form of a riddle (e.g., Riddle: I am a foot in length but I am not a part of your body—What am I? Answer: Ruler. Riddle: A sleeping caterpillar you will find hiding inside; soon it will become a beautiful butterfly—What am I? Answer: Cocoon).

Knowing: Fantasy or Fact?

As new information is constantly being generated and added to what is already known, it becomes increasingly important that gifted learners develop skills that enable them to make hypotheses about the future. The purpose of this activity is to allow gifted learners to utilize the knowledge they already have to make valid predictions. The teacher presents the learners with science fiction literature that has now become more factual (e.g., George Orwell's *1984*, or Jules Verne's *Twenty Thousand Leagues Under the Sea*). The teacher shows students how information found in literature that was once considered fiction has now become fact. The students are then presented with current science fiction from writers such as Asimov and asked to analyze the work and make predictions as to what they believe will become fact and why.

Variation. Younger gifted children can exchange ideas on what they believe will happen in the future. Current science fiction movies can be used as a basis for discussion.

Patterning: A Touch of Class

An important skill in the learning of science is the ability to place various plants and animals into higher order classifications. Therefore, in this activity gifted learners are given various plant or animal categories and asked to place them into the appropriate classifications.

Variation. Younger gifted children may be presented with pictures of various animals. The students are to categorize the animals according to shared characteristics. The same animal may be placed in various categories depending on the characteristics the students select.

Valuing: It's Your Future . . .

The purpose of this activity is to increase gifted learners' knowledge of various emotional issues in science, thus developing or modifying beliefs about these issues. In this activity, gifted learners are presented with a continuing situation, such as the future impact of genetic manipulation. In a small group, or as an independent activity, the students must give some ideas as to the possible ramifications of such practices. The students are then asked to present and discuss other scientific or medical issues that will have impact on society in the future.

Variation. To vary this activity, teachers can ask gifted learners to generate their own science fiction for the year 2180. Using existing knowledge, students can generate ideas about what will happen in the future; however, all of their ideas must be based on current fact. Afterward, they might discuss whether or not they would like to live in the kind of futures that they created and why.

Creating: Designing Mr. (or Ms.) Right

Creative activities can be effectively utilized even in the area of science. For example, gifted students can be given the opportunity to create the perfect human by integrating the features of numerous actual humans they would like this being to have (e.g., the mind of Einstein, the strength of Charles Atlas). After completing the activity, students can share their perfect humans with the class.

Variation. To vary this activity, younger gifted learners could be presented with the materials to make a picture collage of their conceptualization of the perfect human.

Arts/Music

Perceiving: Artful Comparisons

In the arts and music field, gifted learners will be exposed to various forms of the arts. In this activity, gifted learners are first presented with art works produced during several periods (e.g., postimpressionism) and they are asked to compare and contrast these works of art, discussing both the obvious and subtle similarities and differences in these pieces. Areas for discussion may include the common elements found in each of the works, the style of presentation, and the artist's manipulation of the medium to produce the outcome.

Variation. As a variation of this activity, gifted learners may be presented with music from various periods. After listening to the music, the students can be asked to identify the instruments used to produce the pieces and relate to their classmates what mood the music conveys.

Communicating: Interpretative Dance

In the classroom, gifted learners should be given many opportunities to express themselves in various ways. One way to assist gifted learners to broaden their means of communication is having them interpret various musical pieces through movement. Examples of appropriate musical pieces include "Danse Macabre" by Saint Saens, or music from "The Nutcracker Suite" by Tchaikovsky. Following the presentation, the students are given the opportunity to use movement to express the feelings the music conveys.

Variation. This activity can also be used with younger gifted learners by altering the musical process. The students might be exposed to the music of the "Baby Elephant Walk" by Mancini and express themselves by role playing elephants.

Loving: Poetic License

One important art form is that of poetry. In this activity, gifted learners are first given the opportunity to examine various pieces of poetry and then are asked to compose their own poems. For example, the students might write poems to inanimate objects:

Ode to a Pencil
Oh, Dear Pencil, I love your grace.
You write so quickly, or erase.
Teacher thinks my handwriting's best,
But I just push and you do the rest.

The students can then be asked to share their poems with the class or make collages of the poems for a class bulletin board.

Variation. To vary this activity, teachers might ask the gifted learners to pretend that they are the inanimate object and write a poem rhyming or nonrhyming describing their feelings.

Decision Making: Who Says It's Art!!

There are many opportunities that can be provided to the gifted learners to develop decision-making skills in the arts and music areas. For example, gifted learners can be guided in developing criteria for evaluating art. Next, they are exposed to various art forms and asked to analyze these according to their criteria.

Variation. Gifted learners, as a variation of this activity, can be exposed to various criteria that are utilized to evaluate art. Afterwards, the students can be exposed to various art works and asked to determine which of the pieces fit the criteria presented.

Knowing: I've Got a Feeling . . .

Art and music may hold special meaning for gifted children and can provide excellent media for self-expression. In this activity, the gifted learner is presented with various musical compositions and asked to interpret through art the feelings the music conveys. The students can then share their work with each other and discuss the type of mood their own art work conveys.

Variation. The gifted learners can be presented with various works of art and asked to comment on the moods these works convey. The students can also be encouraged to read the artists' biographies, looking for clues as to events in their lives that may have influenced the art.

Patterning: Shape Up!

Analyzing art well is a useful skill; thus, this activity focuses on one component of art analysis. In this activity, gifted learners are first presented with various art forms and then, with the teacher's guidance, are asked to identify the different geometric shapes that are present in the art.

Variation. This activity can be varied for younger gifted learners by giving them opportunities to individually create an artistic piece utilizing various geometric shapes. The learners can share their work with others in the class, explaining why they selected the particular shapes focused in their work.

Valuing: The Art of Campaigning

As gifted learners are exposed to various forms of art, they may come to value various art media. In this activity, gifted learners are given an opportunity to enthusiastically promote the type of art they like best. The gifted learners are encouraged to select a piece of art or music and organize a campaign, complete with original posters and slogans, to generate interest for the work they think is best. The teacher may also choose to focus students' attention on one particular art form or period of art. Students then select and campaign for their favorite piece of art.

Variation. A variation of this activity is to have gifted learners bring in art pieces of their own, which may include any type of art the students may have collected. The students then must give their criteria for considering the piece a work of art.

Creating: Let's Dance!

Dance is a form of art that gifted learners should come to appreciate. Therefore, in this activity, gifted learners are given the opportunity to select a piece of art and corresponding music and then are encouraged to interpret the art and music in creative movement and present their creations to the class.

Variation. Sometimes students will be reluctant to demonstrate their creations individually. Therefore, to vary this activity, the teacher can have small groups of students, or perhaps the entire class, design and demonstrate creative movement together.

SUMMARY

The principal aim of this chapter on the gifted curriculum has been to demonstrate that no structured content and no set of behaviorally stated objectives can be passed along from institution to institution, from classroom to classroom, or from individual to individual as the curriculum for the gifted. To produce the most effective instruction possible, initiators of the gifted program must not only consider content to be learned but also the general processes underlying learning and the individuals to whom the content is to be applied. This, in essence, is the nature of the holistic curriculum that relates the elements of learned content, learning processes, and learning style.

While the learning processes presented here were taken from the writings of Berman (1968), perhaps other general yet equally important processes could be established as the focus of the gifted curriculum. Numerous examples were presented, however, to show how these particular processes might appear within certain segments of the instructional content. What is most essential for program developers to remember, however, is that the learner and that learner's style are central to the curriculum. Therefore, maximum effectiveness of the gifted curriculum hinges on its ability to relate to the learner's abilities, needs, and interests.

REFERENCES

Berman, L. *New priorities in the curriculum*. Columbus, Ohio: Charles E. Merrill, 1968.

Dunn, R., & Price, G. The learning style characteristics of gifted students. *Gifted Child Quarterly*, 1980, *24*, 33-36.

Flavell, J. H. *Cognitive-development*. Englewood Cliffs, N.J.: Prentice-Hall, 1977.

Griggs, S., & Price, G. Learning styles of the gifted. In J.W. Keefe (Ed.), *Learning style: An overview in student learning styles: Diagnosing and prescribing programs*. Reston, Va.: The National Association of Secondary School Principals, 1979.

Keefe, J. W. *Learning style: An overview in student learning styles: Diagnosing and prescribing programs*. Reston, Va.: The National Association of Secondary School Principals, 1979.

Rumelhart, D. E. Schemata: The building blocks of cognition. In R. J. Spiro, B.C. Bruce, & W. F. Brewer (Eds.), *Theoretical issues in reading comprehension*. Hillsdale, N.J.: Lawrence Erlbaum, 1980.

Saurerman, D., & Michael, W. Differential placement of high-achieving and low-achieving gifted pupils in grades four, five and six on measures of field-dependence, field-independence, creativity and self concept. *Gifted Child Quarterly*, 1980, *24*, 81-85.

Chapter 8

Financing the Gifted Program

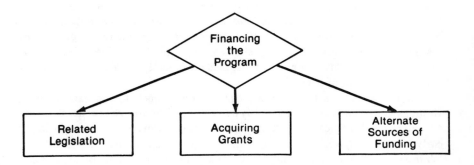

One of the major purposes of all gifted programs is to provide these learners with differentiated education, thus assisting them in identifying and working toward fulfillment of their potential. One important element necessary in reaching this objective is the identification and acquisition of the funds needed to provide gifted learners with the alternate educational experiences so vital to their development.

It is not necessary to spend a great deal of time building a case for the importance of funds to support educational programs, because those educators who have found themselves working in programs without adequate resources realize how difficult it becomes to meet the established objectives. While there are those in education who believe that everyone should rally around a worthwhile project, the realism of the times becomes glaringly apparent—everything costs money. Qualified teachers, materials and resources, facilities, transportation, and new educational experiences every year are drastically increasing in cost. Consequently, as the movement in gifted education begins to surge in this country and the demand for new educational programs for the gifted becomes apparent, the search for funding is, and will continue to be, extremely competitive. Therefore, it is essential that those individuals planning programs at the local, state, and higher educational levels develop both an acute awareness of possible funding sources and the skills to successfully acquire these funds.

Owing to the importance of these factors, the initial purpose of this chapter is to present an in-depth analysis of current gifted legislation, which provides financial assistance for the development of gifted programs. A second purpose is to outline other potential federal and nonfederal sources of funding, and a third purpose is to provide a framework for developing project proposals.

GIFTED LEGISLATION

A Historical Review

Before examining the guidelines of current gifted legislation to which all federally funded gifted programs must adhere, it is necessary first to describe briefly the historical development of the growing national interest in gifted learners. In so doing, focus will be placed on the important legislative milestones that have actively and convincingly demonstrated the federal government's concern for and support of gifted education.

While interest in gifted learners can be traced back to the early work of Hollingsworth and Terman, it has only been within the past two decades that gifted education has become a subject of government concern. Prior to and during the early 1960s very little action was generated in gifted education at the federal level. Williams (1978) reports that outside of a few publications put out by the Office of Education about gifted learners, there was no other interest shown during this time. Whatever gifted programming existed in schools was spurred on by those educators who recognized that gifted children were different in many ways from the child in the mainstream and, consequently, required special adjustments in instruction to meet their needs.

However, in 1969, the tide began to turn with the passing of the Elementary and Secondary Amendments of 1969 (i.e., Public Law 91-230). Section 806 of this law, which specifically focused on the gifted and talented child, stipulated that Title III and Title V of the Elementary and Secondary Education Act, as well as the Teacher Fellowship Provision of Higher Education Act of 1956, should be applied to the gifted. Likewise, the law stipulated that a study be conducted to determine if the needs of the gifted were being met in the nation's schools (Williams, 1978). The resulting study, which is referred to as the Marland Report of 1971, presented startling information depicting the waste of potential in gifted and talented learners owing to the poor educational services being provided for them. The impact of this study brought with it a shifting in the tide in gifted education (and renewed interest in leadership and responsibility for gifted education by the federal Office of Education).

To ensure its leadership role, the Office of Education developed the Office of the Gifted and Talented. One of the purposes of the new office was to rekindle interest in the gifted. The Gifted and Talented Office had no funding appropriated to it and relied heavily on monies obtained under other acts and title programs for which the gifted would qualify.

Then, in 1974, the federal government made a greater commitment to gifted education with the passage of the Special Projects Act (Public Law 93-380). Section 404 of this act specifically referred to gifted and talented learners and provided money that was to be distributed by the Office of the Gifted and Talented directly to public and private agencies.

There are two important aspects of this act that are somewhat different from current legislation. First, all of the allocation of financial resources was under a discretionary grant program. Under this type of system, there were no direct allotments of funds designated for state educational agencies alone. The Office of the Gifted and Talented established funding priorities and reviewed a variety of proposals and projects from which all those who qualified for funding, including states, local education agencies, institutions of higher education, and other non-profit institutions, competed. Second, appropriations were distributed directly through the Office of the Gifted and Talented and not through any state disbursement programs. Furthermore, several important aspects of this law laid the groundwork for future gifted legislation:

- The Office of the Gifted and Talented was officially recognized as coordinator of all projects and programs for the gifted and talented.

- State educational grants and local educational grants were authorized to assist these agencies in the planning, development, operation, and improvement of programs and projects for the gifted and talented.

- Grants to state educational agencies could be awarded to institutions of higher education for preparing pre-service and in-service educators for working with the gifted.

- Grants to higher education and other nonprofit agencies were made to provide leadership personnel for the education of gifted and talented children and youth.

- Funds were transferred to the National Institute of Education to carry on research and related activities that included research training, surveys, demonstration, or dissemination of information about gifted and talented children.

- Contracts with public and private agencies and organizations were authorized for the establishment and operation of model projects for the identification and education of talented children (e.g., career education, bilingual education, and programs for education of handicapped and educationally disadvantaged children).

Gifted and Talented Children's Act (PL 95-561)

In November 1978, Congress restructured the existing act and entitled it the Gifted and Talented Children's Act (Public Law 95-561, Part A, Title IX of the Elementary and Secondary Education Act). Unlike Public Law 93-380, the Special Projects Act, this particular law provided that the majority of allotted funds (75 percent) was to be designated for state-administered programs and distributed directly and competitively by the states to local educational agencies. Only 25 percent would be distributed directly by the Office of the Gifted and Talented under a discretionary grant program. As is evident from the distribution of funds, this law placed much of the responsibility with state educational agencies. While the salient features of Public Law 95-561 are presented in Table 4-1, some important guidelines that are mandated by the law are outlined in Table 8-1.

Framework of the Gifted and Talented Children's Act

Overview of the Law. The Gifted and Talented Children's Act of 1978 provides a wide range of opportunities for both public and private agencies to acquire funds to improve educational services for the gifted and talented. In the state-administered section of the law, states that make applications according to the guidelines set down by the Office of Gifted and Talented, as well as those that meet the assurances stipulated in the law, would receive a direct allotment of at least $50,000 yearly up to a three-year period. (This figure may vary depending on funding.) In addition, states may also take part in developing proposals and compete with other states for additional funds. The intent of the state-administered part of the law is to enable states to assist local school divisions in the improvement of services for the gifted. Consequently, 90 percent of the funds acquired by the states in this portion of the law must be distributed competitively to local school divisions. The remaining 10 percent of funds can be used by the states to assist in their own planning and in providing assistance to those school divisions that do not have the resources to compete in preparing proposals or in planning, developing, and operating gifted programs.

In the discretionary section of the law, 25 percent of the federal funds are distributed on a competitive basis to public and private institutions, with the commissioner selecting certain activities as priorities in any given year.

In the discretionary program three types of programs are supported:

1. *Statewide activities projects.* Funding for these is available for states only and can focus on providing a statewide plan for meeting the needs of gifted and talented. In addition, these funds can be used to develop innovative strategies to provide assistance to local school divisions.
2. *Educational service projects and model projects.* All public and private agencies are eligible for funds, the intent of which is to develop innovative

approaches for gifted and talented, especially for those from special populations.

3. *Professional development.* All public and private agencies are eligible for funds under this section. Emphasis in these projects is placed on providing training and development of materials to be used in preparing educators to meet the needs of gifted.

General Mandates. The law specifically mandates that any project involving gifted and talented children that is submitted for funding must contain two important elements. First, the project must include the utilization of comprehensive and multiple methods of identification of giftedness and talent and assessment of the needs of these special children. The term "comprehensive" focuses specifically on all those children who come within the service category outlined by the project, including children from special populations (e.g., handicapped, culturally different) and who additionally are in the geographic area to be serviced by the project. "Multiple" refers to the use of at least two methods of identifying the gifted and talented and includes teacher nomination, intelligence tests, peer nomination, and measures of creativity, for example. Regardless of what methods are selected, however, it is important that the project developer establish a relationship between the methods selected and the overall purposes of the program. In addition, proposals involving gifted and talented learners must include a component that outlines the provision of differentiated or specialized educational services for the gifted and talented.

A second important provision of this act is that public and private agencies receiving funding must contribute 10 percent as their share in the project either "in cash" or "in kind." This 10 percent contribution applies to all projects except those that involve students from nonprofit elementary or secondary schools as well as those funds supporting clearinghouse activities (i.e., information dissemination), research, evaluation, and related activities.

A third major provision, which will again be mentioned later in this discussion, is the provision of opportunities for gifted and talented children and their teachers in private, nonprofit schools to take part in gifted programs and workshops conducted by local public schools. This requirement is to be carried out unless the state educational agency determines that this procedure cannot legally be accomplished in the state.

State Mandates. There are some additional provisions in the law that outline specifically the state's responsibilities. Overall, one of the most important regulations for the states is that in applying for funds a plan must be outlined and a set of criteria should be developed that will ensure that 90 percent of the money received will be made available to local school divisions on a competitive basis. In addition, this plan must include criteria for ensuring that at least 50 percent of the funds made

Table 8-1 Overview of Gifted and Talented Education Act of 1978

Type of Program	Matching Funds Required	Special Provisions	Guidelines for Local Distribution	Local Duration
State administered program (75% of federal funds)	10% "cash" or "in kind"— except projects involving the participation of students in nonprofit private elementary or secondary schools/clearinghouse activities and research, evaluation, and related activities	States must use at least 50% of funds for programs and projects that include a component for identification and education of disadvantaged gifted and talented children from low income families	1. States must distribute 90% of funds received on competitive basis to local educational agencies 2. States can utilize remaining 10% for statewide planning and coordination/administrative and technical assistance and in-service training	States cannot fund local educational agencies in excess of 5 years
Discretionary program (25% of federal funds)	10% "cash" or "in kind"— except projects involving the participation of students in nonprofit private elementary or secondary schools/clearinghouse activities and research, evaluation, and related activities	20% of funds to conduct directly or by grant or contract a program of research evaluation and related activities (carried out by National Institute of Education) Not more than 20% to be granted to institutions of higher education for the training of national leadership personnel	*Three types of programs funded under discretionary grant program (and examples)* 1. *Statewide, activities, projects* (available for state only): Develop a statewide approach to meet needs of gifted and talented. Involve representatives of parent group and other public and private organizations interested in gifted. Develop innovative strategies for identification and assistance for gifted, specially special gifted. Provide help to private schools, to meet needs of gifted. Provide in-service training. 2. *Educational service projects and model projects:* Provide innovative demonstration or model approaches for education of gifted and talented, targeted toward special populations, e.g., bilingual, handicapped. Focus on particular category of educational service (e.g., early childhood education, arts education). Operate, improve, or expand existing educational projects. 3. *Professional development:* Includes in-service training and leadership training. Other activities include graduate level instruction leading to degree in education of gifted and talented. Short-term courses and instruction seminars, internships, and work training experiences with specialized training materials. Workshops and conferences.	

Eligible	Purpose	Methods of Federal Distribution	Federal Duration
State educational agencies (all 50 states and territories)	To provide support for local educational agencies To plan, develop, operate, and improve programs to meet the needs of the gifted and talented at preschool, elementary, and secondary levels.	1. Direct state allotments ($50,000 to each state, may vary according to funding. 2. Competitve grants to states Budget period for both No. 1 and No. 2 will be 12 months.	States receive funding each year for 3-year period Yearly renewal application
1. State educational agencies 2. Local, educational agencies 3. Institutions of higher education 4. Other public and private organi-zations 5. Combinations of above 6. Contracts with public or private agencies	To assist in establishing and maintaining projects To plan, develop, operate, and improve programs To meet special educational needs of gifted and talented, including the training of personnel engaged in education of gifted and talented children or the supervision of personnel	1. Competitive grants	12-month period (Applicants may apply for multi-year project)

available to local school divisions serve the special educational needs of disadvantaged gifted and talented children from low income families.

A second major mandate that the states must adhere to is providing technical assistance to local school divisions that are unable, because of their size or resources, to compete with other local agencies in the planning, development, or implementation of gifted programs. Funds from this assistance may be utilized from the remaining 10 percent that is not disbursed on a competitive basis. States may also use part of this money for statewide planning, coordination, and in-service training.

As was mentioned, this law ensures that gifted learners and their teachers in nonprofit private elementary and secondary schools receive the opportunity to take part in gifted programs funded at the local school level. Therefore, it becomes the state's responsibility to ensure that the local educational agencies have attempted to equitably involve gifted children and their teachers in the gifted program.

Mandates for Local Educational Agencies. Local educational agencies applying for funds must have as part of their projects provisions that demonstrate how students from the nonprofit private elementary and secondary schools will participate in such programs. Projects that do not have this component cannot be approved by the state educational agencies. This law also allows local educational agencies to use funds initially designed for educational projects or in-service training. In addition, prior to submitting funding applications, local educational agencies must hold an open, public meeting to give the community an opportunity to comment on its application for funding.

As is evident from a review of this law, there are many assurances that must be met before public and private agencies are qualified to receive funds. The review of the law within this chapter only presents the important mandates that must be met when applying for funding. There are, however, other aspects of the law and specific criteria that must also be carefully scrutinized before applying for funds. Project developers who are considering making an application for funding should consult the actual Gifted and Talented Education Act of 1978 (PL 95-561) and the regulations of the law found in the *Federal Register,* Thursday, April 3, 1980, Part VIII.

ACQUIRING FUNDS—A NECESSARY HEADACHE?

There are a variety of sources for funding in this country, and those who have become skillful at convincing such agencies that their projects are worth funding inevitably experience both rewards and headaches. While on the surface it may appear that seeking and acquiring funds is a type of Alice in Wonderland adventure, it soon becomes apparent that the many benefits accrued from this undertaking are accompanied by much hard work and many frustrations. For example, those who are fortunate in acquiring funds face the arduous task of administering the grant in ways that meet the assurances stipulated by the funding agencies while at the same time meeting the objectives outlined in their specific proposals.

A prevailing opinion evident in education is that obtaining funding for a program is to be considered an art because of the many facets involved in obtaining funds and the stiff competition for such monies. Therefore, it is essential that those individuals responsible for program development acquire skills that go beyond the actual preparation of the proposal and seek a broader understanding of the appropriate avenues to funding, as well as the processes necessary to develop and implement an idea. Consequently, those individuals interested in funding must work through a process that is not individual but group oriented and is active, not passive, in nature.

Stages of Proposal Development

As was pointed out earlier, the Gifted and Talented Education Act (PL 95-561) has several sets of criteria by which it evaluates various types of project proposals. Sometimes, as new programs are initiated and new guidelines are set, these criteria may change. However, there are important elements that should be and often are found in all regulations or proposal outlines. These elements will be discussed in the remainder of this chapter.

As is evident from Exhibit 8-1, there are several stages that should be followed in the process of developing a project proposal.

Stage I: Idea Formulation

It is in this stage that the idea for the project is formulated and that the person developing the proposal (preferably the project director) reflects on an area of concern. This stage of formulating the idea is important because it is here that the groundwork is laid for all that will follow throughout this process.

In this stage of idea formulation, it is important that the project developer use the information gained from the needs assessment described in Chapter 3 to pinpoint problem areas that may impede gifted learners from working toward their potential. Most likely, a number of need areas will be generated from this thinking process. While many of these areas may be worth pursuing, it is preferable that the project developer reduce these many areas to a few that not only have educational importance but also are of manageable proportions. Responses to the questions that follow may assist in narrowing the need areas. In addition, the project developer can, by reflecting on these questions, determine if an idea is one that is worth pursuing.

- Is the identified area one that has implications for the psychological, social, and emotional development of gifted learners?

Exhibit 8-1 Stages in Developing a Grant Proposal

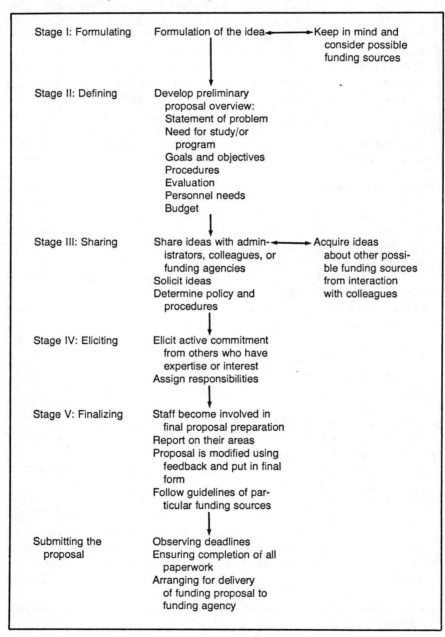

Stage I: Formulating   Formulation of the idea ←→ Keep in mind and
                                                 consider possible
                                                 funding sources

Stage II: Defining   Develop preliminary
                         proposal overview:
                         Statement of problem
                         Need for study/or
                            program
                         Goals and objectives
                         Procedures
                         Evaluation
                         Personnel needs
                         Budget

Stage III: Sharing   Share ideas with admin- ←→ Acquire ideas
                         istrators, colleagues, or   about other possi-
                         funding agencies   ble funding sources
                      Solicit ideas   from interaction
                      Determine policy and   with colleagues
                         procedures

Stage IV: Eliciting   Elicit active commitment
                         from others who have
                         expertise or interest
                      Assign responsibilities

Stage V: Finalizing   Staff become involved in
                         final proposal preparation
                      Report on their areas
                      Proposal is modified using
                         feedback and put in final
                         form
                      Follow guidelines of par-
                         ticular funding sources

Submitting the   Observing deadlines
   proposal   Ensuring completion of all
                         paperwork
                      Arranging for delivery
                         of funding proposal to
                         funding agency

- Is the formulated idea one that has constantly been reviewed throughout the research, or is it one that is timely but relatively undocumented?

- Is the idea one that if developed into a proposal will complement the overall objectives of this school and gifted program?

- Is the idea one that fits into the overall goals and objectives established by the funding source(s)?

- Is the idea one that if funded can be carried out successfully given the types of resources available in our program?

As the project developer focuses attention on identifying a relative problem area, there is constant thought given to the overall goals and specific objectives that will need to be defined, as well as to procedures and strategies that might be applicable to meet these objectives and to the types of specific staffing and facilities that will be needed to carry out the proposed idea. Furthermore, the project developer or those involved in this process should keep in mind possible funding sources.

As was mentioned previously, there are various types of funding available. Some, as will be presented later, are specifically earmarked for gifted education; others encompass academic areas or special populations in which gifted children may be identified (refer to Appendix B for information about alternate funding sources). Funding sources that should be given consideration include federal, state, and local government programs, private individuals, corporations, and foundations. It is important when seeking funding sources that no stone be left unturned. The many funding sources beyond federal, state, and local programs are to a certain degree more difficult to locate and obtain but nevertheless provide alternate sources of aid. To save time and effort and, eventually, frustration, it is vitally important that the project developer carefully research possible funding sources, eliminating as possibilities those whose overall philosophies and goals do not coincide with those of both the gifted program and the proposed idea. An annotated list of alternate funding sources that should be considered is presented in Appendix B.

Once the project developer has given due consideration to the selection of an appropriate problem area and funding source, stage II can effectively be implemented.

Stage II: Defining

In this stage of development, the project developer actually brings some specificity to the idea by developing a preliminary proposal overview. Undergoing this process enables the project developer first to define the idea by specifying the goals and objectives of the project as well as any other needs that will assist in meeting these goals and objectives. Second, this procedure provides a working draft that the project developer can share with others (who may be directly or indirectly responsible for the approval of such an idea) and, in addition, enables the project developer to acquire the feedback of other colleagues. Third, this working draft in its expanded form will later reflect the finished proposal.

In this stage, it is vital that the project developer convey all the necessary aspects of the idea in a clear and concise manner. A lengthy and verbose preliminary proposal will turn others off and thus run the risk of not being read. On the other hand, enough information should be provided so that the reader is not left puzzled about the idea and its implementation process. Additionally, there are several elements that are essential for the development of a good proposal and that should be included in the preliminary proposal. These elements are comprised of the statement of the problem, the need for the study or program, goals and objectives, procedures, evaluation design, personnel needs, cost, and advantages for others. While these elements will be discussed in more detail in stage V, it is important to mention briefly some important points when developing the preliminary proposal.

As the project developer in stage II focuses on the elements that need to be addressed in developing the proposal overview, attention should also be given, as mentioned previously, to the possible funding sources whose philosophies and goals are similar to the idea that will be developed. In addition, it is important that the project developer, while defining the problem in writing, place emphasis on convincing the funding agency that the proposed idea truly identifies a real problem relevant to the agency's own interests and that the proposed study or program in some way either attempts to find a solution to the problem or sheds more light on ways to deal more effectively with the problem. Since all of the many competitors will attempt to convince the funding agency of the superior relevance and worthiness of their particular projects, it is crucial that the project developer present a strong case for the need for a specific project. Likewise, it is important to propose overall goals and specific objectives that focus on what will be accomplished by the study or program, as well as proposing a clear method for evaluating the success of such a program.

Final points that must be considered are the overall cost of the program, as well as its needs. A proposal whose cost is unrealistic and that requires a large staff will meet with skepticism both when presented to the local persons involved in the process and to those who will be funding the proposal itself. Interaction with these individuals constitutes the next stage of proposal development.

Stage III: Sharing

One of the most important aspects of getting a proposal off the ground is soliciting feedback about the proposed idea from immediate administrators, supervisors, and colleagues. This is a very important stage in proposal development for a number of reasons. First, whether it is state, local, or higher levels of education that are being approached for funds, there usually will be a series of procedures that the proposal must go through before it can be submitted. If the institution housing the grant has, as is often the case, a specified procedure to follow, the administrator can provide this information to the project developer. Because this procedure is very often a complicated and elaborate process, the project developer would do well to seek the assistance of the supervisor or administrator, who, in addition to explaining the correct procedures, may also be able to speed up the process. A second benefit of sharing the preliminary proposal is that it enables administrators, supervisors, and colleagues to give their reaction to the proposed ideas as well as to provide any suggestions that would strengthen the proposal. The project proposal developer might, as a guideline, give those reading the proposal a series of questions to think about and react to. Questions such as the following might be presented:

- Is the proposed project one that focuses on an important need, has broad educational implications, and should be pursued?

- Is this project consistent with the overall goals and objectives of our own institution and in line with our present educational philosophy?

- Are the goals and objectives proposed in this project important and realistic?

- Are there any specific funding sources you are aware of whose philosophy and goals would be consistent with this proposed project and may be worth pursuing?

- Are there any specific modifications you would make to strengthen this proposal?

- Are there any particular abilities or interests you have that may be beneficial to this project?

This last question leads us into the next stage, that of eliciting support for the proposal.

Stage IV: Eliciting

While in stage III the project developer attempts to get the reactions and opinions of administrators and other staff, in stage IV the project developer is actually seeking a commitment from the staff to become actively involved in assisting in the development of the proposal and likewise taking part in carrying out the proposed study or program. Staff who have indicated special abilities or areas of interest that would be beneficial to the proposed project might be assigned the specific task of developing a particular area of the proposal that reflects these special skills. While it is possible for one person to develop a proposal, it is certainly not advisable, for there are many different aspects to effective program development that go beyond the formal writing procedure. Depending on the type of project, there is often much leg work and research to be done. Enlisting the aid of other staff, especially those who may eventually become involved in the project, will not only save the project developer much needed time and effort but will also enable those who eventually may be asked to implement the project to give their input into its development. Consequently, the project becomes group oriented, such that all involved take credit for its successes and assume responsibility for its failures. When such cooperation is effectively enacted, the involved individuals are ready to engage in the fifth and final stage.

Stage V: Finalizing

The finalizing stage is one in which the proposal is modified according to the suggestions and put into final form. The finalizing stage is an active group process in which those who have expressed interest in working on the project and have been assigned responsibilities report the results of their findings and assist in the actual preparation of the final document. As was mentioned earlier, all those involved in preparing the project share ideas about possible funding sources. By this time in the process, a particular funding source should have already been decided on and the pertinent information about the agency (its guidelines, goals, and priority areas) should be thoroughly familiar to all of the members. In preparing the document for final form, those involved with developing the proposal utilize the same elements described in the preliminary proposal development, discussed in stage II. These elements are expanded to present an in-depth analysis of the project. Some important points to remember when engaging in this process include the following:

Statement of the Problem. In stating the problem that is to be addressed by the proposed project, it is important that the project deal with a true need and that there is indeed a real problem. It is essential, then, that the importance of this problem and its implicatons for gifted learners be demonstrated adequately. Generally, the broader the implications of the proposed study, the more likely a funding agency, especially those dispensing federal monies, will be impressed by the project and give it support. However, the proposal's presentation of the problem should be narrow enough in scope to be manageable by the proposer and thus convince reviewers that the project developer has a true grasp of the elements of the problem and consequently will be able to carry out the project effectively. Therefore, not only should problem statements focus on a manageable element that has far reaching effects, but it should also present enough evidence to convince the reviewer that the examination of this identified problem is within the capabilities of the institution proposing the project.

Need for the Study. Directly linked to the statement of the problem is the demonstration that there is truly a need to focus on this particular problem. Establishing the need for the study or program is important because it enables reviewers to see that one's grasp of the problem goes beyond the ability to define it. In building a case for the need for the study or program, a review of the literature pertinent to the proposed project should be completed. When reporting the review of literature, it is important to present the information in summary form. Sometimes the technical information related to studies or programs makes for boring reading and may quickly turn off a reviewer to a study or program that otherwise has merit.

Another important factor that must be considered when writing this section is the need to make sure that the summary flows smoothly. At times there are studies and programs that may have some indirect implication and pertinence to the proposed study. While all avenues must be explored when building the need for the study, it is important that studies that indirectly relate to the proposed projects flow smoothly so that it does not appear that these studies were haphazardly inserted as fillers.

Goals and Objectives. The goals and objectives of the proposed project indicate what it is that will be achieved by this particular program. While there may be several goals of the intended project that may be stated in broad terms, the objectives are the specific means by which these goals will be achieved. Preferably, the objectives should be written in measurable terms, because those that deal with realistic and measurable outcomes are more likely to be seen as plausible by grant reviewers. Guidelines for writing effective behavioral objectives are presented in Chapter 4.

Unfortunately, there is a tendency in developing project proposals to believe that the more objectives there are, the more worthwhile and impressive the project. This is an erroneous notion, which, if followed, could lead to the rejection of the proposal. Since there is only so much that can be accomplished throughout the duration of any one project, the specification of many objectives to be attained may make grant reviewers skeptical of the project's ability to effectively accomplish these objectives. Thus, one should bear in mind that the only objectives to be included in the proposal are those that can feasibly be met by the project.

Procedures. The procedures are an important section of the proposal because it is here that the project developer identifies the method or methods that will be used to accomplish the stated goals and objectives of the project. When writing a project for funding, it is essential that nothing be left to the imagination of the grant reviewers. Therefore, it is important for project developers not only to specify exactly what will be done during the course of the project, but also the time frame in which they will be completed and who specifically will be responsible for each element. Very often, a time line is utilized to vividly show the framework within which the program will evolve. This framework is also useful during the project's evaluation phase. In Exhibit 8-2, a time line is shown that presents an example of the major tasks and subtasks to be accomplished.

Evaluation. If the project involves an evaluative study, a description of the appropriate statistical design should be presented (see Chapter 9). What is important in writing this section of the proposal is the need for the project developer to substantiate the particular method chosen to accomplish the stated objectives. The funding agency should feel comfortable that the project proposer has a sufficient understanding of other project developers' previous attempts at similar research, and, in utilizing this information, has based the proposed idea on a sound rationale.

The evaluation model designed will be largely dependent on the project and thus will vary considerably. Those institutions generating project proposals that are of a research nature will most likely use an experimental design that is appropriate for the project proposed. It is important in selecting such a design that the project proposers are either themselves thoroughly familiar with various experimental designs or have access to a resource person who can assist in designing the study and preparing the computer program to analyze the data. On the other hand, most school divisions and state agencies seeking funding will, a large percentage of the time, be proposing projects focusing on some aspects of program development that, in essence, have as their immediate objective the improvement of instruction. Therefore, the evaluation design of such a project will include periodic feedback, which occurs throughout the implementation of the program, and the final evaluation, which measures the outcomes of the proposed project against the stated objectives. To assist in both aspects of the evaluation, a time line, as described and presented in Exhibit 8-2, can be used. Periodic feedback enables project directors and staff to determine how the program is progressing, if the objectives are being met according to the proposed framework, and whether modifications need to be made to ensure the program's continued effectiveness. In completing the final evaluation, the question that is sought is how well did we accomplish what we said we would. More information on evaluation models is presented in Chapter 9.

Personnel Needs. In identifying personnel needs, it is essential that project developers not only identify those who will be directly involved in the program or study but, in addition, show the particular qualifications each of these individuals possesses that are relevant to the success of the proposed project. Very often, funding agencies will request that information on the personnel be presented, but even if they do not, a brief résumé outlining the particular qualifications the person brings to the project should be included in the appendices.

Sometimes some personnel needs will be provided by the institution sponsoring the grant proposal. Even though the funds for these staff members will be derived from the proposed budget, it nevertheless should be listed as "in-kind" services, thus demonstrating the sponsoring institution's support for the project. Probably

Exhibit 8-2 A Sample Time Line for Development of Proposal or Completion of Project

	Person Responsible	May	June	July	Aug.	Sept.	Oct.	Nov.	Etc.
Major Tasks: Staffing the Program									
Subtask 1: Interviewing Candidates	Ms. Kennedy	15th							
Subtask 2: Selection of Personnel	Ms. Kennedy		15th						
Subtask 3: Classroom Assignments	Mr. Johnson			30th					
Major Tasks: _____									
Subtask 1: _____	_____								
Subtask 2: _____	_____								
Subtask 3: _____	_____								

the two most important questions that should be considered in developing personnel needs are the following: (1) Do the personnel selected have the necessary qualifications to take part in this project? (2) Are the personnel needs realistic in terms of the type of project proposed?

Budget. No project proposal would be complete without a detailed analysis of the amount of funds needed to carry out the project. Very often, proposals are submitted either drastically overestimating the cost or inadequately estimating how much will be needed to implement the project. Some project developers believe that a good proposal will sell itself even though the costs are overestimated. These individuals rely on the funding agency to negotiate a workable and agreeable figure for both parties. While this is a possible strategy, and may be to some degree effective, it is inadvisable, in view of the increasing competition for funds, that this strategy be adopted, especially when the very success of carrying out the project is based solely on the possibility of receiving funds.

A more effective strategy for developing a budget should involve not only an itemized analysis of all proposed expenditures but also a budget justification that presents a detailed analysis of how the anticipated expenditures were determined. It is important in preparing a budget to do research to determine specific costs. With prices constantly changing, it is crucial that what is submitted be an accurate description of actual costs that will be incurred. In addition, there is a need to break down various categories. For example, travel may include local as well as out-of-town expenses; telephone costs may include service charges as well as long-distance calls. The more specific the budget analysis, the more likely it is that funding agencies will believe that you have an accurate understanding of what is required to carry out the proposed project. Traditionally, budgets have included all of the direct costs (e.g., personnel, travel, supplies) as well as indirect costs (e.g., usually a fixed rate that is reimbursed to the sponsoring institution for providing certain services). A budget sheet with the suggested categories that should be included in the proposal is shown in Exhibit 8-3.

Submitting the Proposal

Once the project proposal has been put into final form, there are several important things that must be considered. Usually the completed project, along with the necessary forms that accompany the proposal when submitted, must be authorized by an appropriate member or members of the institution sponsoring the project. Project developers should give those individuals as much lead time as possible so that they do not feel rushed to send the authorized project back without first having had the opportunity to review it thoroughly. Likewise, funding agencies will often have specific deadlines that require that the proposal be in their hands by a certain date. Therefore, it will be crucial for project developers to plan

Exhibit 8-3 Sample Budget Categories for Grant Proposals

Personnel
  Program director
  Teaching staff (list individually)
  Aides or assistants/consultants
  Clerical assistance
  Fringe benefits

Communication
  Telephone
    Local
    Long distance
  Postage
  Printing/reproduction

Equipment, materials, and supplies
  Instructional materials
  Office supplies
  Equipment
    Office
    Instructional

Travel
  Local travel
  Conference travel

Other Costs
  Rental of facilities
  Workshops
  Mini-conferences
  Indirect costs

ahead, outlining how much time it will take for the proposal to be approved and authorized by their supervisors and the arrangements for seeing that the project proposal is delivered to the appropriate agency. Once this has been accomplished, the next step is to wait for the funding agency's decision.

SUMMARY

Often, the development of a gifted program is dependent on outside funding resources. The acquisition of funding, however, can at times become a very complex process, which necessitates the development of special skills. The goal of this chapter, then, has been to examine the current federal law that has appropriated funding for gifted education and to outline the procedures necessary to develop a funding proposal.

In addition, an important factor in obtaining funding for gifted programs is the identification of other government, private, and foundation agencies that may provide possible resources. Because in the search for funds the importance of these agencies cannot be overlooked, a pertinent list of sources and the types of funding they provide is also presented in Appendix B.

REFERENCES

Williams, J. The federal role in education of the gifted and talented. In Goldstein, H. (Ed.), *Readings in gifted and talented education*. Connecticut: Special Learning Corporation, 1978.

Chapter 9

Evaluating the Gifted Program

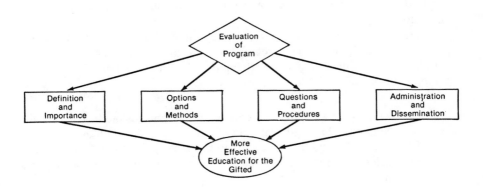

Throughout this text a parallel has been drawn between initiating a gifted program and undertaking an extensive journey. Continuing that analogy, let us note that at points during a trip, and certainly at its conclusion, it is important for the travelers to look back and assess the value of their journey. Was their trip, in general, a success or failure? Did they accomplish what they set out to accomplish? Was their undertaking worth the time and expense? In gifted programming, those involved in its development and implementation must also stop and reflect on the worth of their project. They, too, must judge the overall successes or failures of their task. They, too, must balance its cost, in terms of time and expense, to the educational benefits that have been reaped. It is through the process of evaluation that this assessment can be effectively and efficiently accomplished.

Indeed, evaluation is one of the most critical facets of program development, but it is also one of the least employed. Perhaps it is used so little because many in education lack a clear understanding of what evaluation is, what it has to offer, or how it can be applied. In this chapter we will address those areas by exploring what evaluation is and why it is necessary in gifted programming. The principal methodologies that can be employed in assessment and several typical questions to which those methodologies can be applied will be considered.

269

EVALUATION: ITS DEFINITION AND ITS IMPORTANCE

What Is Evaluation?

There are many ways that the process of evaluation can be defined to convey the purposes it is intended to fulfill. Mason and Bramble (1978), for example, describe evaluation as "the process of determining the adequacy of a product, objective, process, procedure, program, approach, function or functionary" (p. 111). Stufflebeam (1973), on the other hand, defines evaluation as "the process of delineating, obtaining, and providing useful information for judging decision alternatives" (p. 129).

While there are variations in the terminology applied from one evaluator to the next to delineate the assessment process, there are common elements within these definitions that focus in on the underlying meaning of evaluation. Among these common threads are the following four factors:

1. *Evaluation is the basis for decision making.* The conclusions reached and the judgments made in the gifted program come about as the result of evaluation. Effective evaluation should lead to effective change in the gifted program.
2. *Evaluation is a process.* As such, it is ongoing in nature and requires systematic implementation.
3. *Evaluation is dependent on information.* In evaluation there is the need to collect, analyze, and disseminate data about the gifted program.
4. *Evaluation is a collaborative effort.* No meaningful evaluation can exist unless there is a cooperative, working relationship between the gifted program staff and the evaluation team in collecting and interpreting information.

The presence of these commonalities should not be misconstrued as a sign of complete agreement among evaluators as to the purposes and methods of assessment. As in gifted education, there are controversies that can be underscored by the way in which the central concept is defined, by what is highlighted or deemphasized. For example, there are those who will equate evaluation with measurement. These individuals might judge the curriculum on the basis of the gifted learners' performance on a standardized test. Others may define evaluation as being synonymous with professional judgment, and for them the curriculum of the gifted program should be assessed by experts. Finally, there are those who view evaluation as a comparison between learners' performance and program objectives. For these individuals, assessment would focus on the behaviorally stated objectives of the gifted curriculum. Several of these controversies will become more apparent throughout this chapter.

Again, what these differences suggest to those involved in gifted education is that how one chooses to define evaluation is important because it will have impact on the way assessment is conducted. Therefore, when approaching evaluation, developers should analyze carefully the philosophy and focus of their gifted programs and select or construct a definition of assessment that complements these aspects. The definition of assessment that becomes part of the educational package should reflect what program initiators seek to demonstrate through evaluation and how they plan on achieving their goals.

What Is the Importance of Evaluation?

When discussing the value of evaluation in gifted programming there are two key issues that must be considered in some detail: accountability and cost vs. benefit.

Accountability

Education by its very nature is a decision-making process. Those involved in teaching are being called on daily to make choices in the learning environment that have an effect on students. Generally, these decisions are of limited scope and come about as the result of some intuitive process. This intuitive form of judgment may function adequately for many of the decisions made in the classroom setting but definitely not for all.

When the choices to be made are broad based, deeply affecting the educational experiences of many learners, as in the development and maintenance of a gifted program, decisions must arise from adequate information gathered in some systematic way. Educators and the public are entitled to know how choices come about. The public has the right, if not the duty, to call on educators to demonstrate if the goals established for the gifted program have been achieved and if these goals have been shown to be worthwhile for the gifted. The time has passed when those in education can create and maintain instructional policy merely on the basis of some "gut" reaction. They must be able to substantiate their decisions on the basis of evidence.

Consequently, without a disciplined approach taken in the assessment of the gifted program there is little assurance that the determinations have been arrived at objectively through an analysis of sufficient amounts of information assembled in some organized fashion. Guba (1978) illustrated the link between evaluation and decision making in this way:

> Evaluation has come to be widely viewed as the handmaiden of decision-making and social policy development. Congress has mandated that evaluation shall be an integral part of almost every Federally

supported social action program—whether in education, health, justice, or welfare—both to assist in the development and refinement of these programs as well as to render some judgment about their worth. (p. 1)

As has been shown, educators will be held accountable to others for the programs they organize for gifted learners. Therefore, educators must evaluate carefully the choices they make and must have the data available to them that demonstrate the strengths of their actions. Evaluation can also furnish program developers with an awareness of those areas where change or modification is called for.

Cost vs. Benefit

In the realm of education, time and change equate to money, and as those in gifted education realize only too well, there is only a limited amount of financial assistance available. What this creates is an intense competition among educational groups for the dollars that exist. To keep the gifted program afloat financially, planners must be able to demonstrate to those who hold the purse strings that the project itself or various aspects of that project are worth the investment. Proving that the gifted program is of sufficient benefit to its student, and perhaps the educational community, is a difficult task, which is made more manageable through evaluation.

It is through evaluation that gifted programming can be shown to have the desired effects on learners. The benefits can be ascertained through students' scores on some standardized tests, by the judgment of experts as to the value of the program, or by the comparison of learners' behaviors to program objectives. Data are compiled and shared with those who are less committed to the project and less assured of the benefits it reaps. These individuals, whether at state, local, or national levels, then weigh the evidence against the cost of the program. From this position they must decide whether to maintain, modify, or eliminate the program in question.

This issue of cost vs. benefits is not restricted to decisions arising outside the gifted program. Within the program as well it is important for staff members to assign priorities to their needs and goals. This action should also incorporate some analysis of the benefits that certain facets of the project produce in comparison to the financial burdens they place on educational resources. Also, cost can be looked on as more than direct monetary investment. For example, it incorporates the number of hours required, the allocation of personnel and materials, and more.

This cost vs. benefits analysis, especially when externally applied to the gifted program, is not without its problems. First, it is difficult for those within and outside the gifted program to come to some consensus on both the value and the measurement of benefits. Certainly "benefits" is a value-laden term, the meaning of which may not be agreed on easily. Second, when accurately determining the costs and benefits of gifted projects, it is difficult to isolate those conditions that existed before program development that may have had some effect on its outcome.

However, given the strong link between instructional changes and monetary factors the issue of cost vs. benefits cannot be overlooked. As a consequence, program developers will need to demonstrate to those less convinced of the project's worth how their innovations and modifications have been to the benefit of gifted learners. They will have to show those who are cost conscious that they did indeed get their money's worth. Evaluation is the tool by which the information required to state one's case can be effectively and efficiently accumulated.

EVALUATION: THE OPTIONS AND THE METHODS

With some ideas in mind as to what evaluation is and why it is important in gifted programming, the focus can shift to the principal options and methodologies available to educators within the assessment process. As is illustrated in the flow chart in Figure 9-1, there are, simplistically stated, two major directions evaluators can take in the assessment process. First, they can determine whether their instructional program for gifted learners warrants formal or informal evaluation. Second, if the path of formal evaluation is considered to be more appropriate, program developers must then choose whether a naturalistic or experimental approach should be applied.

The flow chart also shows that there are certain terminal points within the evaluation process. At these various points in the assessment, information is compiled and analyzed. Then, judgments about the gifted program are based on the data result. The judgments that arise in educational evaluation can ultimately have one of three effects on the gifted program in operation: *maintenance, modification,* or *elimination.* In maintenance, no changes in the existing program are deemed necessary and the educational format is left intact. If the data suggest that some alterations in the the gifted program are called for, the judgment would be for modification of existing conditions. After examining the available information, staff and evaluators may decide that the program is not meeting their expectations and is not worth maintaining or modifying. In such a case the judgment may be to eliminate the program. Generally, the decisions that result from evaluation fall somewhere between the two extremes of maintenance and elimination. Most programs can be improved and most have something to contribute to the education of the gifted learner.

It should also be noted that the judgments made in the gifted program do not have to occur only at the conclusion of the operating term. Because evaluation is a

Figure 9-1 Display of Principal Options within the Evaluation Process

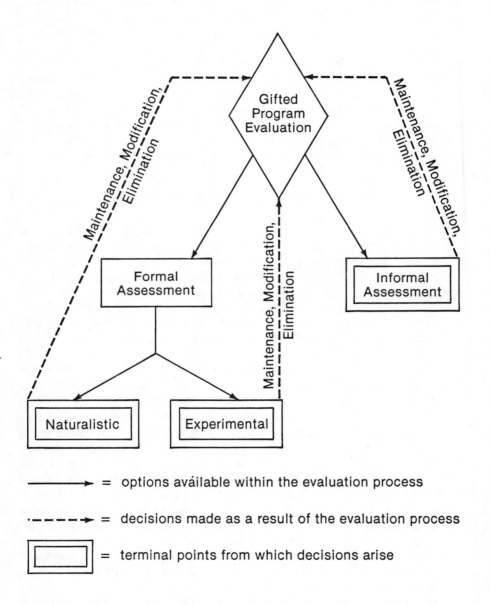

→ = options available within the evaluation process

·— — —► = decisions made as a result of the evaluation process

☐ = terminal points from which decisions arise

continuous process there is always a flow of information. There are periods during gifted program development when staff members can use the knowledge or insights they gain from assessment to make changes in the emerging curriculum. This is the type of evaluation identified as *formative* (Scriven, 1967). Feedback can be furnished during the development of the gifted program, and appropriate revisions in the curriculum can be made prior to project completion.

Summative evaluation (Scriven, 1967), on the other hand, is the consideration of the gifted program after all or much of the work has been finished. It is more likely that a decision to maintain or eliminate would be made in the summative stages of assessment. Then, evaluators can fairly judge a project that has had time to operate in and adjust to its surroundings. Both formative and summative assessment can function whether the decision is made to pursue formal or informal evaluation or naturalistic or experimental methodologies.

Formal vs. Informal Evaluation

When the gifted program staff enters into the evaluative task, their first key decision comes in the commitment to either formal or informal assessment. This represents one of the most basic issues in evaluation. Informal assessment, as described by Stake (1973), is more dependent on casual observation, intuitive norms, subjective judgments, and implicit goals. On the other hand, formal evaluation involves the use of checklists, controlled comparisons, standardized testing, and structured visitations.

A general point of contrast between these two evaluative options is the area of objectivity and subjectivity. While informal assessment is more subjective in nature, formal evaluation is more objective. It should be cautioned that the quality of evaluation that results from the more subjective, informal assessment is of a variable quality—sometimes good and sometimes weak or distorted.

Why conduct an informal evaluation, then, if the judgments to be made about gifted programming are based on results that are perhaps questionable? Building on some ideas expressed by Stake (1973), there are several potential explanations for why dissatisfied educators may choose to overlook formal evaluation in favor of its informal counterpart.

- Many formal evaluation reports turn out to be either highly irrelevant or highly unreadable to gifted program staff.

- Formal assessment frequently carries with it the burden of added expense for the gifted program.

- Even when completed, formal evaluation may not furnish the gifted program staff with the answers they need.

- Formal evaluation calls for special training that may be lacking in the gifted program staff.
- Some of the instruments applied in formal assessment may prove ambiguous, as in the case of checklists.
- Psychometric tests used in certain formal evaluations are not particularly useful in assessing instruction, only in discriminating among students.
- Formal evaluation may appear as formal criticism to some educators who are "turned off" by the process.

Even in light of the difficulties and dissatisfactions that formal evaluation might have for those involved in gifted programming it may have one rather large advantage over informal assessment. Informal evaluation, encompassing more personal judgments, furnishes little testable evidence that the decisions made are well grounded in reality. Consequently, program planners must consider their situations carefully. They must determine the importance of assessment within their program's framework, and they must specifically consider what kinds of questions they wish to have answered through the evaluation process. Several sample questions will be posed later in this chapter.

It should also be noted that programs receiving state or federal support may be required to submit their curriculums to more formal evaluation. These governmental agencies, and certan private foundations, are concerned with the accuracy of program evaluation. They want some assurance that their investments can be justified and that the programs, as outlined, are having the desired effect on gifted learners.

Finally, without formal evaluation there is little opportunity for program developers to identify those aspects of their respective projects that have been most beneficial to the educational growth of the gifted. Likewise, the less effective innovations cannot be modified or eliminated if they are not accurately isolated. While no evaluation process, formal or informal, can be totally accurate or comprehensive, those more systematically and objectively conducted have perhaps the better chance of being so.

Naturalistic vs. Experimental Methodologies

Once the determination of formal evaluation has been made, program developers must then direct their attention to a second issue—What methodology should be employed? In the most basic structure of evaluation there are two methodological approaches to assessment that can be implemented. These two modes of evaluation are naturalistic and experimental.

The experimental approach is by far the most widely implemented type of formal assessment in gifted program evaluation. An experimental investigation briefly can be described as one in which the evaluator attempts to control treatment conditions and extraneous factors that could exert influence on that treatment (Mason & Bramble, 1978). Without the presence of these controls, the evaluator has no means of showing a causal link between what occurred in the gifted program and the effects on gifted learners. An evaluation conducted experimentally must involve some form of planned intervention with manipulation of selected aspects in the gifted program.

Also, the evaluator employing an experimental design first must focus on a particular aspect of instruction that would be valuable to investigate. Once this important aspect, or variable, is identified, the evaluator must set about formulating the specific question to be investigated. The question that is posted is the heart of the evaluation process, within either methodology, and must be stated carefully to reflect what educators really want to know about their programs.

When the question has thoughtfully been put forth, evaluators must then determine the best procedure for testing it. As previously stated, evaluators in establishing procedure must be sure to control for any extraneous influences that could render their findings invalid. They must impose strict standards on their investigation, such as random assignment of gifted learners to treatment and control groups, to make this possible. If some but not all, of the requirements of an experiment design are met, the evaluation is often referred to as quasi-experimental (Campbell & Stanley, 1963). Because of the rigors of the experimental approach, evaluators must be knowledgeable in this mode of investigation or able to bring someone into the evaluation process who can design and conduct assessment in this way.

An alternative to the experimental approach in evaluation is naturalistic inquiry (Guba, 1978). In the naturalistic mode of assessment, the evaluator has no desire to isolate a particular aspect of the curriculum and investigate it apart from the instructional context in which it occurs. To the naturalistic evaluator, it is essential to consider the behaviors of gifted learners in relation to the actual classroom experiences and not separate from it. When assessment is conducted in the naturalistic framework, there is also no attempt made to manipulate or intervene in the instruction that is taking place. The goal of the evaluator would be to describe as accurately and objectively as possible what is occurring in the gifted program and how this reflects positively or negatively to what program developers had anticipated.

Another point of comparison between experimental and naturalistic inquiry is that the focus of the naturalistic evaluator tends to be broader and less predetermined than the experimental counterpart. When entering a situation the naturalistic inquirer, as an impartial observer, often lets patterns of behaviors emerge freely and does not enter the gifted program with the notion of finding *proof* that a certain type of behavior is present. The experimentalist, by contrast, is more like the horse wearing blinders so that the attention can be purposely directed in one way or another.

While naturalistic evaluation, at first glance, may have more appeal to gifted programmers because of its less rigorous appearance, there are several cautions that must be presented. First, if the goal of the evaluation is a list of clear-cut statements of cause and effect, then naturalistic inquiry may not be the most appropriate approach. Naturalistic evaluation, as noted, is more descriptive and less judgmental in nature. It does not attempt to establish a cause and effect relationship between gifted program and gifted learner only to report what is actually taking place in the program. It is this descriptive reporting that is to furnish evidence of the worth of the program as a whole.

Second, naturalistic assessment requires great amounts of observation time and objectivity on the part of the evaluator. It cannot be as rapidly completed as some of the quick pretest and posttest experimental designs. Third, synthesizing the vast amounts of information obtained is a tremendous task that must be considered in selecting a naturalistic approach. Finally, as with the experimental design, naturalistic evaluation should be performed by someone with knowledge and experience in that area. Assessing the value of the gifted program is no place for beginners to cut their teeth on naturalistic or experimental evaluation.

Participant vs. Professional Evaluators

This brings up another issue that is directly related to the topic of evaluation methodologies. Both naturalistic and experimental investigations should be undertaken by individuals with training and experience. Many gifted programmers must wrestle with the problem of whether or not to bring in someone from the outside to assist them in the formal evaluation of their projects. As with many of the other questions in evaluation, this one has no clear, yes or no, answer. There are, however, several factors that program initiators can consider when making their decision.

First of all, the need for outside evaluation will depend, in part, on the complexity of the design to be implemented. An informal assessment, of course, and perhaps some of the simpler experimental designs, once carefully outlined, could be carried out by educators who are participating in the gifted program. However, more detailed or sophisticated assessment procedures may demand the expertise and training that can be supplied only by professional evaluators.

The main purpose, then, in bringing in outside evaluators is that they have expertise in an area unfamiliar to participants in the gifted program. Should there be those who are active in the gifted program who also are knowledgeable in various assessment procedures the focus of the question would shift to the level of their involvement and its effect on their objectivity. Objectivity is the distinguishing characteristic of formal evaluation. Therefore, it would be meaningless to conduct formal assessment if care is not taken to maintain the objectivity of the evaluator.

While the main thrust for professional judgment in assessment is this investment in assumed expertise, there are several disadvantages to the employment of outside evaluators:

- Professional evaluators may not have knowledge of the specialized subject area. For example, individuals brought in to assess the gifted program may have expertise in evaluation but may know little about gifted education and the uniqueness of gifted learners.

- Professional evaluators generally mean added expense for the gifted program. Consequently, their input must be balanced carefully against the expected benefits.

- Professional evaluators may unintentionally exude a skeptical spirit on the otherwise creative fires of the gifted program's leadership (Scriven, 1967).

One way to lessen the potential gap between professional evaluators and the gifted program staff is to bring these individuals together early in project development. Make each group aware of its respective role in, and its importance to, the success of the gifted program. In addition, the expert appraisers should be made aware of the philosophy, goals, materials, and strategies that are part of the instructional approach so that this knowledge can be incorporated into their evaluation designs. By making sure that evaluators are kept abreast of what is occurring in the gifted program, more accurate assessments are more likely to be obtained.

Regardless of whether the program staff makes the decision to use professional or participant evaluators, one fact remains. It is imperative that the staff define the framework in which the evaluator is expected to operate. By taking time to establish a policy statement about the "who," "what," "when," "where," and "how" of assessment, the program staff can provide structure and clarity to the process for those directly or indirectly involved in the evaluation.

Among the basic points to be addressed in this statement are:

- WHO—the make-up of the evaluation team according to positions or competencies
- WHAT—the instruments and methods for gathering information
- WHEN—the time schedule for information collection
- WHERE—the source of the information
- HOW—the methodology, design, and sampling procedures to be employed.

This policy should be developed with the input of the evaluation team who will be functioning under its constraints.

EVALUATION: QUESTIONS, METHODOLOGIES, AND PROCEDURES RELATED

Earlier in the chapter it was stated that questions are the heart of the evaluation process. Before educators set out to collect and analyze information about their gifted programs, they must ask themselves exactly what it is that they wish to know or want others to know about their projects. What program participants want to know determines the kinds of questions that are asked in the evaluation process. In turn, it is these questions that help determine the assessment procedure to be employed. By examining several questions that are common examples of the ones posed in gifted program assessment, it can be demonstrated how various procedures may then ensue within the framework of a particular methodology. These questions will center in three areas: student performance, program objectives, and curriculum diversity.

Student Performance

The principal goal of developing and implementing a gifted program should be to produce positive change in those learners who take part. Yet, how do staff members begin to demonstrate that the educational programs they have established for the gifted result in this positive change? In examining this issue the gifted staff may pose a question such as:

- What effect does the gifted program have on the performance of those learners who participate?

Looking at this question from the perspective of the experimental evaluators, the idea of performance evaluation could possibly be equated to the area of measurement. Within this framework, the evaluator would set out to select a standardized test that could be used to measure student performance. The instrument would be administered to all gifted students prior to their participation in the instructional program. Through a process of random selection, some of those gifted tested would participate in the planned program while others received an alternate form of instruction (e.g., regular class instruction). At the end of the prescribed period (perhaps a term, perhaps a year) all gifted students would be administered the same or similar form of the pretest. It would be the hope of project developers that those gifted learners participating in the special program would score significantly higher from pretest to posttest than those gifted students who remained in regular classrooms.

Of course, this is only one procedure that an evaluator employing an experimental methodology might design to address the question of student performance. An equally acceptable but quite diverse approach might be taken by the evaluator who favors a naturalistic mode of assessment. That evaluator may decide to look at the effect of the gifted program on learners' performance through an in-depth case study method.

In the case-study approach, the observer documents detailed information about a single or few program participants. Data relevant to the individual's condition prior to entrance in the gifted program can be documented along with elaborate descriptions of what occurs within the instructional period and the learner's reactions to those occurrences. The chronicle that results may possibly demonstrate incidents, behaviors, or verbalizations that evince positive change or growth in that particular learner. These descriptions would have to be both comprehensive and well written to reveal the kind of evidence usable in the evaluation process.

A variation of this type of case study is the longitudinal investigation in which several participant-learners are followed over an extended period of time. The purpose of such an extensive study would be to ascertain whether those who took part in the planned program exhibited behaviors over time that were of a uniquely positive nature and that might be attributable, in part, to their participation in the gifted program. The difficulty with such studies, however, is in providing any clear link between what transpired in the gifted program and the later actions of the gifted learner. Also, many programs do not have the luxuries of time, money, and personnel to invest in such long-range investigations. What is often required is some quick feedback. This cannot be supplied by a longitudinal evaluative study.

What case studies do furnish in the assessment process is much detailed information about the gifted learner, as well as the interactions between the learner and the instructional program. This kind of personal, comprehensive description is not possible within the experimental scheme of evaluation. Furthermore, it accounts for the active involvement of the learner with the surrounding educational environment, describing that involvement rather than controlling it, as in the case of the experimentalist.

Program Objectives

Those who devise special educational programs for the gifted have specific purposes for doing so and goals they wish to achieve through the implementation of these aims. The program goals and the various group- and learner-specific objectives that emerge from these goals must be moved in a thoughtful and systematic way from ideas into print (see Chapter 4). It is these goals and objectives that indicate the path that is to be followed by the particular institution in the quest for effective education for the gifted. These objectives and goals also function as the markers by which the progress of that project can be calculated. In essence, these objectives are what program initiators say they are going to do, and the issue is whether it is done. A question that addresses this concern in the assessment process may be stated something like this:

- Are the objectives set forth in the gifted program evidenced in the behaviors of those learners who participate?

As was discussed at the outset of this chapter, there are several views of evaluation that can be reflected in procedure. In the first question considered, the evaluators approached the concept of evaluation from a "measurement" perspective. However, there are also those individuals who relate evaluation to a comparison between learner's performance and program objectives. It is the kind of question just posed that would best be investigated by evaluators with this viewpoint.

How might an assessment procedure be designed to investigate this question within the experimental methodology? One possible approach would be for the evaluator, with the support of the staff, to designate a specific objective area worthy of study. For example, the program staff may indicate that one of the main goals of their gifted curriculum has been the active participation of learners in decision making. A group objective developed from this goal might be that learners be given frequent opportunities to make choices within the instructional program that reflect their personal needs and interests. The evaluation team, then, may select this characteristic of "learner choice" and may seek to ascertain its presence in the behaviors of gifted program participants.

From this point the evaluator would have to clearly describe, or operationally define, exactly what will be meant by the term "learner choice." To verify the existence of "learner choice" in the gifted program, the experimental evaluator may decide to administer a questionnaire to all gifted students that is constructed to assess the degree of input these learners had in various facets of their education. At the conclusion of the program term, this questionnaire would be administered again and the scores of those participating in the designated project could be compared with those who remained within the regular curriculum. A questionnaire could also be constructed to include several objective areas.

The naturalistic evaluator concerned with the comparison of learner's behaviors with stated objectives would approach this question from a different direction. Perhaps the evaluator, again with the aid of the program staff, would formulate a list of learner outcomes based on group- or learner-specific objectives (e.g., learner choice). With this list in hand, the evaluator would spend much time in the program observing and recording relevant information. From the extensive description that results, the evaluator could address the question of whether the objectives set forth in the program plan are evidenced in the behaviors of participating learners.

A variation of this procedure would be for the assessment team to go into the instructional setting blind. Rather than observing classroom activities in relation to a list of desired outcomes, the evaluator would first observe and describe patterns of behaviors operating in the gifted program. Then, these patterns would be compared with the objectives to be sought within the gifted curriculum. In this way, evaluators may seem less influenced by their knowledge of what is expected to transpire within the program and more able to maintain their objectivity.

Curriculum Diversity

One of the driving forces in gifted education is the expressed belief that gifted learners, as a consequence of their unique abilities, are in need and deserving of differentiated instruction. Furthermore, if the existing instructional program were sufficiently diversified to meet the needs of the gifted learners there would be no purpose in designing and implementing a special project. Consequently, it is logical for those evaluating the gifted program to question the degree or manner to which the curriculum outlined for the gifted varies from the regular instructional offering. A question that might be posed in this regard is:

- Does the gifted program provide educational experiences markedly different from those experiences offered within the regular instructional program?

The evaluator employing an experimental methodology may wish to approach this particular question from the perspective of expert judgment. This link between evaluation and the opinions of experts is the third viewpoint of assessment mentioned at the beginning of this chapter. Within this context, the evaluation team might set out to identify the dimensions on which both regular and gifted curriculums can be contrasted, for example, materials, personnel, and content. Once these various dimensions have been delineated, an evaluator with expertise in curriculum could be called on to rate these programs along some continuum. It will be up to the expert then to judge the degree to which the gifted curriculum deviates from normal instruction and in which areas this diversity is more or less apparent.

Experts may also be brought in to assess the objectives set forth in the planned curriculum. These expert evaluators can make the determination as to whether the objectives are worthwhile in themselves and whether these objectives demonstrate some marked contrast to the stated purposes of the regular curriculum.

To the evaluator working in the naturalistic mode of inquiry, this question of curriculum diversity would be best addressed by an appropriate description of what is actually taking place within both curriculums. While the naturalistic evaluator may not be an expert in curriculum, this individual might feel the need to become familiar with the language and focus of curricular investigations. If the goal of the evaluation process is a statement of variation between the gifted and regular programs, then the evaluator operating within the naturalistic framework would need to be well acquainted with the practices of both. Although the naturalistic evaluators could not make a judgment about the gifted curriculum like the expert appraisers, they could furnish descriptive evidence of activities or behaviors visible in the gifted curriculum but not evident in regular instruction.

While the questions presented here are by no means the only ones that could be asked of the gifted program in the process of evaluation, they do serve as suitable examples. By considering these examples of assessment questions, we have demonstrated how evaluators working within a particular methodology might develop a procedure for answering these questions. As there are many questions that could be asked in the evaluation process; there are also numerous procedures that could be designed to investigate each question posed. It is for the evaluator or evaluation team, with the support and assistance of gifted staff members, to make the determination of procedure based on a clear understanding of the uniqueness of the program to be assessed.

EVALUATION: ADMINISTRATION AND DISSEMINATION

Now that the general topics of evaluation definition and importance, options, and methods have been surveyed, it is useful to discuss some of the practical elements in the administration of the assessment process and the dissemination of the information it provides. The administration of the evaluation may fall to several individuals within the gifted program. Perhaps the program coordinator who oversees the many other facets of the gifted program may wish to assume responsibility for monitoring the evaluation component. On the other hand, this duty could be delegated to another who has demonstrated administrative competency and is willing to undertake the added responsibilities.

Whoever will be assigned the task of administering the evaluation of the gifted program should be provided with an outline of the potential duties that frequently accompany this position. In the monitoring of the evaluation, one of the duties that would be included is identifying the major level(s) to be served in decision making, whether local, state, or national. This would exert some influence on the depth and purpose of the evaluation because of the extensive guidelines that often are passed down from the state and national levels.

Among the other responsibilities suggested by Stufflebeam (1969) that fall in the administrative category of the gifted project are the following:

- Summarizing the schedule for the evaluation procedure. It will help the entire process to outline exactly what needs to be accomplished and the time frame for its achievement.

- Defining and planning for the staff and resource requirements. When it has been determined what must transpire in the evaluation process and when it should occur, the next step is to identify who and what are needed to complete these various tasks. An administrative match between goals, personnel, and resources is what must develop.

- Specifying the means of assessing the required tasks in the evaluation process. Determining and assigning various tasks in assessment are only one dimension with which administrators must be concerned. It is also critical for those in charge to be able to determine if those given certain responsibilities carry them out as requested. Administrators must have some systematic way of keeping abreast of the progress being made by members of the evaluation team.

- Establishing criteria for the assessment of the evaluation design. Those serving on the evaluation team must be able to accurately assess not only the separate components in the process but the information that emerges. Are the data produced from the evaluation valid, reliable, and credible?

- Specifying and scheduling some means for updating the evaluation design periodically. Keeping a check on the effectiveness and appropriateness of the evaluation design permits the modification of established procedure if necessary. Thus, no flawed design is permitted to operate to the end of the evaluation, resulting in a less useful or perhaps meaningless product.

- Budgeting for the total evaluation program. In gifted education, as in other phases of instruction, it is always wise to consider the monetary ramifications of what is proposed. Therefore, the administrators should plan carefully for the estimated cost of materials, personnel, and procedures involved in the designed assessment.

These are but a few of the administrative considerations that are part of the evaluation of the gifted program. Those involved in the design and implementation of gifted instruction must also be able to compile the information that is acquired and present it in a format that is clear, comprehensive yet concise. Stake (1969) offers one outline for the final evaluation report that contains the key aspects of the assessment process (Exhibit 9-1).

The objectives of the evaluation, which should parallel the objectives of the gifted program according to Stake, include a statement as to the intended audience. As noted previously, the language, depth, and purpose of this report should reflect the audience who is to be served by the information contained. Also included in this section is a statement of what gifted staff members feel they will do with the knowledge gained from the assessment process. In addition, to establish the credibility of the evaluators, themselves, it is mandatory that their own biases and beliefs be clearly set forth at the outset of the presentation. Those who read the evaluation report have the right to know the perspective of those who design, collect, and analyze the information about the gifted program.

Section II of the evaluation report is a layout of the gifted project. It is an attempt to portray as completely and briefly as possible the design of the program. This

Exhibit 9-1 Table of Contents, or Format, for a Final Evaluation Report

Section I— OBJECTIVES OF THE EVALUATION
    A. Audiences to be served by the evaluation
    B. Decisions about the program, anticipated
    C. Rationale, bias of evaluators

Section II— SPECIFICATION OF THE PROGRAM
    A. Educational philosophy behind the program
    B. Subject matter
    C. Learning objectives, staff aims
    D. Instructional procedures, tactics, media
    E. Students
    F. Instructional and community setting
    G. Standards, bases for judging quality

Section III— PROGRAM OUTCOMES
    A. Opportunities, experiences provided
    B. Student gains and losses
    C. Side effects and bonuses
    D. Costs of all kinds

Section IV— RELATIONSHIPS AND INDICATORS
    A. Congruencies, real and intended
    B. Contingencies, causes and effects
    C. Trend lines, indicators, comparisons

Section V— JUDGMENTS OF WORTH
    A. Value of outcomes
    B. Relevance of objectives to needs
    C. Usefulness of evaluation information gathered

Source: Reprinted from The Countenance of Educational Evaluation by R. E. Stake. In B. R. Worthen & J. R. Sanders (Eds.), *Educational Evaluation: Theory and Practice,* by permission of Wadsworth Publishing Company, Belmont, Calif., 1973.

design is contrasted to the outcomes realized by the gifted project that are displayed in Section III of the report. In the following section of the final evaluation report is the analysis—the discrepancies that are evidenced between the program specifications and its outcomes. Congruencies come from the horizontal analysis of differences between intended and real outcomes, while contingencies refer to the vertical consideration of apparent causes and effects within the development of all outcomes, real or intended.

Up to this point, the evaluation report has been the objective presentation of information about the design and observed results of the gifted program. While section IV considers the imbalance between program goals and program outcomes, it does so in an empirical way, reserving judgment on what is evidenced. These more subjective decisions are made in section V of the final report, in which the outcomes, objectives, and evaluation process itself are submitted to judgments of their relative worth. It is from the information provided in this concluding section that those in authority can make the determination of whether to maintain, modify, or eliminate the gifted program under evaluation.

SUMMARY

Perhaps many of the other facets of the gifted program have more appeal to the educational innovators than the evaluation of the gifted program. It is often more stimulating to build a new project, moving it from idea to action, than it is to criticize one already in operation. However, no project can be considered complete without this evaluative element. If educators want others to appreciate that program and support its continuance, then they must be able to demonstrate its value. They must also be able to view the program objectively throughout its development. In this way, changes in the format can be made when and if they are needed. Indeed, through the evaluation process, educators have increased the likelihood of producing a more effective instructional program for the gifted and of alerting others to the success they have enjoyed. No program should be planned without careful consideration given to how it will be assessed. Evaluation is not the culmination of comprehensive and practical education for gifted learners, it is but the beginning of a revitalized program.

REFERENCES

Campbell, D. T., & Stanley, J. C. Experimental and quasi-experimental designs for research on teaching. In N. L. Gage (Ed.), *Handbook of research on teaching*. Chicago: Rand McNally, 1963.

Guba, E. G. *Toward a methodology of naturalistic inquiry in educational evaluation* (CSE Monograph Series in Evaluation, No. 8). Los Angeles: Center for the Study of Evaluation, University of California, 1978.

Mason, E. J., & Bramble, W. J. *Understanding and conducting research: Applications in education and the behavioral sciences*. New York: McGraw-Hill, 1978.

Scriven, M. The methodology of evaluation. In R. E. Stake (Ed.), *Curriculum evaluation* (AREA Monograph Series in Evaluation, No. 1). Chicago: Rand McNally, 1967.

Stake, R. E. Evaluation design, instrumentation, data collection, and analysis of data. In J. L. Davis (Ed.), *Educational evaluation*. Columbus, Ohio: Ohio State Department of Public Instruction, 1969.

Stake, R. E. The countenance of educational evaluation. In B. R. Worthen & J. R. Sanders (Eds.), *Educational evaluation: Theory and practice.* Belmont, Calif.: Wadsworth Publishing Company, 1973.

Stufflebeam, D. L. Evaluation as enlightenment for decisionmaking. In W. H. Beatty (Ed.), *Improving educational assessment and an inventory of measures of affective behavior.* Washington, D.C.: Association for Supervision and Curriculum Development, NEA, 1969.

Stufflebeam, D. L. Educational evaluation and decisionmaking. In B. R. Worthen & J. R. Sanders (Eds.), *Educational evaluation: Theory and practice.* Belmont, Calif.: Wadsworth Publishing Company, 1973.

Appendix A

The Renzulli-Hartman Scale for Rating Behavioral Characteristics of Superior Students

Name_____ Date_____

School_____ Grade_____ Age $\overline{\text{Yrs. Mos.}}$

Teacher or person completing this form_____

How long have you known this child? _____Months.

DIRECTIONS. These scales are designed to obtain teacher estimates of a student's characteristics in the areas of learning, motivation, creativity, and leadership. The items are derived from the research literature dealing with characteristics of gifted and creative persons. It should be pointed out that a considerable amount of individual differences can be found within this population; and therefore, the profiles are likely to vary a great deal. Each item in the scales should be considered separately and should reflect the degree to which you have observed the presence or absence of each characteristic. Since the four dimensions of the instrument represent relatively different sets of behaviors, *the scores obtained from the separate scales should not be summed to yield a total score.* Please read the statements carefully and place an X in the appropriate place according to the following scale of values.

1. If you have *seldom* or *never* observed this characteristic.
2. If you have observed this characteristic *occasionally*.
3. If you have observed this characteristic to a *considerable* degree.
4. If you have observed this characteristic *almost all of the time*.

Space has been provided following each item for your comments.

SCORING. Separate scores for each of the three dimensions may be obtained as follows:

289

Add the total number of X's in each column to obtain the "Column Total."

Multiply the Column Total by the "Weight" for each column to obtain the "Weighted Column Total."

Sum the Weighted Column Totals across to obtain the "Score" for each dimension of the scale.

Enter the Scores below.

Learning Characteristics . . . . _____

Motivational Characteristics . . . . _____

Creativity Characteristics . . . . _____

Leadership Characteristics . . . . _____

PART I: LEARNING CHARACTERISTICS

	1*	2	3	4
1. Has unusually advanced vocabulary for age or grade level; uses terms in a meaningful way; has verbal behavior characterized by "richness" of expression, elaboration, and fluency.				
2. Possesses a large storehouse of information about a variety of topics (beyond the usual interests of youngsters his age).				
3. Has quick mastery and recall of factual information.				
4. Has rapid insight into cause-effect relationships; tries to discover the how and why of things; asks many provocative questions (as distinct from information or factual questions); wants to know what makes things (or people) "tick."				
5. Has a ready grasp of underlying principles and can quickly make valid generalizations about events, people, or things; looks for similarities and differences in events, people, and things.				
6. Is a keen and alert observer; usually "sees more" or "gets more" out of a story, film, etc., than others.				

---

* 1—Seldom or never
2—Occasionally
3—Considerably
4—Almost always

7. Reads a great deal on his own; usually prefers adult level books; does not avoid difficult material; may show a preference for biography, autobiography, encyclopedias, and atlases.

8. Tries to understand complicated material by separating it into its respective parts; reasons things out for himself; sees logical and common sense answers.

Column Total

Weight	1	2	3	4

Weighted Column Total

TOTAL

PART II: MOTIVATIONAL CHARACTERISTICS

	1	2	3	4

1. Becomes absorbed and truly involved in certain topics or problems; is persistent in seeking task completion. (It is sometimes difficult to get him to move on to another topic.)

2. Is easily bored with routine tasks.

3. Needs little external motivation to follow through in work that initially excites him.

4. Strives toward perfection; is self-critical; is not easily satisfied with his own speed or products.

5. Prefers to work independently; requires little direction from teachers.

6. Is interested in many "adult" problems such as religion, politics, sex, race—more than usual for age level.

7. Often is self-assertive (sometimes even aggressive); stubborn in his beliefs.

8. Likes to organize and bring structure to things, people, and situations.

9. Is quite concerned with right and wrong, good and bad; often evaluates and passes judgment on events, people, and things.

Column Total

Weight	1	2	3	4

Weighted Column Total

TOTAL

PART III: CREATIVITY CHARACTERISTICS

	1	2	3	4

1. Displays a great deal of curiosity about many things; is constantly asking questions about anything and everything.

2. Generates a large number of ideas or solutions to problems and questions; often offers unusual (''way out''), unique, clever responses.

3. Is uninhibited in expressions of opinion; is sometimes radical and spirited in disagreement; is tenacious.

4. Is a high risk taker; is adventurous and speculative.

5. Displays a good deal of intellectual playfulness; fantasizes; imagines (''I wonder what would happen if. . . ''); manipulates ideas (i.e., changes, elaborates upon them); is often concerned with adapting, improving, and modifying institutions, objects, and systems.

6. Displays a keen sense of humor and sees humor in situations that may not appear to be humorous to others.

7. Is unusually aware of his impulses and more open to the irrational in himself (freer expression of feminine interest for boys, greater than usual amount of independence for girls); shows emotional sensitivity.

8. Is sensitive to beauty; attends to aesthetic characteristics of things.

9. Is nonconforming; accepts disorder, is not interested in details; is individualistic; does not fear being different.

10. Criticizes constructively; is unwilling to accept authoritarian pronouncements without critical examination.

Column Total

Weight	1	2	3	4

Weighted Column Total

TOTAL

PART IV: LEADERSHIP CHARACTERISTICS

	1	2	3	4
1. Carries responsibility well; can be counted on to do what he has promised and usually does it well.				
2. Is self confident with children his own age as well as adults; seems comfortable when asked to show his work to the class.				
3. Seems to be well liked by his classmates.				
4. Is cooperative with teacher and classmates; tends to avoid bickering and is generally easy to get along with.				
5. Can express himself well; has good verbal facility and is usually well understood.				
6. Adapts readily to new situations; is flexible in thought and action and does not seem disturbed when the normal routine is changed.				
7. Seems to enjoy being around other people; is sociable and prefers not to be alone.				
8. Tends to dominate others when they are around; generally directs the activity in which he is involved.				
9. Participates in most social activities connected with the school; can be counted on to be there if anyone is.				
10. Excels in athletic activities; is well coordinated and enjoys all sorts of athletic games.				
Column Total				
Weight	1	2	3	4
Weighted Column Total				
TOTAL				

Source: From Scale for Rating Behavioral Characteristics of Superior Students by J. S. Renzulli and Hartman, *Exceptional Children, 38,* 1971, 243-248. Copyright 1971 by The Council for Exceptional Children. Reprinted with permission.

Appendix B

Alternate Sources of Funding

The Gifted and Talented Children's Act (PL 95-561) was presented and discussed in Chapter 8. As is evident from the discussion, this law provides a large part of the funding for the development and implementation of gifted programs and is, therefore, a natural outlet for project developers seeking funds. However, in addition to principal funding agencies, there are other private and governmental sources that may also furnish resources to support gifted education. Therefore, it is imperative that project developers investigate all possible resources at the local, state, and national levels. To assist project developers in identifying alternate sources of funding for gifted programs, a sample list of agencies with a description of the type of projects they fund is provided.

I. *General Sources*

The Alvord Foundation
200 World Center Building
Washington, DC 20006

Purpose: Broad
Nature: Grants primarily for higher and secondary education and cultural arts

Carnegie Corporation of New York
437 Madison Avenue
New York, NY 10022
(212) 371-3200

Program Name: 1. U.S. program
                    2. Commonwealth program
Nature: In the U.S. program, grants are made primarily for research and demonstration projects in certain aspects of early childhood education, elementary and secondary education, and higher and professional education. In addition, the corporation gives a few grants for policy research and

monitoring projects designed to advance the cause of social justice and equal opportunity in education. Assistance through the Commonwealth program focuses largely on Southern Africa, the South Pacific, and the Caribbean and emphasizes projects designed to facilitate communication and leadership development.

Purpose: To promote the advancement and diffusion of knowledge and understanding.

Candidates: Qualified schools, colleges, universities, educational groups, professional associations, and other organizations with appropriate interests are eligible to apply.

The Educational Foundation of America
16250 Ventura Boulevard
Suite 445
Encino, CA 91436

Nature: Grants to qualified organizations for specific projects in the broad area of undergraduate higher education. A very limited number of proposals will be considered in the medical field, particularly dealing with cancer and heart disease research and care. In general, the foundation makes grants only for specific projects and does not provide funds for endowment or building programs, for grants to individuals, or for annual fund-raising campaigns.

Candidates: Programs sponsored must fall within the foundation's area of interest.

Contact: Executive Director

Charles A. Frueauff Foundation, Inc.
70 Pine Street
New York, NY 10005

Nature: Grants in the fields of higher education, hospitals, health-related services, and community services to children, the indigent, and handicapped.

Candidates: Grants are made only to nonprofit, tax-exempt institutions within the United States.

William T. Grant Foundation
130 East 59th Street
New York, NY 10022
(212) 752-0071

Nature: The foundation gives support to programs that give promise of contributing new knowledge on the psychological and behavioral development of children and youth.

Purpose: To discover and support imaginative and sound projects that will contribute to the healthy psychological development of children and youth.

Candidates: Qualified institutions or organizations with appropriate interest are eligible to apply. No grants are made to individuals.

Spencer Foundation
875 North Michigan Avenue
Chicago, IL 60611
(312) 337-7000

Nature: Grants and fellowship for research in the behavioral sciences to expand knowledge and understanding of the problems and processes of education.

Purpose: The foundation has a broad interest in research which shows promise of improving educational science or practice.

Candidates: Special emphasis is placed on behavioral sciences, but consideration will be given to any research aiding the identification or solution of fundamental problems in education.

The Charles Stewart Mott Foundation
Mott Foundation Building
Flint, MI 48502
(313) 238-5651

Nature: Grants for improvement of the quality of living in the community through pilot ventures in community educational affairs. Emphasis is on improving opportunity for the individual, partnership with the community, effectiveness of community systems, and leadership.

Candidates: Organizations and institutions with the appropriate interests are eligible. Tax-exempt status is required.

II. *Sources for Special Populations of Gifted Learners*

American Library Association
50 East Huron Street
Chicago, IL 60611
(312) 944-6780

Program Name: Louise Giles Minority Scholarship Program
Nature: Scholarship for graduate work at the master's level at an
                ALA-accredited library school.
Candidates: Applicant must demonstrate academic excellence, leader-
                ship, and evidence of a commitment to a career in librari-
                anship, must enter a library school offering an ALA-
                accredited program, and must be a member of a principal
                minority group (American Indian or Alaskan Native,
                Asian or Pacific Islander, Black, or Hispanic).
Contact: Staff Liaison

Cherokee Nation of Oklahoma
P.O. Box 119
Tahlequah, OK 74464
(918) 456-8887

Nature: In the Department of Education the following federally
                funded programs are available:
                (1) Adult Education Program
                (2) Indian Adult Education Learning Center
                (3) Bilingual Early Childhood Education Program
                (4) Consumer Education Program
                (5) Health Careers Program
                (6) Stilwell Academy
                (7) Elementary Resource Center
Purpose: Social services and economic development.
Candidates: Requirements vary depending on funding agency.

Compton Foundation, Inc.
10 Hanover Square
New York, NY 10005
(212) 747-2530

Purpose: Particular regard for equal educational opportunity; support
                for disadvantaged students through grants to selected
                schools, colleges, and related research programs, and for
                research and teaching; support of culture and the arts to
                improve the quality of cultural institutions, to promote
                community participation in cultural affairs, and to en-
                courage the development of creative talent.
Candidates: Grants are made only to organizations which qualify under
                the requirements of the Tax Reform Act of 1969. No
                grants are made to individuals.

J. M. McDonald Foundation, Inc.
2057 East River Road
Cortland, NY 13045
(607) 756-9283

Nature:	Grants for a variety of projects in the areas of education, children and youth, hospital and medical care, religious and church activities, safety and health, and the aged, blind, deaf, and handicapped.
Purpose:	To provide greater educational opportunities for youth through the support of educational institutions; to assist in projects related to the problems of mentally and physically handicapped children as well as the aged; and to aid in research for the general betterment of the human condition.
Candidates:	Nonprofit organizations with appropriate interests are eligible for support. Applicants must be located in the United States. No grants are made to individuals.

National Scholarship Service and Fund for Negro Students
1776 Broadway
New York, NY 10019

Program Name:	Supplementary scholarship fund
Nature:	Scholarships for black juniors and seniors to help fill the gap between students' total resources and college costs.
Contact:	Scholarship Committee

National Science Foundation
1800 G Street, N.W.
Washington, DC 20550
(202) 282-7150

Program Name:	Physically handicapped in science program
Nature:	Projects supported are conferences, workshops, studies, and science training models that directly involve groups of handicapped students.
Purpose:	To identify and provide information on problems of the physically handicapped in becoming scientists and ways to overcome these problems and to develop student science training models directly involving handicapped students at the secondary and college level.
Candidates:	Proposals from colleges, universities, schools for the handicapped, and nonprofit organizations are accepted.
Contact:	Division of Scientific Personnel Improvement

Office of Education
400 Maryland Avenue, S.W.
Washington, DC 20202
(202) 245-2181 or (202) 472-2795

Program Name: Women's Educational Equity Act Program
Nature: Funding for projects designed in one of three ways:
              (1) To change the educational system to eliminate sex role
                  stereotyping that limits the aspirations and options of
                  women.
              (2) To create changes in educational institutions to over-
                  come discriminatory practices that may be in violation
                  of federal laws, executive orders, or regulations.
              (3) To provide special training for individuals to remedy
                  the limitations of opportunities resulting from past or
                  continuing discriminatory practices against women.
Purpose: To promote educational equity for women and assist in
              eliminating sex discrimination in education.
Candidates: Public agencies, nonprofit organizations, and individuals
              may apply.
Contact: Women's Program Staff

Office of Education
Office of Bilingual Education
400 Maryland Avenue, S.W.
Washington, DC 20202
(202) 245-2609

Program Name: Bilingual education
Nature: Grants to support programs to stimulate and encourage the
              development and operation of new and imaginative pro-
              grams, services, and activities that meet the special edu-
              cational needs of children 3 to 18 years of age who have
              limited English-speaking ability and who come from
              environments where the dominant language is other than
              English.
Purpose: To develop and carry out elementary and secondary school
              programs, including activities at the preschool level, to
              meet the educational needs of limited English-speaking
              ability, and to demonstrate effective ways of providing
              such children instruction designed to enable them, while
              using their native language, to achieve confidence in
              English.

Candidates: Proposals may be written by all states including the District of Columbia, Puerto Rico, Guam, American Samoa, The Virgin Islands, the Trust Territory of the Pacific Islands, and the Department of the Interior. Grants may be made to a state education agency, a local public education agency, by a combination of such agencies, or by an institution of higher education (including junior and community colleges) applying jointly with one or more local education agencies. Schools to benefit must be eligible under Title VII specifications.

III. *Sources for Experiences in Visual and Performing Arts*

Academy of Vocal Arts
1920 Spruce Street
Philadelphia, PA 19103
(215) 735-1685

Nature: Scholarships for operatic singers covering full tuition at the academy.

Candidates: Admission is by competitive auditions.

Berkshire Music Center
Boston Symphony Orchestra, Inc.
Symphony Hall
Boston, MA
(617) 266-1492

Program Name: The Fellowship Program

Nature: Fellowships to aid young musicians (composers, conductors, singers, and instrumentalists) who have completed their formal training and are interested in undertaking intensive work on performance.

Purpose: To further the musical training of exceptional students under the guidance of members of the Boston Symphony.

Candidates: Active performers between the ages of 18 and 30 may apply. An audition is required. No academic requirements.

The Curtis Institute of Music
1726 Locust Street
Philadelphia, PA 19103
(215) 893-5252

Program Name: Music scholarships
Nature: Training of young performing musicians, admitted by competitive audition, for a tuition-free musical education.
Purpose: To hand down through contemporary masters the great traditions of the past; to teach students to build on this heritage for the future.
Candidates: There are no educational prerequisites. All are eligible for the competitive audition regardless of race, origin, or geographic distribution. All students are on a scholarship basis exclusively and pay no tuition fees.

National Association of Teachers of Singing
250 West 57th Street
New York, NY 10019

Program Name: Artist awards
Nature: Awards to select young singers whose artistry fits them to embark on professional careers now and to encourage these young artists to carry on the tradition of fine singing as professional artists. Selection will be made on present accomplishment rather than on potential.
Purpose: To encourage the highest standards of the vocal art and of ethical principles in the teaching of singing and to promote vocal education and research at all levels, both for the enrichment of the general public and for the professional advancement of the talented.
Candidates: (1-a) Applicant's most recent teacher must be a NATS member in good standing.
               (1-b) Applicant must have studied with a NATS teacher continuously for at least one year.
               (2)   Applicants must be at least 21 years of age but not more than 32 by the deadline entry date of October 1.
               (3)   NATS members in good standing for at least one year prior to the deadline date who meet the age requirements are eligible.
               (4)   First-place winners in the national audition may not compete again, but second- and third-place winners are encouraged to do so.

National Endowment for the Arts
Columbia Plaza
2401 E Street, N.W.

Washington, DC 20506
(202) 634-6369

Program Name:	Work Experience Internship Program
Nature:	Internships tenable in an office of NEA, to gain a working view of the agency's operations with time also provided to attend seminars on subjects ranging from managing cultural centers and state arts agencies to how to fill out a grant application. Activities provide detailed knowledge of the endowment's programs including policy development, grant-making procedures, and internal administration.
Purpose:	To acquaint arts administrators or potential arts administrators with the policies, procedures, and operations of the National Endowment and to give them an overview of arts activities in this country.
Candidates:	Participants are selected on a competitive basis on their academic background and prior professional experience. To qualify, candidates must be sponsored by an organization, university, state arts agency, or other professional nonprofit arts organization.
Contact:	Intern Program Office

National Endowment for the Arts
Washington, DC 20506
(202) 634-6369

Nature:	Grants to organizations, state, regional, or local arts agencies, and individuals in the fields of architecture and environmental arts, dance, education, expansion arts, folk arts, literature, museums, music, public media (radio, television, and film), theater, and the visual arts.
Purpose:	To encourage broad dissemination of highest quality arts across the country; to assist major cultural institutions to improve standards and to provide greater public service; and to give support that encourages creativity among our most gifted artists and advances the quality of the life of our nation.
Candidates:	U.S. tax-exempt nonprofit institutions are eligible to apply, as are appropriate state, regional, or local arts agencies and individuals. Grants may be made to a group only if no part of its net earnings is for the benefit of a private stockholder or individual and provided donations to such

groups are allowable as charitable contributions under Section 170(c) of the Internal Revenue Code of 1954, as amended. Individuals must be of exceptional talent to qualify for grants, and ordinarily individual grants are made to U.S. citizens.

National Endowments for the Humanities
806 15th Street, N.W.
Washington, DC 20506
(202) 382-5862

Program Name:	Youth grants in the humanities
Nature:	Grants to support humanities projects developed and conducted by students and other young people. Projects may concern education, of either a formal, institutional, or informal, public nature; study or research of a specific problem; or activities aimed at disseminating humanistic knowledge or disseminating it through film, exhibitions, public presentations, and other media.
Purpose:	To support humanities projects developed and conducted by students and other young people.
Candidates:	College and university students, high school students, and young persons not in school may submit applications, either directly or through nonprofit organizations. Consideration will be given first to projects by persons who have not completed professional training. Projects must relate in a clear way to the humanities, must have a specific purpose and scope and high promise of helping individuals develop critical faculties, and must be designed primarily for implementation by young people.
Contact:	Youth grants in the humanities

Scholastic Magazines, Inc.
50 West 44th Street
New York, NY 10036

Program Names:	(1) Writing awards scholarships
	(2) Art awards scholarships
	(3) Photography awards scholarships
Nature:	Scholarship grants offered through scholastic awards programs to college-bound high school seniors demonstrating outstanding artistic ability and high academic standing.
Candidates:	These awards are for high school seniors only.

Ludwig Vogelstein Foundation, Inc.
340 Haven Avenue
New York, NY 10033

Purpose: To aid meritorious individuals and scholarly projects
                primarily in the humanities and the arts; in general, no
                grants in excess of $5,000 to any individual.

Contact: Manager

FUNDING RESOURCES

Annual register of grant support, (12th ed.). Chicago: Marquis Who's Who, Inc., 1978.

The guide to federal assistance. LaJolla, Calif.: Wellborn Associates, Inc., *1*, 1980.

Kurzig, C. M., et al., (Eds.). *Foundation grants to individuals*. New York: The Foundation Center, 1977.

Lewis, M. O., (Ed.). *The foundation directory*. New York: The Foundation Center, 1979.

Turner, R., (Ed.). *The grants register, 1977-1979*. New York: St. James Press/St. Martin's Press, 1976.

Index

A

Abbreviated Binet for the
  Disadvantaged (ABDA), 53
Ability and giftedness, 13
Abstract reasoning, 28
Academic achievement records, 24.
  See also Achievement tests
Academic grade-point average, 21
Academic load as acceleration, 147
Academy of Vocal Arts, 301
Acceleration format, 127, 139,
  144-148, 160
  advantages and disadvantages of,
    145-146
  types of, 137, 146-147
  vs. enrichment, 156-159
  vs. exclusive grouping, 156-159
Accountability, 109, 271-272
Achievement and giftedness, 11
Achievement tests, 21, 24, 60
Acquiring funds, 256-267
Activities. *See* Enrichment activities
Adamson, G., 207
Adjustment, burden of. *See*
  Adjustment, center of

Adjustment, center of, 156-157, 160
Administration of tests, 31-32
Administrative abilities, personnel,
  82, 88
Administrator(s), 261
  competencies and responsibilities,
    165-173
  as disseminator of information,
    166, 170-171, 175
  district, 168
  as evaluator, 166, 172-173, 176
  as information seeker, 166, 169,
    174
  as motivator, 166-169, 174
  national, 168
  and needs assessment committee,
    68-69
  as partner in program planning,
    166, 172, 176
  responsibility of counselors to,
    182-183, 184
  role in assessment process, 84
  role in gifted programs, 163-173,
    174-176, 214
  state, 168
Adult Education Program, 298

Advanced placements, 147
Advisors, community, 75, 87
Advisory councils, state, 92
Affective learning, 220, 222, 223
Age, program population, 72, 73
Alexander, P., 33, 34-36, 40, 105, 206
Alexander and Muia Behavioral
    Checklist, 33, 34-36, 40, 105
Alice in Wonderland, 256
Alpha Biographical Inventory, 54
Alternate sources of funding,
    295-305
Alvino, J., 37
Alvord Foundation, The, funding
    source, 295
American Association of Curriculum
    Development (AACD), 107-108
American Cancer Society, 239
American Library Association,
    funding source for gifted,
    297-298
Analogies in intelligence testing, 28
Anastasi, A., 6, 45, 55
Arithmetic, 106, 110
    in gifted curriculum, 217, 219, 226,
    240-242
Art, 106, 110
    in gifted curriculum, 217, 219, 226,
    245-247
Arthur, G., 55
Arthur Adaptation of the Leiter
    International Performance Scale,
    55
Artistic talent and giftedness, 11
Asian American learners, 31, 54
Asimov, Isaac, 244
Assessment, 69-89. *See also*
    Evaluation of special children.
    devices, nontraditional, 21, 52-55
    of needs, 65-97
    of needs and format selection, 129,
    130, 137
    of needs and goals/objectives, 99,
    100, 100-103, 105, 112, 120
    process, summary of, 84-89
Atlas, Charles, 245

Attitude assessment, 24, 84
Awareness:
    administrator, 164
    community/cultural, 82

B

"Baby Elephant Walk," 246
Baldwin, A. Y., 40, 41, 115, 206, 208,
    209
Baldwin Identification Matrix
    (BIM), 41
Banks, G., 145
Barbe, W. B., 42
Behavior, 105, 106, 107, 110, 122
    and evaluation, 281, 282.
    terminal (or desired), 113-115
    See also Behaviors
Behavioral checklists, 22, 33, 34-36,
    60
Behaviorist movement, 16
Behaviorist theory of learning, 101.
    See also Learning, theories of
Behaviors, conceptual and
    perceptual, 221-222. *See also*
    Behavior
Berman, L., 225, 248
Bernal, E. M., 37, 38, 45, 54, 206,
    207, 209
Bilingual Early Childhood
    Education Program, 298
Bilingual intelligence tests, 54
BIM. *See* Baldwin Identification
    Matrix
Binet, A., 3, 5
Binet-Simon Intelligence Test
    (1905), 5
Bish, C. E., 42, 145, 146
Bishop, W. E., 206, 207, 208, 209
Black, H., 52
Black Intelligence Tests of Cultural
    Homogeneity (BITCH), 53-54
Blind or partially blind learners, 55
Bloom, B. S., 104
Bondi, J., 107

Boothby, P. R., 46
Bradley, R. C., 42
Bramble, W. J., 270
Brodbelt, S., 206, 207
Bruch, C. B., 53
Brunner, J. S., 101
Budget, 266
  analysis, 266
  estimated, 131-133
  sample, 267
  strategy, 266
Building, school, as facility for gifted
  programming, 70-71
Burden of adjustment. *See*
  Adjustment, center of

C

Cangemi, J. P., 206, 207
Capacities, personnel, 80, 81-82
Captain Ahab, 236
Caring, 196
Carnegie Corporation of New York,
  funding source, 295-296
Cartoon Conservation Scales, 54
Case studies of learning styles,
  224-225
Case-study methodology of
  evaluation, 281
Casual observation and evaluation,
  275
Cattell, R. B., 25
Cattell Culture Fair (intelligence
  test), 6
Cause and effect relationships, skills
  in identifying, 238-239
Center of adjustment, 156-157, 160
Certification, gifted teacher, 81, 88
Charles A. Frueauff Foundation,
  Inc., funding source, 296
Charles Stewart Mott Foundation,
  The, funding source, 297
Checklists, 275. *See also* Behavioral
  checklists
Cherokee Nation of Oklahoma,

  funding source for gifted, 298
Child development programs,
  fundings for, 297
Children with special needs, 69-70
Christmas Carol, A, 236
Cities , planning programs for, 74-75
Classroom, gifted programming in,
  77, 265
Cleland, D. L., 206, 207, 208, 209
Closed space school structure, 78
Cobb, P. H., 207
Cobb, S. G., 297
Cognitive development, 9, 10, 184
Cognitive mode of learning, 220, 222,
  223
Cognitive theory of learning, 101.
  See also Learning, theories of
Columbia Mental Maturity Scale,
  26, 55
Commitment and support of
  program, 93, 182, 184
Committee, needs assessment, 68-69
Communicating:
  in curricular areas, 234, 237, 240,
    243, 245-246
  as learning process, 219, 226-227
Communication, 234
  as budget category, 267
  counselor, 182-183, 184, 185-186
  parents and, 189-192
  skills, 82, 88
Community, 137-138, 160
  and administrators, 166-168, 171
  as assessment area, 71-76, 85-87
  demographic data, 72-76
  representation, 56, 68
Community educational affairs,
  funding for, 297
Community planning level, 89, 90,
  92, 96
Community service, funding for, 296
Competencies, personnel, 80, 81
Completion of project, time line for,
  265
Comprehension and intelligence
  tests, 28

Comprehensive information
strategy, 39-42, 61, 68, 253
Compton Foundation, Inc., funding
source for gifted, 298
Conceptual behaviors, 221
Concrete operational stage
(cognitive development), 9
Conferences, 92, 267
Confidentiality, 178
Consistency in program planning,
89, 90
Consultants:
community, 75, 87
counselors as, 182-183, 184
in format selection, 135-136
Consumer Education Program, 298
Contact, counselor
Contact list, community, 74
Content:
and evaluation, 283
and goals and objectives
development, 100, 103-105, 106,
112, 120, 122
Content areas, 105, 118-119, 217,
218, 219, 220, 225, 227, 229, 232,
233-248
Continuous progress, 147
Contracting, 152
Controlled comparison and
evaluation, 275
Cooper, J. M., 207, 209
Cooperation, counselor, 183, 184
Coping, parental, 189-192
Cost vs benefit analyses, 143, 269,
271, 272-273
Council for Exceptional Children
(CED), 91
Counseling, 180, 181, 183-186
Counseling in the Elementary and
Middle Schools, 181
Counselors, 177
in gifted program, 163, 173,
177-186
roles and responsibilities, 177-186,
214
Coursework, gifted, for teachers, 81,

88
Creating as learning process, 219,
232
in curricular areas, 236-237,
239-240, 242, 245, 247. See also
Creativity
Creativity, 12, 13
characteristics of superior
students, scale for, 292
measures, 253
tests as information, 25
Cultural heritage, community, 75-76,
87
Culturally different gifted students,
44, 45-47, 52-55
Culture as assessment area, 66, 71,
72, 73, 74, 75, 76, 87, 96
Culture-fair tests, 24, 52
in needs assessment model, 68
vs culture-free and culture-bound
tests, 53
Culture-sensitive evaluation, 47
Cumulative test scores, 25
Curiosity as gifted trait, 46
Curricular objectives, national, 89
Curriculum, 77
as assessment area, 66, 76-80, 87
characteristics, 218-219
diversity and evaluation, 280,
283-284
and format selection, 156-158
graded and nongraded, 78
holistic approach and, 217-248
influence on teaching style, 200,
201, 202
key elements of, 76-77, 218
materials, 133-134
timeliness, 218
Curtis Institute of Music, The,
funding source, 301-302

D

Dance, funding programs in, 303-304
"Danse Macabre," 245

Data collection, 66-67, 68, 91
Davis, A., 52
Deaf learners, 55
DeAvila, E. A., 54
Decision making, 235, 238, 241,
    243-244, 246
    and evaluation, 271-272, 282
    as learning process, 219, 228-229
    policies, 87
    process, 78
Defining (stage II) proposal
    development, 258, 259-260
DeHaan, R. F., 11
Demographic data, 72-76, 85-87
    presentation of, 72, 73
Demonstration and enrichment, 148
Demonstration programs, funding
    for, 295
Descriptive research, gifted, 81
Detail recognition in intelligence
    tests, 28
*Developing Understanding of Self
    and Others (DUSO): D-1 and D-2,*
    182
Development, proposal, 257-268
    time line for, 265
Developmental theory of learning,
    101
Diagnosis by supportive personnel,
    188
Differentiation of instruction, 111
Dinkmeyer, D. C., 180, 181, 182, 183
Direct costs in budgeting, 266
Disabled, education for, 47-49
Disadvantaged students, support for,
    298-299
Discrepancy model, 78, 80, 83
Discrimination in intelligence tests,
    27
District planning level, 89, 90, 92, 95
Divergent-productive abilities and
    creativity, 25
Dow, C. M. E., 207
Drop-out trends, 83, 88
Dunn, R., 221
Durr, W., 148

E

Early admissions programs, 193
Earp, E., 61
Economic characteristics,
    community, 72-76
Economic support of program,
    community, 74
Education, 128-129, 160
    characteristics, 66
    differentiated, 249
    holistic, 182, 184
    years of, as demographic data, 73
Education for All Handicapped
    Children Act (PL 94-142), 121
Educational Evaluation, 286
Educational Foundation of America,
    The, funding source, 296
Educational institutions,
    community, 75, 86, 96
Educational programming, 99
Educational science, 297
Educational service projects, model
    projects, funding for, 252-253
Egalitarianism and the gifted
    movement, 14
Effectiveness, program, and
    evaluation, 264
Einstein, Albert, 245
Eisner, E., 115, 117
Elementary Resource Center, 298
Elementary and Secondary
    Amendments of 1961 (Public Law
    91-230) Section 806, 250
Elementary and Secondary
    Education Act (Public Law
    91-230), 250
Eliciting reactions and support, 258,
    261-262
Elimination of gifted program, 273,
    274
Ellison, R. E., 54
Employment patterns, community,
    74, 86
Encouragement, counselor, 180-181,
    184

English language competence and
   group intelligence tests, 24, 52
Enrichment, 151-153
   activities, 135, 151
   compared, 156-159
   horizontal, 148, 149
   as program format, 127, 139,
      148-153, 160
   supplementary, 148, 149
   vertical, 148, 149
Enrichment triad model, 148, 150
*Enrichment Triad Model: A Guide
   for Developing Defensible
   Programs for the Gifted and
   Talented, The,* 150
Environmental stimulation and
   intellectual growth, 14
Equipment, 77, 267
Erickson, E. H., 101
Evaluation, 286
   administration and dissemination
      and, 172-173, 269, 284-287
   as component of SLIP, 125
   defined, 269, 270-271
   experimental approach, 273, 274,
      276-279, 280, 281, 283
   formal, 273, 274, 275-276, 278
   formative, 275
   and goal development, 108
   importance of, 269, 271-273
   methods, 269, 270, 276-279
   naturalistic approach to, 273, 274,
      276-279, 280-281
   by objectives, 109-111, 188
   objectivity, 275-276, 278, 283
   options, 269, 273-275
   procedures, 269
   and proposal development, 264
   questions, 269, 280-284
   summative, 275
Evaluation model design, 264
Evaluators, 278-279
   community, 75, 81
   experimental, 280
   naturalistic, 280, 282, 283
Exclusive groupings, 154-155

compared, 156-159
   as program format, 127, 129, 139,
      140, 153-156, 160
Experiences in the visual and
   performing arts, funding sources
   for, 301-305
Expert judgment and evaluation,
   270, 283
Extracurricular interest groups, 152

F

Facilities, 69, 70, 77, 85, 249, 267
Factor analytic model of
   intelligence, 7
Family size, 72, 73
Federal funding, 91, 251, 268
Federal Register, 256
Feedback and evaluation, 264
Feldhusen, J. F., 206, 209
Field dependence/independence and
   gifted learners, 221, 222
Field trips, 135
Finalizing as program development
   phase, 258, 262-266
Financial support, 69-71, 85
   as commitment, 70, 74
Fixed intelligence conception of
   intelligence, 2, 3, 5
Flanders, N. A., 196
Flavell, J. H., 4, 9, 101
Flexibility, 89, 90, 165
Fliegler, L. A., 42, 145, 146
Floating teachers, 152
Folk arts, funding, 303-304
Follow-up evaluation, 58, 188
Form, needs assessment
   information, 67
Formal operations stage (cognitive
   development), 9
Format selection, 126-160
   categories, 144-159
   compared, 156-159
   considerations toward, 127-143
   costs of, 131-136, 160
   individual student and, 140-143

physical setting of, 136-138
requirements and, 138-140
Foundation funding, 268, 295-305
Frasier, M. M., 208, 209
French, J. L., 56, 206, 207
Funding, federal, 91
  as distributed by Office of the
    Gifted and Talented, 251
Funding sources, 268
  alternate, 259, 295-305
  general, 295-297
  nature of programs for, 295-305
    passim
  program purposes of, 295-305
    passim
  qualified candidates for, 295-305
    passim
  for special populations, 297-301
  for visual and performing arts,
    301-305
Funds acquisition, 249, 256-267
Furst, N., 196
Future Shock, 102

G

"G" factor, 6
Gallagher, J. J., 51, 146
Galton, F., 2, 3, 5
Gardner, B., 52
Gardner, M., 52
Gay, J. E., 38
Gear, G. H., 37, 206, 208, 209
General information and
  intelligence tests, 28
General Intellectual ability and
  giftedness, 12
Generalizations in intelligence tests,
  28
Genetic theories of giftedness, 9
Geographic design of community, 74,
  96
Geography as assessment area, 66
Gibson, J. T., 207, 208, 209
Gifted, 42, 44-52, 61
  characteristics (and concomitant

problems) of, 43-44
  culturally different, 44, 45-47
  handicapped, 44, 47-50
  identification of, 21-61
  operational definition of, 22
  problems of, 43-44
  typical, behaviors of, 42-44
  as white, middle-class America, 45
Gifted curriculum, 217-248. *See also*
  Curriculum
Gifted education, overview, 23
Gifted handicapped, assessing, 55-56
Gifted learners, 179, 220
  and curriculum, 218, 219, 220-225,
    229
  funding sources for, 297-301
  and program goal development,
    101-102
  responsibility of counselors to,
    177-181, 184
  and school administrators, 168
  and teaching style, 200, 201,
    202-203
Gifted legislation, 250-256
Gifted movement:
  egalitarianism and, 14
  government support of, 14-15
  history of, 1-10
  solidification of, 13
  specialization and, 14
  supportive personnel awareness
    of, 186
Gifted opinionnaire, 79
Gifted performance criteria, 210-213
Gifted population assessment, 66,
  84, 88
Gifted program, 69
  development, personnel role in, 83
  financing, 249-268
  goal, 21
  nonisolationist character of, 65-97
  roles and responsibilities in,
    163-214
  supportive personnel familiarity
    with, 186
  vertical oganization of, 90

Gifted and Talented, Office of, 250-251

Gifted and Talented Children's Act (PL 95-561), 252-256, 295
provisions of, 252-253

Gifted and Talented Education Act of 1978 (PL 55-561), 256, 257
guidelines for local distribution, 254
special provisions of, 254

Gifted underachievers, 44, 50-52

Giftedness, 1-10
defined, 2, 3-4, 10-17, 18
government support of, 14-15
and the learning process, 100-102, 112, 120

Goal(s), 100-103
areas, 107-108
development, 99, 100, 105-108, 109, 110, 112
and evaluation, 281
and grant proposal, 259, 263
and objectives, development of, 99-126
program planning by, 65
and teaching style, 200, 201, 202

Grade-point average, 21

Grade skipping, 137, 146

Grade telescoping, 137, 147

Graded curriculum, 78, 87

Grant(s)
administration, 257
development, states in, 258
to individuals, 300, 301, 302, 303, 304, 305

Griggs, S., 221

Grinch Who Stole Christmas, The, 236

Group-directed teaching style. See Teaching styles

Group intelligence tests, 22, 24

Group planning and learning style, 221-222

Guba, E. G., 271

Guidance pesonnel. See Counselors

Guidelines, national curricular, 89, 91

Guilford, J. P., 4, 7, 10, 17

Guilford's structure of the intellect, 6-9

H

Handicapped, 49
assessment, 55-56, 61
funding, 299
gifted learner, 44, 47-50
students' science program, 299-300. See also Disabled

Haptic Intelligence Tests for the Adult Blind, 55

Harmin, M., 182

Hartman, R., 33

Havassy, B., 54

Havighurst, R. J., 11, 101

Hayes-Binet intelligence test, 55

Health Careers Program, 298

Health-related services, funding for, 296

Hearing impaired learner, 55

Henjum, A. E., 209

Heredity and intellectual measurement, 2

Heritage, cultural community, 75-76

Higher education, undergraduate, funding for, 296

Hilliard, A. G., 54

Hiroshima, 238

Hiskey, M., 55

Hoffman, D., 52

Homogeneity of student population, 78, 87

Hospital funding, 296

Humor, sense of, as gifted trait, 46

I

Idea formulation (stage I), 257

Identification of the gifted, 21-61
comprehensive methods of, 253
counselors' responsibilities in, 177-178, 184

process, model for, 39
process, strategies for, 16, 17,
    21-42
Identity, learner, 275
Implicit goals and evaluation, 275
Income as demographic datum, 73
Independent studies, 152
Indian Adult Education Learning
    Center, 298
Indirect costs as budget category,
    266, 267
Individual differences in
    intelligence, 13-14
Individual grants, 300, 301, 302, 303,
    304, 305
Individual intelligence tests, 21, 22,
    25-29
Individual planning level, 89, 90,
    93-94
Individual student cases and format
    selection, 140-143
Individualization and learning
    styles, 222
Induction and intelligence tests, 28
Information, 103-105
    counselor, 180-181, 184
    demographic and community,
        71-76
    federal, 91
    and goal development, 100,
        103-105, 112, 120
Information collection, methods of,
    66, 67, 68
Inhelder, B., 9
Inner-city children, 46
Inputs (cognitive development), 9
In-service programs, 135-136
Instruction, 81, 111
Integration, curricular, 218
Intellectual evaluation, 5-10
Intellectual structure (cognitive
    development), 9
Intelligence, 2, 3, 5
    defined, 3-4
    factor analytic model of, 7
    and gifted movement, 18

scales of (Galton), 5
social, 6-7
Intelligence quotient. *See* IQ
Intelligence tests, 22, 25
    group, 22, 24
    as identification technique, 253
    individual, 21, 22, 25-29
    item analysis of, 25-26
Interaction:
    curricular, 218
    as learning style, 220-225
    between student and counselor,
        178-180, 184, 185, 196
Interaction Analysis Scale, 196
Interactionist theories of giftedness,
    9-10
Interviewing, 265
Intuitive norms, 275
Involvement, 93
    counselor-parent, 184-185
IQ, 3, 60
    deficiencies of, 52
    group test, 22
    as indicator of giftedness, 10-11,
        12
Isaacs, A. F., 42
Item analysis, intelligence test, 25-26

J

Jakubovie, S., 52
Johns Hopkins University, 144-145

K

Kaufmann, P., 207, 208, 209
Kirk, S. A., 42
Klineburg, O., 52
Knowing, 219, 229
    in curricular areas, 235-236,
        238-239, 241, 244, 246-247
Knowledge:
    in goal development, 100, 103-105
    schematization of. *See* Patterning
    types of, 103-104. *See also*
        Information

Kohlberg, L., 101
Kolloff, M. B., 206, 209
Kuhlman Anderson group
    intelligence test, 22

L

Labor and industry data and
    planning, 74
Lacoste, R. J., 46
Language arts, 106, 110, 122
    in gifted curriculum, 217, 219,
        233-237
Leadership and giftedness, 11, 46
    scale for, 293
Learned content. *See* Content areas
    of learning
Learner(s), 29
    choice and evaluation, 282
    gifted, atypical, behaviors of, 42,
        44-52
    gifted, typical, behaviors of, 42-44
    identity, 76
    organization, 78
    "right to review," 60. *See also*
        Gifted learners; learning styles;
        student(s)
Learning:
    affective, 220, 222, 223
    goals, 217, 218
    theories of, 101
Learning centers, 152
Learning characteristics of superior
    students, scale for, 290-291
Learning packets, 152
Learning processes, 217, 219, 220,
    225-232, 233, 248
    and goals and objectives
        development, 100-102, 112, 120
Learning styles, 217, 219, 220-225,
    233, 248
    case studies, 224-225
    levels of consideration, 221, 222
Lectures, 148
Lehman, H., 146
Leiter International Perfomance

Scale and handicapped learners,
    55
Lewis, J. F., 46, 54
Lewis, Meriweather, 106
Libraries, 75, 87, 148
Library school scholarships, 298
Liker-type questionnaire, 78, 79
Listening, active, 182, 183
Local educational agencies,
    mandates for, 256
Longitudinal study and evaluation,
    281
Louise Giles Minority Scholarship
    Program, 298
Loving:
    in curricular areas, 234-235,
        237-238, 240-241, 243, 246
    as learning process, 219, 227-228
Lucito, L., 11, 42, 206, 208, 209
Ludwig Vogelstein Foundation, Inc.,
    funding souce, 305

M

Mager, R., 113
Mainstreaming, 129
    and exclusive grouping, 154
Maintenance of gifted program, 273,
    274
Maker, J. C., 47, 196, 209
Mancini, Henry, 246
Mandates. *See* Mandates for local
    educational agencies; state
    mandates
Mandates for local educational
    agencies, 256
Maria (case study in intelligence test
    item analysis), 26
Marland Report of 1972, 11
Marland, S., 11, 12
Martinson, A., 46
Mason, E. J., 270
Matching funds, 254-255
Materials, 188, 220
    costs of, 249, 267

curriculum, 133-134, 137
and evaluation, 283
professional, 136
Math. *See* Arithmetic
Measurement and evaluation, 270, 280, 282
Mechanical skills and giftedness, 11
Media, 239
Meeker, M., 9, 54
Meeker, R., 9, 54
Memory, 6, 28
Mentorship, 156
Mercer, J. R., 46, 94
Michael, W., 222
Mini-conferences as budget category, 267
Moby Dick, 236
Models, evaluation, 264
Models, identification process, 21-42
Modular scheduling, 148
Mona Lisa, 232
Motivational characteristics of superior students, scale for, 291
Motor behaviors, 5, 28
Muia, J., 33, 34-36, 40, 105, 206
Multiple-factor structure theory, 6, 7
Muro, J. J., 180, 181, 183
Museums, 75, 87
Music, 106, 110
in gifted curriculum, 217, 219, 226, 245-247
programs, funding for, 301, 302

N

National Association for Gifted Children, 91
National Association of Teachers of Singing, funding source, 302
National Endowment for the Arts, funding source, 302-304
National Endowment for the Humanities, 304
National Institute of Education, 251
National planning level, 89, 90, 91, 94
National Scholarship Service and Fund for Negro Students, funding source for gifted, 299
National Science Foundation, funding source for gifted, 299
National Society for the Study of Education, 11
Native American learners, 31, 54
Nebraska Test of Learning Aptitude, 55
Need for study, and proposal development, 263
Needs, personnel, 264-266
Needs assessment, 65-69
areas, 100-103
committee, 68-69
and format selection, 129, 130, 137
and goals and objectives development, 99, 100, 105, 112, 120
information form, 67
model, 67, 68
organization, 65, 66-69
and proposal development, 257
questions, 85-88
Nelson, J. B., 206, 207, 208, 209
Nettleship, R. L., 1
New Priorities in the Curriculum, 225
Newland, T. E., 25, 206, 208
1984, 244
Nongraded class structure, 78, 87
Nongraded curriculum, 78
Nonprofit schools, state funding of, 256
Norm-referenced tests, 21. *See also* Standardized tests
Number factor in ability testing, 6
Nutcracker Suite, The, 245

O

Objective(s), 65, 109-113
behavioral, 113-115

benefits of, 109-113
development of, 99, 109
and evaluation, 280, 281-283
expressive, 113, 115-117
and format selection, 128, 129, 130
as goal of needs assessment, 67
and goals, 99-126
and grant proposal, 259
group-specific, 99, 109-122, 125,
    281, 282
identification of, 188
instructional, 113-115
Objective information strategy,
    22-25
advantages of, 29-31
disadvantages of, 31-33
of identification, 22-33, 60
Objectivity, 275-276, 278, 283
Observational checklists, 33, 34-36
Occupations, as demographic data,
    186
Office of Bilingual Education (Office
    of Education), funding source for
    gifted, 300
Office of Education, 250
as funding source for gifted, 300
Office of Education, Office of
    Bilingual Education, funding
    source for gifted, 300
Office of the Gifted and Talented,
    the Office of Education, 250-251
Open Environment, 78, 87
Open-spaced school structure, 78, 87
Operational definition, 16
Opinion, assessment of, 78, 79
Opinionnaire, gifted, 79
Organization and use of objectives,
    111-113
Orlosky, D. E., 103-104
Orwell, George, 244
Otis Lennon Group Intelligence
    Test, 22
Outcomes, project, and evaluation,
    264
Outputs (in interactionist theory of
    cognitive development), 9

P

Parent nominations as gifted
    identification, 37
Parent support groups, 193-194
Parents of gifted learners:
    and administrators, 166-168,
        170-171
    in assessment process, 84
    and counselors, 183-186
    and evaluation, 60
    in gifted program, 163, 189-194,
        214
    and needs assessment committee,
        68-69
Parliament, 238
Pascales, P., 52
Pattern completion and intelligence
    testing, 28
Patterning, 219, 229-230
    in curricular areas, 236, 239,
        241-242, 244, 247
Peer counseling, 178-179
Peer nomination identification
    technique, 37, 60, 253
Perceiving, 219, 225-226
    in curricular areas, 233-234, 237,
        240, 242-243, 245
Perceptual behaviors, 221-222
Perceptual speed as factor in ability
    testing, 6
Performance as included in
    definition of gifted, 11
Performing arts, 12, 301-305
Periodic feedback and evaluation,
    264
Periodic review (of gifted
    placement), 57, 59-60
Personality, 205
Personality checklist:
    example of, 206-207
    inappropriate uses of, 203-205
Personalized instruction, 222
Personnel, 70-71
    and administrators, 170
    as assessment area, 66, 80-83, 88

as budget category, 267
concerns, 80, 82
and evaluation, 283
and placement committee, 56
in program development, 83, 261
requirements, 132, 138-140
selection, 264-266
Philosophy, educational:
  and gifted programming, 76-77,
    87, 92-93
  and teaching style, 200, 201, 202
Physical setting:
  and needs assessment, 66
  and format selection, 136-138, 160
Physical skills as indicator of
  giftedness, 1
Physiology and learning style, 220,
  222
Piaget, J., 4, 9, 10, 101, 230
Pictorial Test of Intelligence, 56
Pinocchio, 236
Placement committee, 21, 56-61
Placement evaluation, continuous,
  57-59
Placement information, sources of,
  58
Plato, 1-2
Policy statements, national, 89, 96
Population, general, as assessment
  area, 66, 86
Population, school, stability of, 88
Porteau Mazes, 55
Positive attitude of administrators,
  165
Potential ability, 12
Preexisting gifted programs, 70,
  77-78, 85
Preliminary proposal, 261
Preoperational stage (of cognitive
  development), 9
Pressey, S., 146, 148
Price, G., 221
Primary Mental Abilities Test
  (Thurstone), 6, 22
Principal, role in program
  conceptualization, 78. *See also*

Administrator(s)
Private agency funding, 268
Problem defining in grant proposal,
  260
Procedures:
  and proposal development, 263
  and strategies, grant proposal, 259
Process abilities as factor in
  giftedness, 12
Process-product items, intelligence
  tests, 25
Professional development, funding
  for, 253
Professional judgment in evaluation,
  270, 283
Proficiency, teacher, 81
Program content. *See* Content
Program coordinators. *See*
  Administrator(s)
Program development, 257, 262
Program evaluation, federal, 91. *See
  also* Evaluation
Program format. *See* Format
Program goals. *See* Goals
Program objectives. *See* Objectives
Program philosophy. *See*
  Philosophy, educational
Program planners and funding, 249
Program planning, 89-96
  levels of, 90
  by objectives, 65
  summary and pertinent questions
    for, 94-96
Program supervisors. *See*
  Administrators
Project, time line for, 265
Proposal development, stages of,
  257-268
Psychometric movement, 5-10
Psychometric tests, 276
Psychomotor ability as factor in
  giftedness, 12, 220, 222
Public assistance recipients, 74, 85
Public Law 55-561, 256, 257
Public Law 91-230, Elementary and
  Secondary Education Act, 250

Public Law 93-380, 251, 252
Public Law 94-142, 121
Public media, funding for programs
in, 303-304

Ryan, K., 207, 209

S

"S" factor, 6
Saint-Saens, Camille, 245
Salvia, L., 27
Sanders, J. R., 286
Sauerman, D., 222
Scale of Intelligence (Galton), 5
Scale for Rating Behavior
Characteristics of Superior
Students, Renzulli-Hartman
(Appendix A), 289-293
Schermann, A. A., 42
Scholarships, 193. *See also* Funding
sources; individual grants
Scholastic Magazines, Inc., funding
source, 304
School, 137, 160
boards and administrators, 170
curriculum as assessment area, 66,
76-80, 87
district as assessment area, 66,
69-71, 88
objectives and program
development, 259
officials, attitudes toward gifted,
70
personnel. *See* Personnel
philosophy, 76-77, 87, 92-93, 200,
201, 202
planning level, 89, 90, 92, 96
population, characteristics of,
83-84, 88
psychologists, 28
records, as information source, 72
staff. *See* Personnel
Science, 106, 110, 122
in gifted curriculum, 217, 219, 226,
242-245
Science program for handicapped
students, funding for, 299-300
Scientific methodology and

R

Race, as factor in planning, 72, 73, 88
Rapid pacing, 137
Raths, L. E., 182
Raven, J. C., 6
Raven's Progressive Matrices, 6, 26,
54, 55
Reading, 46
Reasoning as factor in ability
testing, 6
Recommendations, 22
Referral process, 22, 77
Reliability, test, 32
Renzulli, J. S., 12, 29, 33, 37, 38,
148-149, 150
Renzulli-Hartman Scale for Rating
Behavioral Characteristics of
Superior Students (Appendix A),
289-293
Reports and studies, federal, 91
Research and demonstration,
funding for, 295
Research studies, gifted, 81
funding for, 295
Residence as demographic data, 73
Resource people, district, 71
Review, learner right to, 60
Revolutionary War, 238
Reyna, J., 37
Rice, J., 145
Risk-taking, 229, 232
Roles and responsibilities in gifted
program, 163-214
Rosenshine, B., 196
Round table discussions and
assessment of gifted, 84
Rural areas, planning programs for,
74-75

understanding giftedness, 2
Scrooge, Ebenezer,.236
Seagoe, M., 43, 44
Self-directed teaching style, 200
Self-evaluation questionnaire for
  teachers, 203, 204, 208-209
Self-expression, 246
Self-nominations as gifted
  identification, 37
Self-perpetuation as aspect of
  curriculum, 219-220
Sensimotor stage (of cognitive
  development), 9
Sequencing as assessed by
  intelligence tests, 28
Services, supportive, 74
Sex, school population data on, 88
Sex role stereotyping, funding for
  programs against, 300
Sharing as part of grant proposal
  process, 258
Shelby, M. E., 207, 209
Simon, S., 182
Sincerity, counselor, 177
Sisk, D., 206, 207
Situational assessment and
  underachievement, 51
*SLIP. See Specific Learner
  Instructional Plan*
Slosson Intelligence Test, 28, 29, 30
Small group instruction, 148
Smith, B. O., 103-104
Smith, L. H., 29, 37, 38
Social-Emotional Climate Index,
  196, 197-200
Social intelligence, 7-8
Social science. *See* Social studies
Social studies, 106, 110, 122
Social superiority and definition of
  gifted, 11
  in gifted curriculum, 217, 219,
    237-240
Social theory of learning, 101. *See
  also* Learning, theories of
Societal influence on goals and
  objectives development, 100,

102-103, 112, 120
Socioeconomy as assessment area,
  66, 71-76, 96
SOI-LA. *See* Structure of the
  Intellect-Learning Abilities Test
SOMPA. *See* System of
  Multicultural Pluralistic
  Assessment
Space relations as factor in ability
  testing, 6
Spanish-speaking population, needs
  of, 68
Spanish-surname populations,
  testing, of, 54
Spearman, C., 3, 5-7, 9, 17
Spearman's Two-Factor Theory, 7
Special Classes, 155-156
Special educational needs, funding
  programs for, 300-301
Special populations of gifted
  learners, funding sources for,
  297-301
Special Projects Act (Public Law
  93-380), Section 404, 251, 252
Specialists, 163, 186-188, 214
Specialization and giftedness, 14
Specific academic aptitude as factor
  in giftedness, 12
*Specific Learner Instructional Plan
  (SLIP),* 121-125, 177, 183, 188, 222
  and parental input, 190, 192-193
Spencer Foundation, funding source,
  297
Staff. *See* Personnel
Staffing. *See* Personnel
Stake, R. E., 275, 285, 286
Standardized tests, 21, 275, 280
Stanford-Binet Intelligence Test, 5,
  17, 22, 28, 29, 45, 53
Stanley, Julian, 144-145
State:
  conferences, 92
  funding, 91
  gifted program development,
    11-12
  mandates, 253, 256

planning level, 89, 90, 91-92, 94-95
services to localities, 91-92
Statement of the problem, 262
Statewide activities projects,
    252-253
Stigmatization, 155
Stilwell Academy, 298
Structure of the Intellect-Learning
    Abilities Test (SOI-LA), 9, 53,
    54
Structured class, 87
Structured visitation, 275
Student(s), 177
    and assessment, 84
    confidentiality, 178
    culturally different and gifted, 44,
        45-47, 52-55
    disabled, 47-49
    disadvantaged, 298-299
    and format selection, 140-143
    performance, 280-281, 282
    population, 78, 83-84
    profiling, 57, 59. See also Learner,
    gifted
Study, need for, and proposal
    development, 263
Stufflebeam, D. L., 270
"Subdominant cultural," 47
Subjective information, 33-37
    strategy, 33-39, 60
Subjectivity in evaluation, 275-276
Sullivan, A. R., 52, 208, 209
Summer school, 155, 193
Superintendent. See Administrators
Superior Students, The Renzulli-
    HXRTRTN Scale for Rating
    Behavioral Characteristics of
    (Appendix A), 289-293
Supplemental activities, 135, 151
Supplies, 70-71, 85
    as budget category, 267
Support, eliciting staff, 261-262
Support personnel, 163, 186-188, 214
Survival skills as gifted trait, 46
System of Multicultural Pluralistic
    Assessment (SOMPA), 53, 54

T

Task commitment as factor in
    giftedness, 12, 13
Taylor, C. W., 54
*Taxonomy of Educational
    Objectives,* 104
Tchaikovsky, Petr, 245
Teacher(s), 195, 203-209, 210-213
    as change agent, 196
    cost of, 249
    and counselors, 182-183, 184
    experienced with gifted, 71, 88
    floating, 152
    and gifted program, 163, 194-213,
        214
    as learning facilitator, 195-203
    and needs assessment, 68-69, 84
    and personality, 200, 201
    and project development, 261
Teacher-directed teaching style, 200
Teacher Fellowship Provision of
    Higher Education Act of 1956, 250
Teacher nomination as gifted
    identification, 37, 60, 253
Teaching proficiency, 81, 88
Teaching styles, 200-203, 204
Telephone costs and budgeting, 266
Tenacity as gifted trait, 46
Terman, L. M., 3, 5, 42, 43, 250
Test data, methods of reporting, 77,
    88
Test release forms, 77
Test selection criteria, 31, 32
Testing, 32-33
    and gifted identification, 77, 88
    limits of, 32
    special, 132, 188
Theater, funding for programs,
    303-304
Thomas, D., 207, 208
Thurstone, L. L., 4, 6, 17
Time frame, 263
Time line sample, 265
Toffler, Alvin, 102
Torrance, E. P., 9, 42, 207, 208, 209

Torrance Tests of Creative Thinking, 9, 25, 54
Total illumination (Plato), 2
Transportation, 136, 249
Travel as budget category, 267
Trial model of counseling interaction, 179
Trust and communication, 196
Twenty Thousand Leagues Under the Sea, 244
Two-Factor Structure Theory (Spearman), 5-6

U

Underachievers, 44, 50-52, 61
Unemployment, community, 74, 85
Unit-specific goals, 100-108

V

Values. *See* Valuing
Values Clarification, 182
Valuing, 219, 230-231
    in curricular areas, 236, 239, 242, 244-245, 247
Verbal factor in ability testing, 6
Verbal skills (Binet-Simon Intelligence Test), 5
Verne, Jules, 244
Vernon, D. F., 207
Vernon, P. E., 207
Vinci, da, Leonardo, 232
Visitations, structured, 275
Visual art as factor in giftedness, 12
Visual and performing arts, funding sources, 301-305
Vocabulary and intelligence tests, 28
Vocal arts, funding sources for, 302
Volunteer aides, 77
Volunteers, parental, 193-194

W

WAIS. *See* Wechsler Adult Intelligence Scale
Wechsler Adult Intelligence Scale (WAIS), 22
Wechsler Intelligence Scale for Children-Revised (WISC-R), 17, 22, 26, 28
Wechsler Intelligence Scales, 22, 29, 45-46, 55
Wechsler Preschool and Primary Intelligence Scale (WPPSI), 22
Weekend school, 155, 193
Whitmore, J. R., 207, 209
Wieler, J., 37
Wiles, J., 107
William T. Grant Foundation, funding source, 296-297
Williams, J., 250
WISC-R, sample profile of, 27. *See also* Wechsler Intelligence Scale for Children-Revised
Withall, J., 195, 196, 203, 206
Witty, P., 42
Women's Educational Equity Act Program, 300
Word fluency as factor in ability testing, 6
Work Experiences Internship Program, funding for, 303
Work force stability, 74
Workers, types of, and community assessment, 86
Workshops as budget category, 267
Worthen, B. R., 286
WPPSI. *See* Wechsler Preschool and Primary Intelligence Scale
Writing scholarships, 304

Y

Ysseldyke, J., 27

About the Authors

PATRICIA ALEXANDER received her Ph.D. from the University of Maryland and is presently an Assistant Professor in Curriculum and Instruction at Texas A & M University. In addition to research and publications in the area of gifted education, Dr. Alexander has made presentations at national and regional conferences on the topic of the gifted. Her educational experience also includes years as an elementary and middle school teacher with instructional emphasis on gifted learners.

JOSEPH MUIA received his doctorate in Academic Curriculum and Instruction from the Pennsylvania State University. He has taught at the elementary school level and spent six years teaching at James Madison University, where his work focused on children with diverse needs. Dr. Muia has published widely in professional educational journals and is presently director of his own educational consulting company.

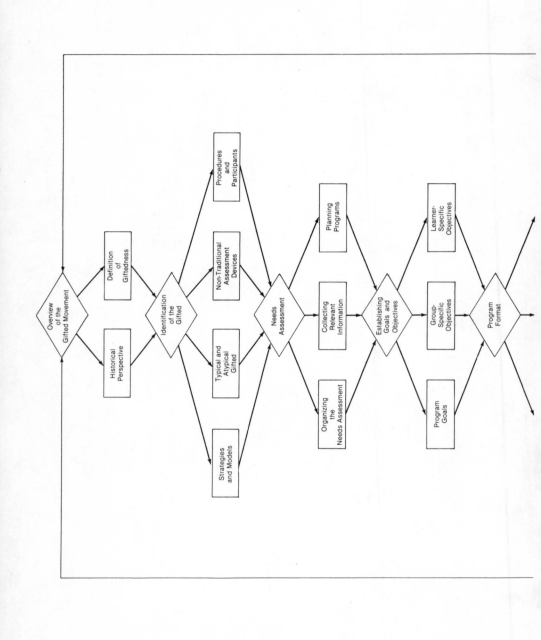